A History of Israel
from Alexander the Great to Bar Kochba

by the same author

A History of Israel
in the Old Testament Period

A History of Israel
from Alexander the Great
to Bar Kochba

Henk Jagersma

Fortress Press   Philadelphia

Translated by John Bowden from the Dutch
Geschiedenis van Israël van Alexander de Grote tot Bar Kochba,
published 1985 by Uitgeversmaatschappij J. H. Kok, Kampen.

© Uitgeversmaatschappij J. H. Kok, Kampen 1985

English translation © John Bowden 1985

First Fortress Press edition 1986

Library of Congress Cataloging-in-Publication Data

Jagersma, H.
   A history of Israel from Alexander the Great to Bar
Kochba.

   Translation of: Geschiedenis van Israël van Alexander
de Grote tot Bar Kochba.
   Bibliography: p.
   Includes index.
   1. Jews—History—586 B.C.–70 A.D.   2. Jews—History—
168 B.C.–135 A.D.   I. Title.
DS121.65.J3413   1986   933   85–45497
ISBN 0–8006–1890–4

   1823185   Printed in the United Kingdom   1–1890

CONTENTS

PREFACE

Six years after my account of the history of Israel up to 330 BC, here is a sequel which continues it further, up to and including the period of Bar Kochba.

The aim of the present volume is almost the same as that of its predecessor. However, those familiar with its subject-matter will know that the problems with which we have to deal during the history of Israel in this period are often very different from those of earlier times. The mere fact of the greater variety in the sources available makes the writing of the history of Israel from Alexander the Great to Bar Kochba a demanding venture. I was and am well aware of this. That is one of the main reasons why this book has taken longer to appear than I originally planned.

The interest and encouragement of my wife and children, students and many colleagues here and abroad have been a considerable help in working on and completing this book.

Brussels, Spring 1985

ABBREVIATIONS

AASOR	Annual of the American Schools of Oriental Research
AB	The Anchor Bible
ABLA	M.Noth, *Aufsätze zur biblischen Landes- und Altertumskunde 1 and 2*, Neukirchen-Vluyn 1971
AGAJU	Arbeiten zur Geschichte des Antiken Judentums und des Urchristentums
AJBI	*Annual of the Japanese Biblical Institute*
AJSR	*Association for Jewish Studies Review*
ALGHJ	Arbeiten zur Literatur und Geschichte des Hellenistischen Judentums
ANRW	*Aufstieg und Niedergang der Römischen Welt*
AJ	Josephus, *Antiquitates Judaicae*
AOTS	*Archaeology and Old Testament Study*, ed. D.Winton Thomas, Oxford 1969
ARNa	Aboth de Rabbi Nathan, version A
ARNb	Aboth de Rabbi Nathan, version B
ASTI	*Annual of the Swedish Theological Institute*
b	Babylonian Talmud
BA	*Biblical Archaeologist*
BAR	*The Biblical Archaeologist Reader*
BA Rev	*The Biblical Archaeologist Review*
BB	Tractate Baba Bathra
BeO	R.de Vaux, *Bible et Orient*, Paris 1967
Ber	Tractate Berakoth
BH	*Bijbels Handboek*
Bikk	Tractate Bikkurim
BJ	Josephus, *Bellum Judaicum*
BKAT	Biblischer Kommentar Altes Testament
BM	Tractate Baba Metzia
BOT	De Boeken van het Oude Testament
BWAT	Beiträge zur Wissenschaft vom Alten Testament
BZ	*Biblische Zeitschrift*

BZAW	Beihefte zur Zeitschrift für die Alttestamentliche Wissenschaft
CAH	The Cambridge Ancient History
CAT	Commentaire de l'Ancien Testament
CBC	The Cambridge Bible Commentary
CBQ	*Catholic Biblical Quarterly*
CD	Damascus Document
CPJ	*Corpus Papyrorum Judaicarum* I-III, ed. V.A.Tcherikover, A.Fuks and M.Stern, 1957-1964
CRINT	*Compendium Rerum Iudaicarum ad Novum Testamentum* I 1,2, ed. S.Safrai and M.Stern, 1974-1976
Dio Cassius	Dio Cassius, *Historia Romana*
Diodorus Siculus	Diodorus Siculus, *Bibliotheca Historica*
DJD	*Discoveries in the Judean Desert*, 1955ff.
EAEHL	*Encyclopedia of Archaeological Excavations in the Holy Land*, I-IV, ed. M.Avi-Yona and M.Stern (1975-1978)
EdF	Erträge der Forschung
ETL	*Ephemerides Theologicae Lovanienses*
FS	*Festschrift*
FWG	*Fischer Weltgeschichte* 5-8, 1965-1966
GCS	Die griechischen christlichen Schriftsteller der ersten Jahrhunderte
Gitt	Tractate Gittin
GLAJJ	M.Stern, *Greek and Latin Authors on Jews and Judaism* I,II, Jerusalem 1974-1980
GS	*Gesammelte Studien*
HA	*Historia Augusta*
HTR	*Harvard Theological Review*
HUCA	*Hebrew Union College Annual*
IEJ	*Israel Exploration Journal*
IJH	*Israelite and Judaean History*, ed. J.H.Hayes and J.Maxwell Miller, London and Philadelphia 1977
j	Jerusalem Talmud
JAOS	*Journal of the American Oriental Society*
JBL	*Journal of Biblical Literature*
JEOL	*Jaarbericht Ex Oriente Lux*
JJS	*Journal of Jewish Studies*
JNES	*Journal of Near Eastern Studies*
JQR	*Jewish Quarterly Review*

JRS	*Journal of Roman Studies*
JSHRZ	Jüdische Schriften aus hellenistisch-römischer Zeit
JSJ	*Journal for the Study of Judaism in the Persian, Hellenistic and Roman Period*
JSOT	*Journal for the Study of the Old Testament*
JSS	*Journal of Semitic Studies*
JTS	*Journal of Theological Studies*
KAT	Kommentar zum Alten Testament
KS	*Kleine Schriften*
m	Mishnah
Meg Taʿan	Megillat Taʿanit (Fast scroll)
Mur	*Documents from Murabbaʿat*, ed. J.T.Milik
Ned	Tractate Nedarim
NF (NS)	Neue Folge (New Series)
NT	*Novum Testamentum*
NTT	*Nederlands Theologisch Tijdschrift*
NTS	*New Testament Studies*
OBO	Orbis Biblicus et Orientalis
OLZ	*Orientalische Literaturzeitung*
OTS	*Oudtestamentische Studiën*
p	Pesher (commentary)
par.	parallels
PEQ	*Palestine Exploration Quarterly*
PNT	De prediking van het Nieuw Testament
Polybius	Polybius, *Histories*
PsSol	Psalms of Solomon
Q	Qumran
1Q, 2Q, etc.	First, second, etc. Qumran cave
1QpHab	Habakkuk Commentary
4QpNah	Nahum Commentary
RB	*Revue Biblique*
RBPH	*Revue Belge de Philologie et d'Histoire*
RGG	*Die Religion in Geschichte und Gegenwart*
RHR	*Revue de l'histoire des religions*
RivBib	*Rivista Biblica*
RQ	*Revue de Qumrân*
Sanh	Tractate Sanhedrin
SB	Sources Bibliques
SBS	Stuttgarter Bibelstudien
Schürer	E.Schürer, *The History of the Jewish People in the Age of Jesus Christ (175 BC – AD 135)*, I,II, revised and

	edited by G.Vermes, F.Millar and M.Black, I 1973, II 1979
SJLA	*Studies in Judaism in Late Antiquity*
SPB	Studia Post-Biblica
Strabo	Strabo, *Geographica*
SVT	Supplements to *Vetus Testamentum*
Ta ͑an	Tractate Ta ͑anith
TLZ	*Theologische Literaturzeitung*
TR	*Theologische Rundschau*
VT	*Vetus Testamentum*
WdF	Wege der Forschung
WMANT	Wissenschaftliche Monographien zum Alten und Neuen Testament
WUNT	Wissenschaftliche Untersuchungen zum Neuen Testament
ZAW	*Zeitschrift für die alttestamentliche Wissenschaft*
ZDPV	*Zeitschrift des Deutschen Palästina-Vereins*
ZNW	*Zeitschrift für die neutestamentliche Wissenschaft*

Chapter 1

Introduction

1.1 *An explanation*

This book attempts to reconstruct the history of Israel[1] between c.330 BC and AD 135. The choice of this period is determined on the one hand by the fact that the book is intended as a sequel to an earlier work[2] which covered the history of Israel up to about 330 BC. On the other hand, it is logical to choose the year AD 135 as the end of this history because in that year Israel ceased to exist as a state.

In reconstructing this period of the history of Israel we have often to struggle with a great many uncertainties and hypotheses. The most important reason for this is that the sources at our disposal often do not set out to write history in our sense of the word or – in other cases – certainly cannot be said to be objective historiography (see 1.2). Moreover, more than once we are confronted with the fact that for a particular period we have few sources or none at all, and no other data at our disposal. The result of all this is that on many points there is virtually no agreed opinion in academic discussion of this period in the history of Israel. The aim of this book is to indicate the various diverging views within reasonable limits. The way in which I shall do this is to indicate as far as possible divergent and alternative perspectives and make regular use of words like 'perhaps' and 'probably' in connection with subjects on which there is uncertainty. Such an account is much preferable to the so-called 'consecutive narrative' in which the reader often wrongly gets the impression that everything happened 'just like that'.

However, what I have just said certainly does not mean that the sources I have mentioned are of no help at all in a reconstruction of the history of Israel between 330 BC and AD 135. These sources are often written against a historical background or contain allusions to particular historical events. Our task is therefore to deal carefully and critically with the sources and thus try to establish what in fact happened. Here we must not limit ourselves to political history, but pay just as much attention to religious life, the various trends in this period, cultural and literary aspects, and social questions. Especial attention needs to be paid to the economic background. As so often, this background in particular is of decisive significance for the course of history and the most important events which took place in it.[3] Before we move on to that, I want to make some comments on the area and the people with which the book deals. The question of terminology must also be given special attention in this particular connection. First of all, however, I shall give a brief account of the most important sources that we shall be using.

1.2 *Sources*

1.2.1 *The Old Testament*

Only a few parts of the Old Testament are related to the period of the history of Israel which is to be described here. The most important of them is without doubt the book of Daniel. This book, which is usually dated to about 165 BC,[4] has an apocalyptic part (7-12) as well as a series of narratives (Dan.1-6). It is written in order to glorify God and to encourage those who continue to trust in this God – in very difficult circumstances – by announcing the coming of the kingdom of God. As will emerge in due course, this does not mean that we must *a priori* deny the book any historical character. Historical accuracy is not, however, the main concern here. The accuracy improves the nearer we come to the time in which the book must have been written (see also 7.6.1).[5]

In addition to the book of Daniel, the book of Koheleth (Ecclesiastes, *c.* 250 BC) can also be consulted for our period. Koheleth seems above all to provide some information about the social and economic situation of its time (see also 4.4).[6]

1.2.2 *Apocrypha and pseudepigrapha*

The historical value of most of these works must be assumed to be very small. Of course they often give us some insight into the religious developments and situation at the time when they were written.[7] One notable exception to this lack of historical value is I and II Maccabees. The final redaction of these two books took place in *c.* 100 BC.

I Maccabees describes the period from about 175 to 135 BC. The book gives the impression of having been written along the lines of books like I and II Samuel and I and II Kings, aiming to demonstrate the legitimacy of the Hasmonaean dynasty. As such, it has a polemical character.[8] Its historical value must also be judged in that light.

The author of II Maccabees, who probably came from Alexandria in Egypt, calls his book a summary of a five-volume work by a certain Jason of Cyrene (see II Macc. 2.23). There are no good reasons why such a book should not have existed. The central features of II Maccabees are divine protection, the important role of the temple and the cult, and trust in the Torah. Despite the fact that Judas occupies a prominent place in his work, the author of II Maccabees is much more critical of the Maccabees than that of I Maccabees.[9] II Maccabees deals with the same events as I Maccabees with the difference that the prehistory in II Maccabees (= II Macc.3-5) is much more detailed than in I Maccabbees (= I Macc.1.1-9). When there are differences, I Maccabees is usually regarded as the more trustworthy tradition.[10] I shall discuss this problem in more detail when we come to the period in question. I shall also discuss later the authenticity of the many documents which have been preserved in I and II Maccabees and of the specific historical events that can be inferred from the rest of the apocrypha and pseudepigrapha.

1.2.3 *Philo of Alexandria*

Philo (*c.*20 BC – AD 50) was a member of the Jewish community in Alexandria. It emerges from his works that he had a very broad and good Greek education and he can be regarded as the most important Jewish philosopher of classical antiquity.

In about AD 40, Philo was entrusted with the leadership of a delegation from Alexandria to plead the interests of the Jewish community there with Caligula (the emperor Caius Julius Caesar Germanicus, AD 37-41) in Rome. He described his experiences on this occasion in a book entitled *Legatio ad Gaium*. In this work we also find much information about Agrippa I, who was tetrarch of Galilee and Batanaea from AD 37 and king of Judaea from AD 41-44. In the rest of his work we only find sporadic information which is relevant to our purpose.

1.2.4 *Flavius Josephus*

The works of Josephus are without doubt the most important source for our knowledge of the history of Israel in the years between 330 BC and AD 135. At the beginning of the First Jewish War, this Jewish historian, who lived from about AD 37-100, was a commander in Galilee, where in 67 he went over to Vespasian. He wrote *De bello judaico* ('On the Jewish War'), in which, after discussing the prior history from 175 BC to AD 66 (Books I and II), he gives an account of this struggle with Rome, above all from his own experience (Books III-VII). He also wrote *Antiquitates Judaicae* ('Jewish Antiquities'), a history of the Jewish people from creation to about AD 66. In addition he wrote *Contra Apionem* (Against Apion), an apology for Judaism, which is also called 'On the Antiquity of the Jewish people', and a *Vita* (The Life of Josephus), along with another apologia, this time directed against Justus of Tiberias, who criticized Josephus' attitude at the time of the Jewish war.[11] The two first-mentioned works are most important for our purpose.

Like the books of Maccabees, the works of Josephus have been written with a considerable bias. *The Jewish War* betrays considerable sympathy for Vespasian and Titus. For this reason Josephus is rightly regarded as a kind of court historian of the Flavians.[12] At the same time it emerges from his works that his view is also clearly governed by his Pharisaic background and a desire to justify his own conduct during the Jewish War.[13]

In his *Jewish Antiquities* Josephus seems to feel himself under pressure above all to make the Jewish religion accessible to his non-Jewish readers. This may perhaps explain why he tries to describe Judaism as a 'philosophy',[14] and describes groups like the Sadducees, Pharisees, Essenes and Zealots as 'philosophical trends'.

In composing his works Josephus had both written sources and oral information at his disposal. The first category included not only the Old Testament but I Maccabees, a 'World History' (now lost) in 144 volumes by Nicolaus of Damascus, the secretary of Herod the Great, the works of Polybius and Strabo, and many others. He did not always use his sources very carefully, particularly the non-biblical ones.[15] Moreover, his use of them was governed by his motivation for writing his works,[16] which has already been mentioned. Josephus must have had help from Greek assistants in completing his work.[17] However, he was not so modest as always to make this clear.[18]

1.2.5 *Greek and Latin authors*

In general it can be said that these writers paid relatively little attention to what happened in Palestine. The country was only the object of their concern when their own land was affected. However, in this connection their information can often be useful to us.[19] The most important of these authors are as follows.

Polybius (*c.*203-120 BC) wrote a world history in forty volumes (some of which has come down to us), covering the years from 220 to 146 BC. Convinced of the inevitability of Roman rule over the world, he tried to analyse events in order to explain the rise of Rome and the decline of the Hellenistic kingdoms.

Diodorus Siculus (first century BC) wrote a historical survey (part of which has been preserved), the value of which is markedly dependent on the sources which he used (some of which are unknown to us).

The works of Strabo (*c.* 64 BC to AD 21), some of which are lost, seem above all to have been written for leaders and statesmen. They include descriptions of various areas including Palestine.

Livy (*c.* 59 BC – AD 17) is particularly concerned with the foreign policy and the growth of Rome. Palestine is mentioned twice in his *Periochae* (brief summaries of the history of the last century BC).

Plutarch (c.AD 46-120) gives a number of biographies of figures including Gracchus, Marius, Sulla, Pompey and Caesar. Here he stresses character and pays little attention to political circumstances.

Tacitus (born *c.*AD 55) is a supporter of the republic and has little sympathy for the emperors. In his *Annals* he covers the period from the death of Augustus (AD 14) to that of Nero (AD 68). Of his *Histories*, only the books about the year of the four emperors (AD 69) and the year AD 70 have been preserved. In V, 1-13 Tacitus gives a survey of Jewish history up to the First Jewish War.[20] The book breaks off in the middle of the account of the siege of Jerusalem by Titus.

Suetonius (AD 69-140) wrote a number of biographies including lives of the Roman emperors from Augustus to Domitian (AD 81-96). In these works the stress lies on the personal lives of the emperors concerned.

All the works of Appian (second century AD) which deal with the period between *c.*133 and 27 BC have been preserved. Although his work is not always historically reliable, it must be taken into account because of the overall picture he gives of the first century BC.

That part of the history of Rome by Dio Cassius (*c.* AD 155-235) which deals with the period from 69 BC to AD 46 has been preserved. His expertise in the historical sphere must not be rated too highly. His work is valuable simply as a supplement to other sources.

1.2.6 *The Dead Sea Scrolls*

Since 1947, a large number of scrolls, fragments, papyri and ostraca with writing on them have been found by the Dead Sea, dating from the last centuries before the beginning of the Christian era to AD 135. What is unique about them is that they give us information about a group through documents actually produced by the group.[21] In addition, they give us insights into the religion of Israel, above all when the Hasmonaeans were in power. Although none of the writings discovered can be regarded as a historical document in the strict sense of the term, they certainly contain allusions to historical and political events.[22] However, they should be used with great care.

1.2.7 *The New Testament*

The writings of the New Testament were not composed to serve as historical documents, but to bear witness that Jesus is the Christ (cf. John 20.30f.). So the evangelists described the life and message of Jesus in this light. Such an aim does not, however, meant that they give us no historical information. But it is particularly valuable that there are four evangelists, each of whom gives a selection of stories about Jesus. In particular, the differences between the three Synoptic Gospels and that of John are striking. One good example of this is the difference over the length of Jesus' ministry. In the Synoptic Gospels this period seems to cover one year, but in John it covers two or three. The fact that there are differences of this kind is an indication that where the Gospels agree about historical circumstances they may well go back to a real event. Thus both Matthew and Luke give Bethlehem as the place where Jesus was born and according to all four evangelists the crucifixion took place in the time of Pontius Pilate. These and other instances give us a basis for reconstructing the history of Israel in this period.

The Acts of the Apostles and the other writings in the New Testament give us less information in this respect, not least because these books are not as concerned with events in Palestine as are the Gospels.[23]

1.2.8 *The rabbinic literature*

The rabbinic literature came into being after AD 70. Here I shall only mention what is most relevant for us. It consists of extensive collections which in their present form have come down to us after a process which sometimes lasted for several centuries. The term is used to cover the Mishnah, the Tosephta, the Talmuds, the Midrashim and the Targums.[24]

The Mishnah (final redaction about AD 200) contains a collection of laws, regulations and casuistry derived from the Old Testament. According to rabbinic tradition it goes back to Moses through oral tradition. The whole work consists of six parts, sub-divided into tractates which are arranged by themes.

The Tosephta (final redaction about AD 500) has the same division as the Mishnah and contains sayings by rabbis from the time of the Tannaim, which were not incorporated into the Mishnah. The Tosephta (= Supplement) can therefore be regarded more or less as a supplement to the Mishnah.

After the period of the Tannaim (*c.* AD 200) there begins that of the Amoraim, learned men who were primarily concerned with the interpretation and exposition of the Mishnah. Their written works are known as the Gemara. It came into being in two collections, one in Palestine and one in Babylon. The combination of Mishnah and Gemara is known as the Talmud; the two collections are known respectively as the Jerusalem or Palestinian Talmud (final redaction about AD 500) and the Babylonian Talmud (final redaction about AD 700). The latter is regarded as the more important.

The Midrashim are ancient rabbinic commentaries on the Old Testament which presumably derive from readings and addresses in the synagogue. The earliest form of the oldest, Mekilta, Sifre and Sifra, which contain commentaries on parts of Exodus, Leviticus and Numbers-Deuteronomy respectively, probably comes from the time of the Tannaim.

The Targums are translations (often paraphrases) of the Old Testament into Aramaic. The existence of such Targums may go back to the inter-testamental period, as is evident from the discoveries by the Dead Sea.[25]

Too much importance should not be attached to the historical value of this rabbinic literature for a reconstruction of the history of Israel in our period. Although it may contain early material, for the most part it is based on later interpretations and traditions. But when there are allusions to historical events, they need to be taken seriously. However, we must remember that this literature has a very strong and one-sided Pharisaic stamp. The Pharisees were the only important group left in Judaism after the fall of Jerusalem, and they were the ones who gave new stimulus to Judaism so that it could surmount the catastrophe.

Finally, mention should be made of the Megillat Taʿanit (the Fast Scroll),[26] which has some importance as a historical source. This scroll, which probably can be dated to the first century AD, contains a summary of memorial days on which fasting is forbidden. These commemorations recall joyful events from the time of the Maccabees.

1.2.9 *The evidence of archaeology*

Through archaeology we can get some insight into the pattern of settlement, living conditions, the structure of cities and buildings, cultural developments, and so on, in particular periods.[27] In addition to excavations, ostraca, inscriptions and finds of coins[28] are very important for the period with which we shall be dealing. Discoveries of documents are also very important indeed. I shall now mention some of the most significant ones.

Wadi ed-Daliyeh lies about nine miles north of Jericho. Samaritan papyri were found here from the time between about 375 and 335 BC. These papyri belonged to people who had fled into a cave in the wadi before the destruction of Samaria in the time of Alexander the Great and were discovered there later by the Macedonians and killed. These papyri tell us about the governors in power in Samaria in the fourth century BC.[29]

The Zeno papyri were found in 1915, in Fayyum, an oasis in Egypt. They represent the archives of a certain Zeno, who had made a tour of inspection through 'Syria and Phoenicia' on behalf of Apollonius, a kind of minister of Ptolemy II Philadelphus (284-246 BC) of Egypt, between 260 and 258 BC. Among other places he also visited Transjordan. These papyri give us some insight into the administrative and economic situation in Palestine during the third century BC.[30]

Material discovered in Masada, the rock fortress built by Alexander Jannaeus (103-76 BC) and extended by Herod the Great (37-4 BC), gives us information about the history of Masada under the rule of Herod and at the time of the First Jewish War, when this fortress was occupied and lived in by the Zealots.[31]

The letters of Bar Kochba were found in the caves of Murabba'at and at Nahal Ḥever, i.e. in the region of the Dead Sea (cf. 1.2.6). The letters and the coins also found there have extended our knowledge about the period of the Bar Kochba revolt in AD 132-135 (see also ch.18).[32]

1.3 *The land and the people*

1.3.1 *The land*

It almost goes without saying that in any study of the history of Israel between Alexander the Great and Bar Kochba, most of the emphasis lies on Judaea and Jerusalem. Not only do the most important events take place in this area – as far as we know – but we also have most information about it in this period. Alongside that, however, other areas are also relevant. Foremost among these are Samaria and Galilee, then the territories on the other side of the Jordan, like Gaulanitis, the Decapolis and Peraea, and finally to a lesser extent Ituraea and Idumaea. Broadly speaking, this whole area corresponds to the kingdom which came under the rule of the Hasmoneans in the time of John Hyrcanus I.

I shall use the name Palestine as a general designation of this territory. This name seems already to have been known to Herodotus,[33] but it came to the fore when it became the name of the Roman province in this area after AD 135. However, the name is already used widely in scholarly literature for the period we are dealing with here.[34]

1.3.2 *The people*

Without any doubt, many Judaeans also lived in the area outside Judaea. However, Samaria and certainly also part of Galilee and the territory on the other side of the Jordan were mainly populated by, among others, descendants of the former kingdom of Israel, and the inhabitants of Ituraea and Idumaea were made up of quite different population groups.[35]

In addition to this population, in both the Hellenistic and the Roman period other groups also settled in the land. Foreign rulers left behind garrisons in various places, and they and their families formed military colonies. Alongside these, Graeco-Macedonian and later also Roman colonies grew up over the course of time in various places, made up largely of citizens drawn from the Hellenistic kingdoms. This eventually led to cities which were inhabited almost entirely by Greeks or Greek speakers. One well-known example of this is the Decapolis. As we shall see later, this was also wholly or partially the case with other cities, including Samaria. Even Jerusalem was not spared in this respect. In both the Hellenistic and the Roman period it constantly had to put up with military colonists of foreign origin.

Chapter 2

The Beginning of the Hellenistic Period

2.1 *Hellenism*

The conquest of the ancient Near East by Alexander the Great (333-323 BC) is regarded as the beginning of a new period, referred to as the Hellenistic period. Hellenism is a term used in connection with the cultural movement after Alexander as a result of which Greek language and civilization came to occupy a dominant position in the then known world,[1] and especially among leading groups in the cities.[2] Even in Palestine we have the phenomenon of the so-called Hellenistic cities. In such cities there was usually an ephebate, a training period for young men in citizenship (Greek citizenship), often lasting for a year, and a gymnasium, a public place for sport where instruction was also given. As well as furthering the Greek language, the main aim of both institutions was to cultivate the Greek way of life and Greek customs.[3]

This does not mean that with the arrival of Alexander in the Near East Hellenism suddenly descended out of thin air. In the coastal areas along the Mediterranean in this part of Asia there were cities which had regarded themselves as Greek colonies long before the coming of Alexander. Greek culture had already exercised its influence to some degree from such places. This process now began to accelerate. Soldiers settled as occupying forces in conquered territory and merchants who, with their caravans, now penetrated it increasingly deeply, largely furthered the breakthrough of Hellenism.

The conquests of Alexander the Great also meant an upsurge of Hellenism in the Greek homeland and especially in Macedonia. The expedition against the Persians was felt there to be a second Trojan war in which Alexander was seen more or less as a new Achilles.[4] All this was a stimulus to many Greeks to reflect again on the sources of their own culture.

2.2 *The general political and economic situation*

2.2.1 *The expansion of Alexander's empire*

After the battle of Issus in 333 BC, Alexander first directed his attention to the coastal cities in Syria and Palestine. He succeeded in capturing them very quickly, with the exception of Tyre, which only capitulated after a siege lasting about seven months.[5] At this same time Alexander must also have conquered Judaea and Samaria (see 3.2). After the fall of Tyre, he moved southwards. There Gaza, an important post and trading centre, offered vigorous opposition which was only broken after a two months' siege (332 BC). After that he hastened to Egypt, which he was able to conquer without too much difficulty. There in 331 BC he founded Alexandria, a city which in a later period was well-known, among other things, for its large and active Jewish population.

Soon afterwards a last and decisive power struggle took place between Alexander and Darius III, the last king of the Persians. In 331 BC Darius was killed at Gaugamela, which lay in the plain of Arbela east of the Tigris. The following year Darius was killed by one of his satraps. His kingdom and all his possessions now fell into the hands of Alexander, as soon did the rest of the Persian empire.

However, there was still no end to Alexander's campaigns. These extended as far as India (327-325 BC). But when the Macedonian soldiers got that far they refused to go any further, so Alexander was forced to withdraw. This did not mean that Alexander now planned to end his campaigns of conquest. In Babylon, which he intended to make the capital of his empire, he began to prepare an expedition to Arabia. Moreover he wanted to create a great port there with the aim of establishing a link with Egypt from the mouth of the Euphrates via the sea.[6] The implementation of Alexander's plans was thwarted by his death, from malaria, in Babylon in 323 BC.

2.2.2 *Alexander's political administration*

The cornerstone of Alexander's policy was undoubtedly his attempt to unite Macedonians and Persians in one kingdom and to make them one people. The great wedding he organized in Susa, in which he himself, his chief generals, and presumably at least ten thousand other Macedonians married Persian wives, also fits into this context.[7] Other ways in which he planned to achieve his goal were by transforming the army into a battle force consisting of Persians and Macedonians, and appointing both Macedonians and native aristocrats to administrative posts in the conquered territories.

Despite all his efforts, however, Alexander did not succeed in making the

Persians and the Macedonians one people. The difference in historical traditions and cultural development between the two people was too great for it to be possible to forge a unity.

By way of administration, Alexander took over the Persian system of a division into satrapies. During his campaigns he also founded Graeco-Macedonian *poleis* (cities) in many places, the best-known of which was Alexandria in Egypt. As garrison cities, these settlements had primarily a strategic purpose.

Like the Persian kings who had gone before him, Alexander also followed a policy of religious tolerance. The change of ruling power which followed his arrival therefore led to hardly any change in the religious community in Jerusalem.

2.2.3 *Economic conditions*

The Greeks will have been well aware of economic circumstances in the new territory because their merchants had already been engaged in trade activities there since the seventh century BC. As so often in history, the merchants were now followed by the soldiers. It is therefore no coincidence that Alexander's first aim in his campaign against the Persians was to secure important ports and trading cities like Tyre and Gaza. By conquering these places he not only robbed the Persian fleet of its bases but at the same time did away with competition for the Greek merchants.

One of the most far-reaching consequences of the Hellenistic period for economics[8] was the way in which the hoards of precious metals gathered by the Persian kings were turned into coinage. This measure, coupled with an adaptation to the Attic monetary standard, represented great progress in economic matters. With coins as a means of payment trade could be much more flexible.

There were also a great many important resources in the conquered territories. Moreover, the people there had long been accustomed to living under an absolute monarchy, so they were easy to govern. This was the area into which the Macedonians now came, with their spirit of enterprise, their trading methods and their banks. The combination of these factors was a powerful stimulus for the economy. Above all, the city economy in the many *poleis* which the Greeks and Macedonians founded in the conquered territories (cf. 2.2.2), and which they later extended to other cities, played an important role here.

2.3 *Palestine in 333 – 323* BC

2.3.1 *Judaea*

In speaking about Judaea, at this period we are talking of an area limited to Jerusalem and its immediate surroudings and governed by a high priest. We have little more than very fragmentary information about what happened there in the time of Alexander the Great.

The Old Testament is virtually silent about the rise of Alexander. Only one allusion, in Dan.8.5 ('A he-goat from the west'), may relate to this king's campaign in the East. Whether Zech. 9.1-8 also refers to Alexander cannot be established with any certainty.[9] The scanty allusions to Alexander in I Macc.1.1-7 also say nothing about Judaea and even less about Palestine in this period.

The reason for this silence may be that at this point in time nothing serious happened in connection with Judaea, because the war did not affect it. Moreover, it may well have been that the transfer of power did not bring any significant changes for the community in Jerusalem except that from then on the taxes had to be paid to a new ruler. Moreover, Alexander's 'religious tolerance' probably meant that the introverted community in Jerusalem could simply let things pass over their heads. The consequences of the advent of the Hellenistic ruler would only be felt in the country much later.

We find accounts of contacts of Alexander the Great with Judaea in Josephus and the Babylonian Talmud. According to Josephus,[10] after the conquest of Gaza in 332 BC, Alexander visited Jerusalem and there had a meeting with the high priest Jaddua. The whole account is markedly legendary in character. Alexander's visit to the temple in Jerusalem may well have a historical nucleus, in the light of his later action in Egypt, but it is equally conceivable that by analogy with this event Josephus created a similar story about Jerusalem. The Talmud[11] mentions a meeting between the high priest and Alexander at Kefar Saba (later Antipatris) in the coastal plain. In favour of the historicity of this account it seems plausible that a ruler should have invited the governor of a small subject country to meet him. However, the problem here is that the high priest is given as Simon the Just, who lived about a century later.

2.3.2 *Samaria*

In his *Jewish Antiquities*[12] Josephus reports that a certain Sanballat of Samaria came to the aid of Alexander at the siege of Tyre with a force of eight thousand men. Soon after this Sanballat died. Now on the basis of papyrus finds in the Wadi ed-Daliyeh it is certainly possible that at the time of Alexander there was a governor in Samaria with the name Sanballat.[13] This must have been Sanballat III. Furthermore, the defection of a local leader to a conquering general was also a regular phenomenon at that time. The report about Sanballat by Josephus therefore sounds very plausible.

Another credible account appears in the biography of Alexander by Curtius Rufus.[14] According to this, while Alexander was in Egypt the inhabitants of Samaria rebelled and burned alive Andromachus, the Macedonian governor of Coele-Syria (i.e. the whole of Phoenicia and Palestine). Alexander thereupon undertook a punitive expedition against the city in which the rebels were put to death. Supplementary information about this event is given by a chronicle of Eusebius.[15] After suppressing this rebellion Alexander is said to have taken a number of inhabitants of Samaria into captivity and then settled a group of Macedonians there. All these reports seem to be confirmed by the information provided by the papyri discoveries in Wadi ed-Daliyeh mentioned earlier. In addition to papyri, about three hundred skeletons were found there. It is now supposed that these are the skeletons of inhabitants of Samaria who attempted to escape the punitive expedition made by Alexander's troops against this city in 331 BC by fleeing to a cave in the Wadi ed-Daliyeh north of Jericho and were later discovered there by the Macedonians and killed.[16]

All this information is connected with a rebuilding of Shechem at this time by inhabitants of Samaria. The old city of Shechem is said to have been uninhabited between about 480 and 330 BC. Archaeological evidence would seem to indicate that there are again traces of habitation after 330 BC.[17] However, there is considerable uncertainty about this. On the basis of the same archaeological material it is also argued that Shechem had already been inhabited again before the coming of Alexander the Great.[18] The former view seems to me to be most convincing.

2.3.3 *The Samaritan temple*

The question of the rebuilding of Shechem also raises the question of the building of the 'Samaritan'[19] temple on Gerizim. It is usually thought to have been in the Hellenistic period,[20] but the date still needs to be made more precise.

In the section of Flavius Josephus' *Jewish Antiquities* mentioned in the previous paragraph, Josephus reports that when Sanballat declared himself subject to Alexander, at the same time he received permission from Alexander to build a temple on Gerizim. However, it is remarkable that in Josephus' description of a later event during Alexander's stay in Palestine, this temple seems already to have been built.[21] The temple certainly could not have been built during the short time that Alexander stayed in the area, so it seems likely that we should not attach too much importance to the report of Alexander's concern with the building of a temple on Gerizim.[22] It is better to assume that the temple came into being about the same time as the rebuilding of Shechem in about 330 BC and the years following, and in conjunction with it. Specialist studies of this area[23] also suggest that the building of the temple on Gerizim must have taken place about the end of the fourth century BC.

The building of this temple need not of itself imply that there was a schism with temple worship in Jerusalem. Despite all the accounts which seem to tell against this, it is clear that until the Hellenistic period several temples quite legitimately existed alongside that of Jerusalem, including one in Leontopolis in Egypt and probably one in ʿAraq-el-Emir in Transjordan.[24] A breach between Jews and 'Samaritans' in which worship on Gerizim began to have more or less a life of its own alongside that in Jerusalem only came about gradually. This process developed in the period from the third century BC to the second century BC[25] or the beginning of the Christian era.[26]

The building of the temple on Gerizim meant in the first place that Shechem – the city which was also so significant from a religious point of view in the Old Testament period[27] - became the centre of the cult of the 'Samaritans'. Here the term 'Samaritans' should not be associated with the city of Samaria. That place, which can rightly be called the first Hellenistic city in Palestine,[28] belongs in quite a different context. Similarly, mention of 'Samaritans' in a later period should suggest the environs of Shechem and the province of Samaria rather than the city of Samaria.

Chapter 3

The Period of the Diadochi
(*c.* 323-301 BC)

3.1 *The general situation after the death of Alexander*

When Alexander died in 323 BC, there was in fact no successor capable of taking his place. Neither the child who was born after his death nor his weak half-brother Philip Arrideus were in a position to take over power. The real power came into the hands of the so-called Diadochi ('successors'). The term Diadochi denotes the generals who after the death of Alexander took over rule of the Macedonian-Persian world empire, which had only been founded in 330, and later divided it among themselves. This happened when in the course of time they had murdered all the legal heirs of Alexander (see above). The three most important kingdoms of the Didadochi, which eventually survived after many internecine wars, were those of the Ptolemies in Egypt, the Seleucids in Syria-Palestine and the Antigonids in the European part of Alexander's former empire.

In these wars among the Diadochi, Palestine, too, was the scene of a long and bitter struggle, first particularly between the Antigonids and the Ptolemies and later between the Ptolemies and the Seleucids.

3.2 *The struggle for the possession of Palestine*

In 322 BC Ptolemy arrived in Egypt. Once there he set himself up as Alexander's successor and ruler of an independent territory. This is the perspective from which we must view the fact that one of his first actions was to bring the body of Alexander the Great with great pomp and splendour to Egypt.[1]

Like the Pharaohs before him, Ptolemy understood that Coele-Syria (like 'Syria and Palestine', a term used to denote the whole of Palestine and Phoenicia) was a very good base for an attack on Egypt. For this reason alone he was concerned to gain control over the area. In 320 BC he was able to achieve his aim through military means. For the moment, Ptolemy held Palestine for only a very short time. Among other things, he first had to reckon with Antigonus Monophthalmus ('the one-eyed'), a powerful opponent, who also had aspirations to appropriate Alexander's legacy.

After the death of Alexander, Antigonus had become governor over Asia Minor. In about 317 BC he was able to drive out Seleucus, who had been appointed satrap of Babylon. Seleucus thereupon fled to Egypt, where he sought and obtained sanctuary with Ptolemy. Meanwhile Antigonus advanced further towards Syria and Palestine, capturing Tyre, Joppa, Gaza and other places in the process. Ptolemy could do little about this since his hands were tied elsewhere. However, Antigonus, too, had to retreat to Asia Minor because of difficulties there. He handed over government of the conquered areas of Coele-Syria and command of the troops there to his son Demetrius. Demetrius was killed in battle in Gaza in 312 by Alexander's experienced former generals, Ptolemy and Seleucus. After this victory Ptolemy was able to establish his rule over Palestine once again within a short time.

After the battle at Gaza, Seleucus advanced with an army to Babylon and captured the city. This happened on 1 October 312 BC. This date forms the beginning of the so-called Seleucid chronology.

However, the victory at Gaza had not brought Ptolemy long-term success. Barely six months later, Demetrius was able to surprise an army of his and defeat it.[2] When after that Antigonus himself invaded Syria with an army and occupied the cities of Acco, Joppa, Samaria and Gaza, all Ptolemy could do was to retreat back to Egypt.[3]

This situation continued until Seleucus and his allies[4] inflicted a decisive defeat on Antigonus in 301 at the battle of Ipsus (in Phrygia). After this victory a new division of Alexander's empire was made, in which among other things Seleucus was assigned Syria and Palestine. However, Ptolemy, who was not affected either by the battle of Ipsus or the division which followed it, succeeded in making himself master of Palestine. He did this while his allies were still entangled in the struggle with Antigonus, and after the battle of Ipsus he refused to give up the area again.

It goes without saying that this course of action caused his former friend and ally Seleucus, who after Ipsus again laid claim to the area, to be very angry. Throughout the whole of the third century BC Palestine was a cause of dispute between the Ptolemies and the Seleucids. We can find a reflection of this in Dan.11.5-6.[5] As far as Palestine was concerned, matters were provisionally settled in favour of the Ptolemies. From 201-198 BC they were able to retain possession of the land.

3.3 *Consequences for the land and the people*

3.3.1 *The period from 323-311 BC*

In this period, land and people suffered appallingly from the struggle that was waged in the area. The constant changes of controlling power and the battles that went with them will certainly have left deep scars. Above all the coastal cities, and especially Gaza (see above), must have suffered heavily.

We can certainly infer this much, even though we have virtually no information at all about Palestine at this time. This need not cause us any surprise. In this period Judaea and Jerusalem in particular were politically and economically so insignificant that Greek writers had no need to pay much attention to them.[6] Jewish sources are also almost silent about this period. In I Macc.1.9 it is simply said that the Diadochi 'caused many evils on the earth', though that statement in itself is evocative enough of the suffering in which the land was involved at that time.

It is also worth noting a report in Josephus[7] taken from a work of Hecataeus of Abdera from the fourth century BC. This reports how after the battle at Gaza in 312 BC many inhabitants of 'Syria' (i.e. Palestine) followed Ptolemy to Egypt because of his 'friendly and humane atittude'. They are said to have included the sixty-six year old Hezekiah, an important priest from this time, with a number of supporters. It is impossible to say how reliable this report is. The attitude of Ptolemy as described here seems difficult to reconcile with his later activity (see 3.3.2). On the other hand, however, we cannot exclude the possibility that on the advance of Antigonus, supporters of Ptolemy took the road to Egypt. These could well have included priests.[8]

The above-named Hezekiah is probably the figure referred to by the name *Yehizqiyyo* on an old coin which comes from the late Persian period.[9] However, there is no certainty about this.

3.3.2 *The period from 311 to 301 BC*

By contrast the next period, at least to begin with, was one of considerable peace and quiet. This was because during it Antigonus had virtually consolidated his position and had obtained a firm footing in Coele-Syria.

Antigonus seems to have had most problems in the first instance during this period with the Nabataeans.[10] The Nabataeans occupied a key position in connection with the important caravan route from Syria to the Persian Gulf. In 312 BC Antigonus sent his general Athenaeus with an army to conquer their territory. This expedition failed.[11] An attempt soon afterwards by Demetrius to take the 'rock', later Petra, by surprise, also achieved no results.[12]

We may, however, suppose that Antigonus will have established military settlements in the area east of the Jordan in order to be able to have some control over the caravan route. At all events there are indications that he was responsible for the foundation or extension of a city like Pella.[13]

Apart from this, the sources are silent about events in Palestine during the time that it was under the control of Antigonus. This changes after the battle of Ipsus (see 3.2), when Ptolemy was again able to get a footing in the land. According to Josephus, who is here quoting from a lost work of Agatharcides of Cnidus,[14] at this period Ptolemy occupied Jerusalem on a sabbath, because the inhabitants of the city refused to take up arms on that day. On this occasion Ptolemy is also said to have taken prisoner many from Jerusalem and its environs, the hill-country of Judaea, Samaria and Gerizim, and brought them to Egypt.[15] This report by Josephus seems to be confirmed by a report in the Letter of Aristeas,[16] which relates that Ptolemy I had about 100,000 inhabitants of Judaea deported to Egypt. This number may be on the high side, but the deportation may well be a historical fact given the different sources which mention it and the large number of Jews who later lived in Egypt.

Although some[17] scholars think that the capture of Jerusalem mentioned here took place directly after the battle near Gaza in 312 BC, it seems more likely that we should put it in 301 BC. After the battle near Gaza Ptolemy returned directly to Phoenicia.[18]

This conquest of Jerusalem in 301 BC and the harsh treatment by Ptolemy of the inhabitants strongly suggests that there were those among the people and especially among the leaders in Jerusalem who had associated closely with the régime of Antigonus. However, we have no more detailed information.

3.4 *The administrative situation*

3.4.1 *The overall division*

In all probability Antigonus Monophthalmus to some degree developed the system of dividing Palestine into toparchies which was later used by the Ptolemies.[19] A toparchy usually consisted of a city, where the seat of government was established, and the territory of a number of neighbouring villages. A toparchy of this kind was the smallest administrative unit and authority which collected taxes. Taken together, a number of toparchies formed the next largest unit, the hyparchy. This administrative unit presumably corresponded roughly with what in Ptolemaic Egypt was known as the *nomos*. The name of these hyparchies have perhaps been preserved in place names ending with -itis, like Gaulanitis and Galaaditis, and in the (Greek) names ending in

-ia, like Iudaia, Idumaia, Samareia and Galilaia.[20] As the smallest administrative unit and authority for raising taxes the toparchy seems to have existed down to the time of Herod the Great.

The most important administrative positions in both the hyparchies and the toparchies were usually occupied by Greeks in the Hellenistic period.

3.4.2 *The administration in Jerusalem and Judaea*

It is almost certain that the government of Judaea and Jerusalem in this period had rather a different structure from that in the rest of the country. As early as the Persian period,[21] this area must have been governed by a council which had its seat in Jerusalem. In rabbinic literature, which in any case sees the assembly of the seventy elders in Num.11.16 as the Sanhedrin of this time, this council is designated the Great Assembly.[22] The term Josephus[23] uses for the period around 200 BC is *gerousia*, 'the assembly of the elders'. Only in Roman times was this institution given the name Sanhedrin ('court of judgment'), which is also known from the New Testament.

The new authorities evidently left unchanged this administrative situation in Jerusalem dating from the Persian period. Of course it is clear that the council only had limited authority primarily relating to legal and executive powers in domestic matters.

The members of this council were prominent priests and 'elders', presumably a reference to the heads of well-to-do families. The whole council was led by the high priest, who thus had a very important position in the administration of the country.[24] As a rule the high priesthood was handed down from father to son, though there were already exceptions to this regular practice in the early Hellenistic period.[25]

The last high priest to be mentioned in the Old Testament is Jaddua (Neh.12.22), a contemporary of Darius III and Alexander the Great (see also 2.3.1). According to Josephus he was succeeded by his son Onias I.[26] Onias was therefore high priest in the period between 323 and 301 BC. In I Macc.12.22-23 (cf. *AJ* XII, 226-7) there is mention of a letter which Onias is said to have received from Arius I, king of Sparta (309-265 BC). This Arius was an important opponent of Antigonus. The presupposition is that the aim of this letter was to prompt him to rebel against Antigonus.[27] However, the authenticity of the letter is difficult to defend.[28] It seems most likely that the letter is based on a later fiction deriving from circles which at a later date wanted to demonstrate that from of old there had been links with Greece.

Nothing is known about the attitude adopted by Onias I in the dispute between Antigonus and Ptolemy, or about his activity as high priest. The only thing we know with certainty is that he was succeeded by his son Simon I, whom Josephus calls 'the Just'.[29] However, this must be a slip or the result of false information. The Simon who bore this epithet must be Simon II, who lived about 200 BC. That would also fit in better with what is said in Sirach 50 and several traditions preserved in rabbinic literature.[30]

When Simon I took over the office of high priest from his father, a new period had already dawned for the land, that of Ptolemaic rule. We know just as little about the activities of Simon I as we do about those of his father. However, it is certain that the high-priestly family of the Oniads was to go on to play a very important role in the further course of history.

3.4.3 *Administration in the rest of the country*

We have even less information about the administration of the rest of Palestine in this period than we do about that of Judaea. In all probability the region of Samaria formed a more or less independent administrative unity (hyparchy).[31] Whether this also applied to an area like Galilee is unknown. We get the impression from *AJ* XII, 154 and I Macc.10.30 that under Seleucid rule Galilee was part of the administrative unit of Samaria, but it is far from certain whether that was already the case in an earlier period.[32]

In Transjordan there were still tribes with native sheikhs who continued to have a large degree of independence. Moreover, an increasing number of Greek cities came into being there (cf.2.2.2) which later formed the Decapolis.[33] Decapolis must of course be regarded purely as a geographical term.[34] Like the large coastal cities and other Greek settlements in the land, those of what was later the Decapolis should be regarded as independent Greek cities.[35] This means that the inhabitants of these cities could regulate their own internal affairs, but in military terms were completely dependent on the Hellenic authorities, to whom they were also obliged to pay taxes. The administration of such a city lay in the hands of a council, which could consist of several hundred members. Thus according to Josephus,[36] that of Gaza numbered five hundred people.

Chapter 4

The First Half-Century of Ptolemaic Rule (301-246 BC)

4.1 *The position of the Ptolemaic king*

The reign of the Ptolemaic kings in Egypt can be seen as a continuation of that of the former Pharaohs. Like the latter, the Ptolemies could rely on a strong central authority and their position as kings was almost unassailable. The divine worship which the Pharaohs allowed to be offered to them in former times was also largely offered to the Ptolemaic kings. The efforts of especially the first Ptolemaic kings were in fact directed towards creating a form of state which went back to old Egyptian institutions, adapted to Greek insights about the state as an institution.[1]

Above all from a social and economic point of view, the power and influence of the Ptolemaic king was particularly great. As with the Pharaohs, all land was in principle regarded as the property of the king.[2] Part of this land was leased out to the temple. Greek mercenaries could also buy land which they then sub-let to the Egyptians. Moreover, a good deal of land was worked by peasants under the strict supervision of royal officials. All this implies that the king had substantial income from this so-called 'royal land'.

Another source of income was provided by the royal monopoly in the most important forms of trade.[3] In fact all means of production and all barter were in the hands of the state, in other words, in the possession of the king.[4] In addition to all this the king also controlled the collection of the various taxes and tolls.

All this income which the Ptolemies were able to acquire made them the richest and consequently the most powerful rulers in the ancient Near East during the third century BC. The reverse side of the coin is, as so often in history, that a large proportion of the population in their kingdom, in this case especially the native Egyptians, suffered harsh poverty. Only the king and his immediate entourage profited to any degree from these riches. Among the latter were the senior Macedonian and Greek soldiers who served in the army of the Ptolemies.[5]

4.2 *Political developments in c. 301-246* BC

4.2.1 *The time of Ptolemy I Soter (323-283 BC)*

Ptolemy I, surnamed Soter, 'saviour', 'deliverer', can be regarded as the founder of the Hellenistic state of Egypt which existed until 30 BC. In 305 BC Ptolemy had taken the crown for himself, although in fact from 323 BC he already had power over the greater part of the kingdom. The capital of this kingdom was the city of Alexandria, founded by Alexander the Great.

The province of 'Syria and Phoenicia', which also included Palestine, was still not completely in the hands of Ptolemy I after the battle of Ipsus (see 3.2). Apart from the claims to this area by Seleucus I, though these were apparently ineffective in the third century BC, Demetrius – the son of Antigonus – still had possession of the cities of Tyre and Sidon. According to Eusebius,[6] in 296 BC Demetrius again devastated the city of Samaria in an attack on Palestine. However, there is considerable uncertainty about the trustworthiness of this account. It is certain, though, that Tyre and Sidon were in the possession of the Ptolemies at the latest in 286 BC. That meant that the whole of the province of Syria and Phoenicia was in their power.

In particular, their rule over Palestine meant that the Ptolemies could continue the policy of the former Pharaohs. Anyone who occupied Palestine controlled the trade and caravan routes like those from Mesopotamia to Egypt and from Syria and Mesopotamia to the Gulf of Akaba.[7] Economically this area was therefore extremely important for Egypt. In military terms, too, Palestine was very important for the Ptolemies. Strategically it formed a frontier post for the defence of Egypt. The whole policy of Ptolemy I was directed towards strengthening and consolidating his position in Palestine as a military and economic base. It could be said that in fact he had achieved this goal by the end of his reign.

4.2.2 *The period of Ptolemy II Philadelphus (283-246 BC)*

During the reign of Ptolemy II the Ptolemies were at the zenith of their power. Both in the First (274-271 BC) and the Second Syrian War (260-253 BC), he succeeded in defending his position in 'Syria and Phoenicia' against the claims of the Seleucids.

After the Second Syrian War it even seemed that the dispute over this area between the Ptolemies and the Seleucids was finally going to come to an end because a marriage had been arranged between Berenice, the daughter of Ptolemy II, and Antiochus II, the Seleucid king. On this occasion Ptolemy II gave his daughter a large dowry on condition that Antiochus II divorced his first wife, but after the death of Ptolemy II Antiochus II sought to be reconciled with the latter. She, however, managed to have Antiochus II, Berenice and their child killed (cf. Dan.11.6). This became one of the causes of the Third Syrian War (see 5.1.1).

About 278 BC, Ptolemy II also defeated the Nabataeans; the result was that the trade route from Petra to the northern part of Syria was cut off. From then on trade with southern Arabia ran through Gaza. In order to keep the Nabataeans further in check, the southern and eastern frontiers of Palestine were fortified.

To strengthen his position Ptolemy had several cities built (or rebuilt) and fortified in Palestine. They probably included Acco, which was now called Ptolemais;[8] Beth-shean, which in the time of the Ptolemies was called Scythopolis and in the time of the Seleucids Nyssa;[9] Philoteria, which can perhaps be identified with the original Beth-jerach;[10] and Rabbah, the old capital of Ammon, which was later called Philadelphia.[11]

All the developments outlined here had consequences for Palestine. On the basis of the information which we have about this period, which is fragmentary and scarce, we get the impression that in political and military terms little happened. The two Syrian wars seem to have left the greater part of the land unscathed. The greatest changes took place in the social and economic spheres.

4.3 *Social and economic consequences in Palestine*

4.3.1 *Social consequences*

The fact that the Ptolemies built new cities or had old and abandoned ones rebuilt had obvious consequences for the population structure of Palestine. Hitherto it had consisted primarily of Judaeans in Judah, and for the most part of descendants of the former Israel in Samaria and Galilee. Alongside that the process which had already begun under Alexander the Great, as a result of which large groups of Macedonians and Greeks came to live in the land, developed to an increasing degree (cf.1.3.2). These groups settled mainly in the cities along the coast and in Transjordan. These particular locations should not come as any surprise to us. They were the areas which were of great signifiance in both military and economic terms, because the most important trade and caravan routes ran through them. The majority of the new inhabitants were soldiers and merchants with their families and following.

All this helps us to understand how Hellenism could be most easily established in these particular cities. For the most part the better off among the indigenous population were the ones who gradually adopted the new (Hellenistic) life-style.[12] In the country, the villages and cities were able to maintain their original character, even in a later period. One exception to this was the city of Samaria, which already had a Macedonian population in the time of Alexander the Great (see 2.3.2). Above all in Judaea and there particularly in Jerusalem, the process of Hellenization developed very slowly among the leading groups. Here we can only demonstrate it with some certainty in the period after Ptolemy II Philadelphus. In all probability in the first instance economic factors were paramount.

In general it can be said that the period of Ptolemy I and Ptolemy II was a time of peace and quiet in Palestine. That makes a report by Polybius[13] that the inhabitants of Coele-Syria were well-disposed to the Ptolemies seem very plausible. And in the circumstances we can well see how Jewish units could at this time make up part of the Ptolemaic army.[14]

4.3.2 *Economic consequences*

Ptolemaic rule had primarily economic consequences. The position of the Ptolemaic king outlined in 4.1 could not fail to have an effect here in Palestine as well.

It is clear that the state became very strong in the economic sphere during the Ptolemaic period.[15] The authorities in Alexandria (i.e. the king) were concerned to exploit all land as far as possible to their own advantage. The introduction of the Greek system of state leasing served this end.[16] Given that the Ptolemies wanted to make their income as high as possible,[17] they had to levy high taxes. Above all the small farmers were the victims of this. Then came the well-to-do farmers, who were able to occupy a quite independent position over against the king.[18]

So-called 'tax farmers' were entrusted with the collection of this state taxation and other taxes. These people were usually members of the population of the city or region where the taxes were raised; however, the income from the taxes did not benefit the city or region concerned, but the central authority in Alexandria.[19] The position of 'tax farmer' was held by the most well-to-do. A good deal of money was needed for it. Moreover, large 'presents' were often given to the king and above all to officials to exclude rivals.

The income which the king received from these taxes from 'Syria and Phoenicia' seems to have been enormous.[20] When we remember that the 'tax farmers' made their own profit out of them as well, it is clear that the population were oppressed by a heavy burden. On the other hand it should also be pointed out that Ptolemy II Philadelphus took steps against an uncontrolled slave trade in 'Syria and Phoenicia'.[21] Even free farmers who could not pay their debts could be sold as slaves.

We get important information about the economic situation in Palestine during this period from the so-called Zeno papyri.[22] These mention a certain Zeno who, on behalf of Apollonius, as it were a finance minister to Ptolemy II, made a tour of inspection to Palestine in about 261-258 BC. Two of these papyri[23] mention a certain Tobias who lived in a kind of fortress in Ammanitis (Transjordan). The papyri detail gifts which Tobias sent to Ptolemy and Apollonius. Such gifts are an indication of the close relations which Tobias must have had with the court in Alexandria. It is not certain whether this Tobias is a descendant of the Tobiah mentioned in Neh.6.17-19 and 13.4-9, but it is clear, as we shall see in the next chapter, that the descendants of the Tobias mentioned in the Zeno papyri played a major role at the time of Ptolemaic rule in Palestine.

One of the aims of Zeno's journey was to introduce as efficient political and above all economic control in Palestine as there was in the mother country, Egypt. There is no doubt that here figures like Tobias in particular had given a helping hand.

We need to pay special attention in this respect to Judaea and Jerusalem. Judaea, i.e. Jerusalem and its immediate environs, can be regarded as a kind of temple state,[24] governed by a high priest with the support of a kind of council (see 3.4.2). It certainly had no political independence. The high priest paid a tax to the Ptolemies in the name of the people, as his predecessors had done earlier to the Persian rulers. This tax was raised from the populace by a special tax on land.[25] It is not clear whether in this capacity the high priest should also be regarded as a kind of tax farmer. That does not seem completely impossible, although it is more probable that the foreign rulers appointed a Judaean temple official alongside the high priest to be specially responsible for financial matters in Judaea and in the temple.[26]

Without any doubt it can be said that the existence of such officials and of tax farmers did a good deal to further collaboration with the Ptolemies in higher circles. However, at the same time this produced much greater alienation between particular aristocratic circles and the rest of the population.[27] Koheleth (Ecclesiastes) in particular seems illuminating in this respect. For that reason we must pay some attention to its content.

4.4 *Koheleth (Ecclesiastes)*

It is almost universally assumed that Koheleth was written in the third century BC.[28] Its place of origin is generally taken to be Jerusalem.

The use of the name Koheleth, usually translated 'preacher', to denote the author, indicates that he was an important official in Judaean society. Furthermore he is also called a 'wise man' (Koh.12.9; cf. also 2.15). These designations typify him as a member of the higher circles which could be found above all in Jerusalem.[29] We get the impression that in many respects Koheleth also expressed the views of this group. Seen in this light it is not surprising that Koheleth constantly calls on people to accept the existing situation – primarily the social and economic situation. All opposition to it is useless (cf. 8.2-4). Criticism of the king and his system is rejected out of hand (cf. 8.2-4). Everything is essentially unchangeable, and therefore according to Koheleth changes are clearly also impossible (1.15; cf. 7.13). And since everything will be as it must be, his advice is to 'enjoy life' (cf. 9.7ff.). However, it should be remembered that this enjoyment is in fact only possible for the well-to-do with the means for it. For the oppressed, death is a way out (cf.4.1-2).[30]

All this does not alter the fact that Koheleth is also critical of the attitude and life-style of those who are involved only in the aimless pursuit of amassing riches (cf.2.4-8; 5.9-10).

These brief comments from Koheleth indicate the background to an opposition between the aristocracy in Judaea (or at least part of them) on the one hand and the ordinary people on the other, which steadily increased over the course of time. This opposition was finally to lead, among other things, to armed conflict in the time of the Maccabees.[31]

Chapter 5

The Second Half-Century of Ptolemaic Rule (246-198 BC)

5.1 *The Third Syrian War (246-241 BC)*

5.1.1 *The course of the war*

This war broke out when Ptolemy III Euergetes (246-221 BC) had only just come to the throne. It arose directly out of the intrigues around Berenice, the sister of Ptolemy III and the second wife of the Seleucid prince Antiochus II (see 4.2.2). Essentially, of course, it was another expression of the old conflict between Ptolemies and Seleucids over rule in this part of the world. It is also clear that the war was an attempt on the part of Ptolemy III to prevent Seleucus II, the successor to Antiochus II, from setting foot in Asia Minor.[1]

At first the campaign against Seleucus II begun by Ptolemy III went particularly well for Ptolemy. Among other things he succeeded in occupying the major part of Syria and advancing as far as the Euphrates. In 245 BC, however, he seems suddenly to be back in Alexandria again. We cannot tell with any certainty what the reason was. It is possible that a rebellion in Egypt compelled Ptolemy to make a personal appearance there.[2] Another factor may have been the defeat at sea which Antigonus, king of Macedon, inflicted on the Ptolemies in 245 BC.[3] Be this as it may, Seleucus seems to have been stronger at a later stage than the beginning of the war might have suggested. So he succeeded in regaining possession of virtually all of his father's kingdom. Despite all this, Ptolemy succeeded in concluding a peace treaty in his own favour in 241 BC. This left him in possession of the enclave of Seleucia, the port of Antioch and important areas in the south of Asia Minor.[4] The reason why Seleucus accepted a treaty at the end of the Third Syrian War which was so unsatisfactory for him was that he had to deal with his brother Antiochus Hierax, who wanted to be independent ruler of part of the Seleucid kingdom.

The course of the Third Syrian War seems to have been followed with interest in Jerusalem and its environs. We find a reflection of this in Dan.11.6-9. This interest is also expressed by the advent of Onias II in the course of this war.

5.1.2 *The situation in Jerusalem during the Third Syrian War*

Towards the end of the Third Syrian War the then high priest Onias II refused to go on paying tribute to the Ptolemies. We find this report in Josephus,[5] but he puts the event wrongly in the time of Ptolemy V Epiphanes, who ruled from 204 to 180 BC.[6] According to Josephus, this action of Onias was prompted by his limited spiritual capacity and great greed. However, we must assume that Onias II embarked on his course of action on the assumption that Seleucus II would come out best from the Third Syrian War. In all probability he reckoned that the war might mean the end of Ptolemaic rule. One might conclude from this that there were people in Jerusalem who more or less welcomed the prospect of the end of this rule. At any rate, it is inconceivable that Onias will have been alone in his opposition to the Ptolemies. One important factor that prompted hostility to the Ptolemies was that the people were heavily taxed by them. The high priest handed over the tax, but the people had to provide it.

Josephus also reports that Ptolemy III now sent a delegation to Jerusalem to put pressure on Onias. If the country persisted in its refusal to pay tribute, it would be put under military rule.[7] Not everyone was happy with this course of events. The most important representative of the opposition was Joseph, the son of Tobias (cf.5.2). Joseph was clearly the leader, or at any rate the spokesman, of a group in Jerusalem which, if not Hellenistic, was at least pro-Prolemaic. Presumably this was a group which accepted Ptolemaic rule, above all from economic considerations.

Joseph saw an opportunity to bring the conflict between Onias II and Ptolemy III to an end. One result of this was that the *de facto* political, social and economic power in Jerusalem now fell into his hands. Onias II remained high priest, but in future he had little or no influence.

Another report, also from Josephus,[8] tells of a visit which Ptolemy III is said to have made to Jerusalem during the course of the Third Syrian War. On this occasion Ptolemy is said to have sacrificed to God in the Jerusalem temple, rather than to the gods of Egypt, to give thanks for the favourable outcome of the war. This report has a markedly legendary character. Josephus has foreign leaders visiting the temple of Jerusalem on many occasions (cf.2.3.1), clearly with the aim of convincing his non-Jewish readers of the exceptional character of Israel's religion. There may be a historical nucleus in his report in that Ptolemy may indeed have been in Jerusalem at that time, but it will have been to settle things in connection with the advent of Onias II.

5.2 Oniads and Tobiads

In the previous section we have seen how Onias II and Josephus, the son of Tobias, can be seen as representatives of a particular group. Behind each was a particular family; the families are designated the Oniads and Tobiads. We must now look more closely at them, since they play a prominent role in the history of Israel over the next decades.

The designation Oniads is derived from the high priests who were called Onias. The first to bear this name was Onias I, who held office as high priest in Jerusalem between *c.*323 and 300 BC. In particular, the high priests from this family come into the foreground with the Oniads. Here, in addition to Onias II, as we shall see, Simon II the Just, Onias III and Onias IV were the main figures. It will subsequently become clear that these high priests and their followers, i.e. the Oniads, certainly cannot be said to be specifically inclined towards Hellenism. At the same time this means that in the leading circles in Jerusalem we can occasionally see two groups, one of which can be described as favourable towards Hellenism and the other not. The Tobiads make up the former group.

We know nothing about their origins. It has been assumed that there was a link between the Tobiads from the Hellenistic period and the 'son of Tabeel' mentioned in Isa.7.6,[9] but no convincing proof of this can be given (see also 4.3.2). We find most information about the Tobiads in Josephus, in the so-called Tobiad romance,[10] though the information there must be read with a very critical eye. Josephus puts the events he describes in quite the wrong context, in 198 BC; moreover, this story gives the strong impression that its main concern is to make Joseph and his son Hyrcanus the great figures of the Tobiads.[11]

It is certain that this Joseph is a son of the Tobias mentioned in the Zeno papyri.[12] We may infer from them that the Tobiads had both land and a residence (fortress) in Transjordan.[13] This fortress was in Ammanitis (cf.4.3.2), and must have been in the neigbourhood of ʿAraq el-Emir.[14] Clearly the Tobiads had an important position there. Later they also seem to have had considerable influence in Jerusalem and Samaria, as is particularly evident from the rise of Joseph.

5.3 *The rise of Joseph the Tobiad*

The controversy between Onias II and Joseph described in 5.1.2 is the first clash we know of between the Oniads and the Tobiads. It emerges from this that Joseph had shifted the activities of the Tobiads to Jerusalem, where he doubtless belonged to the city aristocracy. In 5.1.2 we noted that he considerably strengthened his position through his opposition to the high priest Onias II, whose authority he was largely able to take over.

After these events Joseph also seems to have been appointed as 'tax farmer' for Palestine and perhaps even for the whole of 'Syria and Phoenicia'.[15] This function he performed for twenty-two years, probably between 239 and 217 BC,[16] and he did so with a harshness and cruelty which spared nothing and no one. In cities like Ashkelon and Scythopolis he had the chief citizens killed for the slightest protest against the high taxes and confiscated their properties.[17]

Now for the first time in history Jerusalem, too, becomes an important international city. The rise of Joseph also signified a great economic boom. Hengel[18] rightly points out that from now on Jerusalem also becomes important for classical authors and is no longer seen as a small and insignificant state round a temple.

The example of Joseph shows that the rich began to settle in the city, contrary to what had happened earlier. Thus Jerusalem increasingly became a financial and economic centre. In fact Joseph and his family can be regarded as the first great bankers there. Moreover, they had a patron in Alexandria,[19] something which presumably owes a good deal to the large number of Jews who gradually settled there.

A pro-Hellenistic attitude clearly comes to the fore in the life-style of Joseph and the Tobiads. This affinity emerges from their contacts with Samaria,[20] the payment of bribes to the king and his immediate entourage,[21] and the scant respect they seem to have had for Jewish legislation.[22] Thus Joseph can be regarded as an important forerunner to a Hellenistic trend among the aristocracy in Jerusalem and its environs. This trend becomes increasingly strong, and because the Tobiads, apart from Hyrcanus, chose the Seleucid side in about 200 BC, their influence on the course of events in Jerusalem continued to be great and often decisive, even after the end of Ptolemaic rule.

5.4 *The Fourth Syrian War (221-217 BC)*

5.4.1 *The prelude*

After many internal conflicts[23] Antiochus III became king over the Seleucid empire in 223 BC at the age of twenty. Although he was inexperienced, he was soon able to put things in order. He restored the unity of his kingdom by eliminating some of his rivals. After that he prepared for a campaign against Egypt with the aim of conquering the old disputed area of 'Syria and Phoenicia'.

In the meantime, Ptolemy III Euergetes (246-221 BC) had died in Egypt; he was succeeded by his son Ptolemy IV Philopator (221-204 BC). This king was also very young (seventeen years old) when he occupied the throne. His position was far from enviable. After the Third Syrian War his father had completely neglected the Egyptian army. Moreover the young king in fact had no influence. Everything was in the hands of his vizier Sosibius. Sosibius was principally concerned to establish peace in the land and to avoid or eliminate conspiracies. Ptolemy IV also seems to have been all too ready to delegate such matters to others. He preferred to occupy himself with art and religious problems.[24]

Given all this, circumstances seemed particularly favourable for Antiochus finally to wrest from the Ptolemies this territory which for so long had been in dispute.

5.4.2 *The course of the war*

To begin with, success was wholly on the side of Antiochus III. First of all he captured Seleucia,[25] the port of Antioch, which had remained in the possession of Ptolemy III after the Third Syrian War. Then he moved southwards, where he captured the cities of Tyre and Acco (Ptolemais), virtually without striking a blow. These cities also brought him substantial provisions and about forty ships.[26] After that he spent an unnecessarily long time capturing various small cities in Phoenicia and Palestine and on a long-drawn-out siege of the fortress of Dor, a port on the Mediterranean coast south of Carmel. Had Antiochus III continued his advance, he would certainly have succeeded in inflicting a final defeat on Ptolemy, given the deplorable state of the Egyptian army.

By delaying, he played completely into the hands of Sosibius, who was concerned to gain time. Here he succeeded completely, by persuading Antiochus III to accept a four-month cease fire. After this, fortunes were reversed, because Sosibius used the pause to raise a new army. This army included soldiers from the military settlements and, for the first time in the history of the Ptolemies, native Egyptians.

In 217 BC there was a battle at Raphia, which ended with the defeat of Antiochus III. The Seleucid king then had no alternative but to make peace with Ptolemy IV; here the political situation was restored to what it had been before the outbreak of the Fourth Syrian War. Daniel 11.10b-12 gives a summary of the war.

However, the Ptolemies did not exploit their victory. They allowed Antiochus III to withdraw in peace. This tactical error would soon demand its price.

5.4.3 *Palestine in and after the Fourth Syrian War*

In contrast to the three previous Syrian wars, Palestine suffered a great deal from action during the fourth war.

Polybius[27] reports that Antiochus III conquered Philadelphia – which he gives its old name, Rabbath-ammon – in the territory of Samaria. According to some scholars,[28] Samaria also included the territory of Judah. Be this as it may, it is at any rate certain that Antiochus III directed his main attention to the coastal cities and Transjordan. The fact that he fought in Palestine for more than two years is itself an indication that the sufferings in the area were great.

After the battle of Raphia in 217 BC, Ptolemy III stayed in the country with his sister Arsinoe. They visited various cities and sanctuaries at this time. Inscriptions in Joppa and Marisa (on the border between Judaea and Idumaea) bear witness to these visits.[29]

We do not know whether they went to Jerusalem then. The non-canonical III Macc. 1.7ff. suggests something of the kind.[30] According to III Macc. 2.25ff., after his return to Egypt Ptolemy IV persecuted the Jews in Alexandria. Both passages suggest that there were bad relations between this king and Judaea, but we have no further details. Neither Josephus nor other sources give us any information on these points. However, it does not seem improbable that relations between Ptolemy and Judaea were not at their best at this time, given the sympathy shown for Antiochus III in Judaea and Jerusalem during the Fifth Syrian War, as we shall soon see. For want of enough evidence, however, we cannot do more than guess. Hengel's view that on the visit to Palestine mentioned above Ptolemy carried out an administrative reform which also put paid to Joseph the Tobiad's twenty-two-year activity as 'tax farmer' over 'Syria and Phoenicia' is also no more than a hypothesis.[31]

5.5 *The expulsion of the Ptolemies from Palestine*

5.5.1 *The political situation after the Fourth Syrian War*

Despite the fact that the Ptolemies had finally proved victorious in the Fourth Syrian War, the days of their rule over Palestine were numbered.

The victory at Raphia on the one hand meant a great personal triumph for Sosibius, but on the other it also led to a major revival among the native population of Egypt. Thanks to their contribution, the advance of Antiochus

III had been brought to a standstill and the Seleucid army had been forced to retreat. No wonder, then, that this native population made itself felt after the war. It was clear that the Greek overlords had lost their reputation. And now it also emerged that there had never really been a genuine unification of Greeks and Egyptians.[32]

In addition to all this, moreover, the government of Ptolemy IV can be said to have been extremely weak both in domestic and in foreign policy (cf. 5.4.1). This situation did not improve in the slightest when after the death of Ptolemy IV in 204 BC the five-year-old Ptolemy V ascended the throne., Circumstances were quite different for his opponent who had been defeated in 217 BC.

Antiochus III had spent the first years after the defeat at Raphia in putting the eastern frontiers of his empire in order. He was able to extend his empire and influence there and restore the frontiers of his territory to their at the time of Seleucus I (312-281 BC). He also made a secret treaty with Philip V of Macedon, in which agreements were made over a division of the foreign possessions of the Ptolemaic empire.

5.5.2 *The Fifth Syrian War (202-198 BC)*

In 201 BC, Antiochus III – who had taken the title 'the Great' because of his successes – invaded 'Syria and Phoenicia' at the head of a large Seleucid army. He succeeded in occupying virtually the whole territory in a very short time. Evidently the Ptolemies offered him hardly any resistance. The opposition to Antiochus must have come mainly from the military garrisons in this area, but there was not much of it. One exception was the city of Gaza, which put up fierce resistance for a long time. We need not be surprised that Gaza should have been the city to do this. It was the terminus of Arab trade with Egypt. So the city was economically of vital importance and for this reason was also the strongest in military terms.

We have a report of the battle for Gaza from the historian Polybius,[33] in which he reports the fierce opposition of the city.

In the spring of that year (201 BC), Palestine was virtually completely in the hands of Antiochus III. After establishing garrisons and occupying forces throughout the region, he again left the country.

The Ptolemaic general Scopas took advantage of these conditions to launch a counter-attack. In the winter of 201-200 BC he in fact succeeded in conquering a large number of provinces of the territory he had lost. However, this success was only of short duration. In 200 BC Antiochus inflicted a decisive defeat on Scopas at Panium (Caesarea Philippi, well known from the New Testament), at the sources of the Jordan. Two years later 'Syria and Phoenicia' was under Seleucid rule as far as the frontier with Egypt.

5.5.3 *Palestine at the time of the Fifth Syrian War*

Above all in the winter of 201-200 BC, the land must have suffered under the war. This was the period of the counter-offensive launched by Scopas (see 5.5.2) and, immediately after that, of the conquest of the area by Antiochus III. Josephus[34] makes special mention of Samaria, Abila and Gadara. Even Judaea and Jerusalem were not spared all this.[35] The temple must have been badly damaged in this period.[36] This is evident from reports[37] that the then high priest Simon II later (see 6.3) had considerable restoration work carried out on the city and the temple. Furthermore, in a decree of Antiochus III[38] (see 6.2.1) contributions are asked for, among other things, the temple and city of Jerusalem. All this suggests considerable devastation. The scanty reports about the battle fought against the Ptolemaic garrisons in Jerusalem also point in this direction.[39]

There are indications that during the Fifth Syrian War there was a pro-Seleucid party in Judaea and Jerusalem. We have already recalled that most Tobiads chose the Seleucid side at this time (see 5.3). Furthermore, a fragment of Polybius preserved in Josephus[40] reports that the inhabitants of Jerusalem went over to Antiochus III. Daniel 11.14 also suggests this.

It is certain that for his part Antiochus recognized the privileges that Jerusalem and the Judaeans had enjoyed during Ptolemaic rule and moreover – for the moment – granted them a reduction in the taxes which they had hitherto had to pay.[41]

All this put an end to Ptolemaic rule, which had lasted for more than a century (301-198 BC). As had happened now for centuries, the land again came under the rule of new powers. After the Assyrians, the Babylonians, the Persians and the Ptolemies it was now the Seleucids from their centre of power in Antioch who exercised rule over Palestine. Like the previous rulers, the Seleucids, too, were ready to leave the spiritual authority of the high priest in Jerusalem undisturbed. This fitted in very well with their own interests. It was to emerge all too quickly how their own interests were paramount. The cries of joy with which many had greeted the Seleucids were all too soon to fall silent.

Chapter 6

The Beginning of Seleucid Rule
(198-175 BC)

6.1 *The general political situation*

6.1.1 *The time of Antiochus III (222-187 BC)*

Victory over the Ptolemies and the conquest of 'Syria and Phoenicia' did not put an end to the political aspirations of Antiochus III. His aim was to continue to extend the Seleucid empire to the north and west. We have seen (5.5.1) that Antiochus III had made a treaty with Philip V of Macedon even before the Fifth Syrian War, in which he promised to share with Philip the Ptolemaic possessions lying outside Egypt. Antiochus now wanted to put this treaty into effect.

In the meantime, however, a new power had appeared on the political scene, Rome. At about the time that Antiochus III conquered Palestine, the Romans had finally defeated Hannibal. This not only put an end to the Second Punic War (202 BC), but also considerably strengthened the power of Rome. The Romans now directed all their attention to Philip V, an old ally of Hannibal.

An occasion for a war against the Macedonians was soon found. On the basis of his treaty with Antiochus III, Philip was engaged in making himself master of the Ptolemaic possessions in the Aegean Sea. Some Greek cities called in the help of the Romans, who inflicted a decisive defeat on Philip in *c.* 197 BC. Although the Romans withdrew again from Greece some years later, very few Greek cities came well out of their 'liberation', which was accompanied by all kinds of conditions. Some of them now invoked the help of Antiochus III, who hitherto had remained neutral in the conflict.

Antiochus succeeded in landing in Greece with troops and occupying some of it, but he was driven out again in the following year (192 BC). The Romans then in turn landed in Asia Minor, where in 190 BC they inflicted a major defeat on the troops of Antiochus III at Magnesia (cf.Dan.11.18). After that Antiochus had no other choice than to make peace with Rome.

The peace concluded at Apamea in 188 BC was very damaging to him. Among other things he had to give up all the territory west of the Taurus, let his second son, later to become Antiochus IV Epiphanes, go to Rome as a hostage, and pay an indemnity of 15,000 talents. This tribute, unprecedented in ancient history, had to be paid in twelve annual instalments.[1]

It was this last condition in particular which was to have a great influence on political relations between the Seleucid empire and Judaea in the years to come.

The main task of Antiochus III was now to raise this annual payment. In fact he did not have the means to do so, and therefore attempted to get the money he needed by laying his hands on temple treasures. In antiquity temples were not only sanctuaries but also acted as banks, above all after the invention of coinage. For this reason Antiochus went to rob the temple of Bel in Elam. However, this action aroused the wrath of the population. They rebelled and killed Antiochus and those who were helping him with the robbery.[2] Thus 187 BC brought a sorry end to the ambitious rule of Antiochus III the Great (cf. Dan.11.19).

6.1.2 *The time of Seleucus IV (187-175 BC)*

Antiochus III was succeeded by his oldest son Seleucus IV Philopator. The position which this king came to inherit was far from enviable. During his reign his every policy was dominated by the question how the annual tribute imposed by the Romans at the peace treaty of Apamea was to be paid. This is also the context of his abortive plundering of the temple in Jerusalem (cf.6.5).

During his reign, Seleucus IV was also threatened by Ptolemy V of Egypt, who had aspirations to take over the territory of 'Syria and Phoenicia' which Egypt had lost. However, the death of Ptolemy in 181 BC put an end to this threat.[3]

The rule of Seleucus IV came to an end when he was murdered in 175 BC by his minister Heliodorus. However, Heliodorus did not succeed in seizing power. Antiochus IV Epiphanes, the brother of Seleucus IV, successfully prevented him from doing this.

6.2 *The measures taken by Antiochus III in favour of Judaea*

6.2.1 *The letter of Antiochus III to the governor Ptolemy*

All the signs are that after his victory over Ptolemy, Antiochus tried to treat his new subjects well with a lenient policy. A letter which he wrote to Ptolemy, the governor of Coele-Syria, was also meant to serve this end. This letter has been preserved for us by Josephus in his *Jewish Antiquities* (*AJ* XIII, 138-44). The authenticity of the document is still disputed.[4]

In this letter Antiochus first expresses his thanks to the Judaeans who supported him in his struggle against the Ptolemies. The king also gave orders aimed at encouraging as far as possible restoration work on the city and temple and the repopulation of Jerusalem. In addition, the members of the council of elders (the *gerousia*, see 3.4.2), the priests and the rest of the temple personnel were exempt from paying taxes and it was stipulated that the government of Judaea was to be in accordance with the ancestral laws.

In fact this letter contains little that is new. The stipulations in it largely guaranteed a continuation of the policy which had already been carried out since the time of Persian rule and was largely based on support for the priests.[5] Of course the letter provided support and reinforcement for the pro-Seleucid group in the temple city of Jerusalem. However, the favourable financial provisions in the letter seem soon to have been qualified, wholly or in part, as a result of the burden of the heavy payments to Rome which the Seleucids had to make after the peace of Apamea in 188.

6.2.2 *The degree about the ritual purity of the temple*

In addition to this letter Josephus reports a decree of Antiochus III in which aliens are not allowed to enter the sanctuary in Jerusalem and there is a prohibition against keeping unclean animals in the city or introducing them into it.[6] Those who break these regulations have to pay a very heavy fine to the priests. Despite a variety of problems, this document seems to fit well into this period.[7] However, the report by Josephus that the decree was proclaimed 'throughout the kingdom' is much exaggerated.

In his *Jewish War*,[8] Josephus reports that there was an inscription in the temple giving in Greek and Latin letters the prohibition against aliens entering the sanctuary. This inscription was certainly there in Roman times.[9]

It goes without saying that a prohibition against the introduction of unclean animals in Jerusalem and the keeping of them there was not conducive to trade in the city. This was not unwelcome to strict religious groups in Jerusalem, who were always afraid of contacts which arose above all through trade between Judaeans and Gentiles.

6.2.3 *The Hefzibah inscription*

An inscription has been discovered in the region of Hefzibah, west of Scythopolis (the ancient Beth-shean) in Galilee from the years 201-195 BC,[10] which contains a number of decrees of Antiochus III and Seleucus IV connected with 'Syria and Phoenicia'. In it we find regulations of Antiochus III which are particularly aimed at protecting the inhabitants of villages from the excesses of the Seleucid occupying forces. Seleucid soldiers are forbidden to have quarters in these villages or to drive the inhabitants out of their houses. Very strict penalties are imposed on those who break these regulations.[11]

This suggests that Antiochus II was not just concerned to secure the sympathy of leading groups, like those in Jerusalem; he also tried to win the favour of the country people.

6.3 *The high priest Simon II*

At the time when Judaea came under Seleucid rule, Simon II was high priest in Jerusalem. He held this office from about 220-190 BC.

Simon II was a son of Onias II, who had come into conflict with Joseph the Tobiad and after that had comparatively little influence (cf.5.1.2).

Simon must have been a much more powerful figure than his father. At least, in all probability he succeeded in gaining much more influence. At any rate, he is given high praise by Sirach (50.1ff.) as a very skilful political and religious leader.[12] This Simon is presumably the person who is described in Pirqe Aboth I.1 as 'the Just' and is mentioned there as one of the last of the 'Great Assembly' (cf.3.4.2). If this is correct, it is a further indication of the important position that Simon II had in Jerusalem at that time.

We do not know Simon's political attitude towards the Ptolemies. Certainly he saw at an early stage that it was important to have good relations with the Seleucids. The measures that Antiochus III took in connection with the temple in the decrees mentioned in 6.2.1, 6.2.2 suggest good relations with the high priest. Obviously Simon II also had personal responsibility for the implementation of the various regulations mentioned in it. At least, this is what Sirach 50.1ff. suggests.

All this also implies that Simon II and his followers in Jerusalem took pains to preserve their own religious forms. The content of the decrees mentioned above points very clearly in this direction. This fact also implies that Simon II and his followers were certainly not strongly influenced by Hellenism.

6.4 *The conflict within the Tobiad family*

Conflict arose within the Tobiad family even during the lifetime of Simon II. The cause of this conflict must be sought in the hostility between Hyrcanus, the eighth son of Joseph the Tobiad, and the rest of his sons. Hyrcanus was evidently anxious to occupy the same position of power as his father, and for this reason wanted to displace his brothers. They did not take to it very kindly.

To begin with, Hyrcanus seems to have been successful, thanks to his good contacts with the royal court in Alexandria. The change of power in Alexandria evidently turned the tide, for while the rest of the Tobiads sailed with the wind and courted the favour of the Seleucids, Hyrcanus remained faithful to the Ptolemies.[13] This pro-Ptolemaic attitude was presumably crucial in resolving the conflict, and in all probability they owed the continuation of their position in Jerusalem to it.

Hyrcanus, on the other hand, left Jerusalem and went to Transjordan, to his grandfather's stronghold in Ammanitis (see 5.2). There he succeeded in establishing an independent princedom.[14] He maintained it throughout the reign of Antiochus III and Seleucus IV, though his success must be attributed more to the flexible administration of these two kings than to the powers of Hyrcanus. From his base Hyrcanus among other things undertook forays against the Nabataeans.[15]

According to Josephus, this conflict was more than a family dispute: it produced a split in the people.[16] This gave rise to a pro-Seleucid group, to which the majority and most of the Tobiads belonged, and a pro-Ptolemaic group, in which we can put Hyrcanus and his supporters. The fact that Hyrcanus left Jerusalem indicates that the latter were in the minority.

6.5 *The struggle between Onias III and Simon the captain of the temple*

Simon II was succeeded as high priest by Onias III, who held this office between about 190 and 174 BC. From the information at our disposal it would appear that Onias III was a less strong personality than his predecessor. However, we should remember that in the time of Onias III the high priesthood was open to heavy attacks from the Tobiads and moreover suffered under the changed political circumstances resulting from the peace of Apamea (cf. 6.1.1). From that moment on the Seleucid kings were chronically in need of money. One of the consequences was, of course, an increase in the burden of taxation. Even Judaea was not spared this, as is evident from an allusion to Seleucus IV in Dan.11.20.

We have seen that in his attempts to pay the high indemnity to Rome Antiochus III did not stop short of plundering the temple of Bel in Elam (see 6.1.1). According to II Macc.3-4, an attempt was also made in the time of Seleucus IV to seize the temple treasure in Jerusalem.

According to II Macc.3.4 the occasion for this was a difference of opinion over the supervision of the market in Jerusalem between Onias III and a certain Simon. This Simon, a supporter of the Tobiads, was appointed by the king captain of the temple, a post which presumably meant that he was responsible for its finances.[17] It is not clear precisely what the difference of opinion over the market was about. It is possible that Simon wanted to do away with certain restrictions and that Onias rejected this because it would endanger the ritual purity of the market.

According to II Macc.3.5, the consequence of Onias' refusal was that Simon went to Apollonius, the then governor of Coele-Syria, and told him that there were great riches in the temple. He in turn informed Seleucus IV. It is understandable that because Seleucus was in great financial straits he then attempted to lay hands on this treasure. With that in view he sent his minister Heliodorus to Jerusalem.

When Heliodorus arrived in Jerusalem, Onias III told him that the money in the temple was the savings of widows and orphans and a contribution deposited by Hyrcanus, the son of Joseph the Tobiad who was in Transjordan. The rest of the account in II Macc.3.13-40 has a very legendary character, so that we do not know what happened next.[18]

However, it is striking that according to II Macc.3.11 Onias had business dealings with Hyrcanus. This could mean that the dispute with Simon also had a political background. Further support for the conjecture comes from the fact that because of his contacts with Hyrcanus,[19] Onias III tended towards a pro-Ptolemaic policy, while Simon and the rest of the Tobiads saw salvation more in a pro-Seleucid policy. Such an attitude on the part of Onias III would also be understandable in view of the general political situation (see 6.1). After the peace of Apamea the position of the Seleucids was still far from rosy, and this could have led to the thought that a return of Ptolemaic government was quite possible. However, it seems even more probable that Onias III was hostile to the Seleucids.

At all events, political opposition seems to have come to a climax in Jerusalem. On the basis of II Macc.4.3 we may assume that it was even accompanied by unrest and bloodshed. For the moment the party of Onias came out worst. Again through the intervention of Simon, Onias was forced to go to Antioch to give account of his actions there.[20] His mission failed because just as he arrived, Seleucus IV was murdered by Heliodorus, who in turn was driven out soon afterwards by Antiochus IV Epiphanes. This ushered in a new period for Judaea and Jerusalem and indeed for all Palestine.

Onias III never returned to Jerusalem. Some years later he was murdered in captivity in the region of Antioch.

6.6 *The situation in the rest of Palestine*

From the beginning of Seleucid rule Palestine was part of the administrative district of 'Syria and Phoenicia', which in addition to Palestine also included the southern part of Syria and Phoenicia.[21] The Apollonius mentioned in 6.5 was one of the best-known governors of the region.

It is unclear what the administrative division of Palestine was at this time. In addition to the temple state of Judaea, Samaria must certainly be seen as a separate administrative unit. However, it is problematic, for instance, whether Galilee was part of Samaria[22] or whether it is to be seen as a more or less independent entity.[23] Lack of further information leaves us in the dark here.

We also have very little information for this period about further events and the situation in this part of Palestine. According to Josephus,[24] to begin with, this part of Samaria was generally prosperous. On the basis of Sirach 50.25f. we may conjecture that at that time in Jerusalem, at least in certain circles, there was considerable opposition to the 'Samaritans'. Sirach called them 'the foolish people who live in Shechem'. Kippenberg[25] sees this statement as the earliest evidence of Jewish polemic against the 'Samaritans'. The inhabitants of the coastal plain are also ridiculed by Sirach in these verses.

In 6.4 we already saw that in this period an independent princedom came into being in Transjordan under the leadership of Hyrcanus. It is not impossible that other such miniature states came into being about this time, especially in this area.

6.7 *The work and position of Jesus Sirach*

6.7.1 *The work*

According to Sirach 50.27 the author of the book ('The Wisdom of Jesus Sirach') came from Jerusalem. Given that he must be counted as a wisdom teacher, we may assume that, like Koheleth (cf.4.4), he was an important figure. He calls himself a scribe (38.24). This term here has to some degree the later significance of the word.[26]

Since Sirach presupposes the death of Simon II (50.1ff.) and there is no trace in his book of the turbulent times which began with the accession of Antiochus IV Epiphanes, his work can be dated roughly in the time around 190 BC.[27]

The book begins with a prologue in which the grandson of Sirach acknowledges responsibility for the Greek translation of it which he made in about 135 BC on behalf of the Jewish Diaspora in Egypt. This is followed in 1.1-42.14 by a series of sayings, hymns of praise and instructions about the nature and origin of wisdom. Then in 42.13-43.33 we have praise of God's glory in creation and nature. Folowing this we find a section in 44.1-50.21 which is known as the 'praise of the fathers'.[28] The conclusion consists of a thanksgiving and a prayer by Sirach (50.22-51.21).

6.7.2 *Sirach's position*

It is clear that formal Hellenistic influences have not passed by Sirach. There are certain traces of them to be found in his work.[29] However, such influence must not be over-estimated. Even if Sirach could read Greek it is a different matter to assume that he had consideerable knowledge of Greek literature.

In terms of subject-matter we see that Sirach is very firmly opposed to Hellenism.[30] This opposition is expressed above all in his championship of the rule of the priests based on the Law of Moses.[31] He puts particular emphasis on the figure of the high priest. Among other things, this emerges from the fact that in the 'praise of the fathers' three times as much space is devoted to Aaron as to Moses (45.6-22),[32] while Phinehas, a descendant of Aaron, gets as much attention as Moses (45.23-25). The stress on the figure of the high priest is also evident at the end of the 'Praise of the fathers' (50.1-21) in a brilliant description of the high priest Simon II.

All this implies that, albeit in a cautious way,[33] Sirach takes up a particular position in the political difficulties in Jerusalem. In his perception of the dangers of riches (8.2,12) and in his description of the rich aristocracy which makes unheeding use of its power (9.13; 13.9-13), Sirach can only be thinking of the Tobiads.[34]

For all these reasons and because of his stress on the importance of the high priest, Sirach can best be described as a sympathizer with or supporter of the group around the high priest Onias III. Moreover, this attitude characterizes him as someone in whom the spirit of opposition to Hellenism begins to emerge. Sirach can thus be seen as a forerunner of later public opposition to Hellenism.

Chapter 7

The Prelude to the Revolt

7.1 *Antiochus IV Epiphanes (175-164 BC)*

Antiochus IV was a son of Antiochus III. After the peace of Apamea (6.1.1) he had been sent as a hostage to Rome. However, he was set free again in 177 BC in exchange for Demetrius, the son of Seleucus IV, whereupon he settled in Athens. A short time later Seleucus was murdered by Heliodorus (cf. 6.1.2). Antiochus IV, however, succeeded in rapidly removing Heliodorus from the political scene and himself seized power. Antiochus IV was not yet the legal successor of Seleucus IV. Seleucus' son had that position (cf. Dan.11.21).

Obviously all this happened with the tacit approval of the Romans. After the peace of Apamea, the real power in this part of the world rested to an increasing degree with Rome. Moreover, the successes of the Maccabees and the Parthians which are to be described in the following chapters must also be seen in this light. These successes could only be achieved through the diplomacy and political intervention of Rome.[1] The policy of Antiochus IV Epiphanes must also be seen in this context.

In the first instance Antiochus IV made attempts to restore the Seleucid kingdom in its old glory. The campaigns he undertook against Egypt served this end. These campaigns are also important for understanding the situation in Palestine and, in particular, because of the effect that they had on certain events in Jerusalem.

The first campaign took place in 170-169 BC. According to II Macc. 4.21 the occasion for it was the hostile attitude in Egypt towards the Seleucid king. This campaign was particularly successful. Antiochus IV was able to get as far as Alexandria. He then made a treaty with Ptolemy VI (180-145 BC) on very favourable terms which in fact made Ptolemy VI his dependent.

However, Ptolemy broke this treaty very quickly, so as early as 168 BC Antiochus had begun a new campaign against Egypt. This campaign again went very well to begin with. However, at that point the Roman Senate intervened; it was happy for Coele-Syria and Phoenicia to be in Antiochus' possession, but it would not allow the Seleucid ruler to get great power and influence in Egypt. An embassy from Rome told Antiochus shortly and sharply to leave Egypt.[2] Antiochus had no choice but to obey.

It hardly needs to be pointed out that this was a great humiliation to the Seleucid king. It also meant that a definitive end had now come to the position of power occupied for some time by the Seleucid kingdom in this part of the world.

Antiochus made a reputation not only in the political sphere but also in the sphere of religion. During his long stay in Rome and Athens (from 188-175 BC), Greek culture and religion in particular seem to have made a deep impression on him. All this was certainly significant for his religious policy. Two important innovations by Antiochus IV should probably also be seen in this light. In the first place he assumed the cult name *theos epiphanes* (the manifest god), and secondly he replaced the image of the traditional Seleucid Apollo with that of Zeus Olympius on the reverse of the Antiochene tetra-drachm.[3] All this clearly influenced later events in Palestine.

7.2 *The dispute over the figure of the high priest*

7.2.1 *The emergence of Jason*

After Onias III had gone to Antioch (cf.6.5), his brother Jason made an appearance, ostensibly as his representative.[4] However, soon afterwards Jason (the Greek form of the name Jeshua) obtained the permanent post of high priest from the king.[5] This presumably happened shortly after the accession of Antiochus Epiphanes. Jason voluntarily offered the king an increase in taxes and an extra single contribution (II Macc.4.7-8). He then, according to II Macc.4.9, offered the king more money if he would consent to the establish-ment of a sports centre (*gymnasium*) and a training centre (*ephebeia*) in Jerusalem to instil the Hellenistic spirit in young men. Moreover, he asked the king to regard the citizens of Jerusalem as 'Antiochenes'. This meant that the inhabitants of Jerusalem would enjoy the same privileges as those of Antioch.

Evidently this did not yet mean that from then on Jerusalem was to be seen as a Greek polis. It is also obvious that Jason could not take such initiatives without having a particular group behind him (cf. also I Macc.1.13f.). We cannot establish with any certainty who belonged to this party, but Hengel's view[6] that it consisted of the priests and well-to-do who held the *de facto* power in Jerusalem seems reasonable (see also II Macc.4.14). We even get the impression from I Macc.1.11 (cf. Dan.11.23) that there were a large number of such people. It goes without saying that the old clan of Tobiads belonged to the group.

This 'Hellenistically inclined' group very probably formed a more or less independent community within Jerusalem.[7] Such Greek communities (and other ethnic groups) existed elsewhere among the native population. For example, the Jews in Alexandria formed such a community there,

It is conceivable that landowners and merchants in Jerusalem were particularly sympathetic to this 'Hellenistic' movement, hoping that it would stimulate economic growth[8] and that the city would obtain the right to mint its own coins (a right which Antiochus IV had granted to a number of cities in the Seleucid empire).[9] On some coins the citizens of the cities which minted them are called 'Antiochenes', i.e. the very designation that Jason wanted to secure for the Hellenists in Jerusalem (see above).[10]

All this does not of itself imply that Hellenism in Jerusalem had already assumed a very radical form. It is equally possible that in the time of Jason there was no more than a tendency towards Hellenism.[11]

It is understandable that Antiochus IV, who, like his predecessors, was desperately in need of money, should have gratefully accepted Jason's offer. It is just as understandable that this development should have caused great scandal among particular groups in Jerusalem and in Judaea. For the moment these could probably not give much vent to their indigation. However, it would all too quickly become evident that there was already a spirit of opposition abroad.

Meanwhile, in 171 Jason's high priesthood had already come to an end. In that year Jason sent Menelaus, a brother[12] of Simon, the temple overseer mentioned in 6.5, to the king to pay the usual tribute. However, when Menelaus arrived in Antioch, for the promise of a payment of 300 talents more than Jason had sent, he managed to get Antiochus IV to appoint him high priest in Jerusalem.

In doing this Antiochus was treading on dangerous ground. While Jason could trace back his ancestry to the Zadokites, the only family from which the high priest might come, Menelaus, who came from another priestly family,[13] was a different matter. To nominate such a figure as high priest was in conflict with the tradition and raised the most enormous problems. This course of action shows that Antiochus IV was badly informed about the religious situation in Jerusalem.

At all events, in the meantime the result of all this was that the days of Jason as high priest were numbered. Jason understood this and also that his life in Jerusalem was no longer secure. So he fled as rapidly as possibly to Transjordan (cf. II Macc.4.26).

7.2.2 *Menelaus as high priest*

Menelaus held the office of high priest from about 172 to 162 BC. According to Josephus,[14] in contrast to Jason, he could rely on the support of the Tobiads. This account seems quite trustworthy. In the last resort Jason was still part of the Oniad family and was probably too moderate in his approach for the Tobiads. With the fall of Jason an end had now come to the dominant position which the Oniads had long held in Jerusalem.

In the meantime the high priesthood of Menelaus caused him a great many difficulties. The greatest problem with which he was confronted was how to pay the 300 extra talents he had promised to Antiochus IV. He did not succeed in getting the payment together. Although the king summoned him to explain why, he was evidently able to find an excuse. At all events, he continued to hold office as high priest.

While Menelaus was with the king, his brother Lysimachus had been appointed his replacement in Jerusalem. He did not hesitate to help himself to treasure from the temple, with the result that a raging mob killed him on the spot.[15] When three delegates from Jerusalem sought out Antiochus IV in Tyre to make a complaint about this, they were put to death on the orders of the king (II Macc.4.43-48).

Menelaus again got into difficulties when during an absence of Antiochus IV he was able to bribe Andronicus, his representative in Antioch, with some of the temple treasure to have Onias III murdered in captivity.[16] After his return Antiochus IV had Andronicus executed for this, but he left Menelaus completely untouched. In all probability, the reason why Menelaus again got of scot-free was the mutual financial concern which he shared with Antiochus.[17]

As can be imagined, all these events did not do Menelaus' position in Jerusalem any good. The resistance against him steadily increased. According to Josephus[18] there seems to have been a change in sympathy among the population over politics. In the time of Hyrcanus (cf. 6.4) the majority seems to have taken the side of the pro-Seleucid Tobiads. With the emergence of Menelaus the situation seems to have changed.

Such a change is quite understandable in the circumstances. While it had promised to be light at the beginning, the burden of taxation under the Seleucid government after the peace of Apamea in 188 BC was presumably greater than it had ever been in the time of the Ptolemies. Furthermore, in the religous sphere the Ptolemies were much more cautious and detached than someone like Antiochus IV Epiphanes.

The fall of Jason described in 7.2.1 can also be seen in this light. Jason was probably not only too moderate for the Tobiads, but may also have been suspected of having pro-Ptolemaic sympathies. His flight to what was (at least earlier) the pro-Ptolemaic stronghold of Ammanitis in Transjordan may point in ths direction. For that reason there is something to be said for the view that Menelaus was little more than an unwilling tool in the hands of the Tobiads.[19] At least that made his position as high priest undisputed. But the problems with which he was confronted continued. That will become clear in what follows.

7.2.3 *Jason's revolt*

II Maccabees 5.5ff. describes an attempt by Jason to regain the office of high priest by means of a revolt. According to II Macc.5.5 he went to Jerusalem with about a thousand men and caused a terrible blood-bath. Menelaus had to take refuge in a suburb of the city.

Josephus[20] also mentions a revolt by Jason. According to him the majority of the people were behind Jason. This majority consisted of pro-Ptolemaic Oniads,[21] who here joined forces with Jason against a pro-Seleucid minority.

Thus the picture painted by II Macc. is in some ways differnt from that of Josephus. However, Josephus does not give us any information about the revolt, but simply reports it as a fact.

The only certain conclusion that can be drawn on the basis of these two sources is that there was a revolt by Jason against Menelaus. Given Jason's earlier activity as high priest, when he certainly did not seem to be anti-Hellenistic, we may reasonably suppose that this was primarily a conflict between two rival Hellenistic groups.[22] However, it seems improbable that the majority of the population felt deeply involved. Presumably that is the reason why important sources like Daniel and I Maccabees are completely silent about this event. We are also in the dark about when the event took place. Some scholars have suggested 169 BC, immediately after the first campaign of Antiochus IV against Egypt;[23] others 168 BC, directly after his second campaign.[24]

One thing is clear, though: in this conflict Jason came off worst. According to II Macc. 5.7ff. he had to flee and could not find refuge anywhere. He did not even find sanctuary with Aretas, ruler of the 'Arabians' (which probably means the Nabataeans), or in Egypt. Finally he died in the land of the 'Lacedaemonians', i.e. in Sparta.

It is also unclear who drove Jason out of Jerusalem. Tcherikover[25] suggested a third group made up of the Hasidim (see 8.1.3), who formed a religious rather than a social movement. However, this view has no support in our sources. It seems more likely that Jason fled from the Seleucid troops.

7.3 *Antiochus IV's actions against Jerusalem*

7.3.1 *The plundering of the temple*

We have three reports of a plundering of the temple by or on the orders of Antiochus IV.

The first is in I Macc.1.20-24. This mentions the year 143 by the Seleucid chronology, i.e. 169 BC.[26] II Maccabees 5.15f. also mentions a plundering of the temple, in which Menelaus accompanied Antiochus IV as a guide. This plundering is said to have taken place after Antiochus' second expedition to Egypt and Jason's revolt. The king is supposed to have interpreted the revolt as a rebellion by Judaea (II Macc.5.11) and to have occupied Jerusalem at that time by force. Thousands of inhabitants are said to have been killed, with others being carried away as slaves. The plundering of the temple in 168 is supposed to be set against this background. Josephus also appears to have had the same date in mind in *AJ* XII, 248-50, when he mentions a plundering of the temple by Antiochus IV.

However, the question is whether this information suggests that the temple was plundered on two different occasions. Given that both in Dan.11.28-31 and in *AJ* XII, 246-50 (though this account is somewhat confused in Josephus), two visits by Antiochus IV seem to be mentioned, it would appear that we should suppose that on both occasions the temple was plundered. Since I Maccabees was Josephus' most important source for the period 175-134 BC,[27] he must have taken the information about the plundering of the temple in 168 BC from another source, perhaps the history of Nicolaus of Damascus.[28]

7.3.2 *Measures of Antiochus IV against Jerusalem*

Antiochus IV also took other measures against the city of Jerusalem, probably in close connection with the events just mentioned and his forced retreat from Egypt in 168 BC (see 7.1). The walls of the city were dismantled, and a heavily fortified citadel, the Acra, was set up over against Mount Zion. The Acra was not just a base for a garrison but at the same time a kind of Greek polis with its own institutions.[29] We find an account of the building of this Acra in both I Macc. (1.33) and Josephus (*AJ* XII, 251). In Josephus it is Antiochus himself who goes to Jerusalem, while in I Maccabees an official responsible for taxes is sent by the king with a great army against the city. This official is probably none other than the Apollonius mentioned in II Macc.5.24 (see also 6.5).

It is clear from these measures that Antiochus regarded something like Jason's revolt (7.2.3) as primarily a political dispute. So he treated it as such. Moreover, since the Romans had ruined his campaign against Egypt Judaea became all the more important to him because this area was now frontier territory. Antiochus must have been particularly concerned to maintain law and order there.

7.4 *The religious situation*

7.4.1 *The decree on religion*

I Maccabees 1.41 reports a decree which Antiochus IV is said to have promulgated to make 'all in his kingdom one people', stipulating 'that each should give up his customs'.

One would expect that there would be at least traces in non-Jewish sources of such a decree affecting everyone in the Seleucid empire (cf. also I Macc.1.51). However, this is not the case. Daniel 11 and II Maccabees also make no mention of any such decree for the whole of the Seleucid empire. The same thing also holds for Josephus. So we must infer that Antiochus IV never in fact promulgated a decree relating to all the empire. The only conclusion we can come to is that the decree concerned just Judaea. This also emerges from the fact that of the eleven verses which deal with the decree, only nine refer to Judaea, while just the beginning and the end refer to the Seleucid empire.

All this can only mean that there is no reason for supposing a general religious persecution in the Seleucid realm in the time of Antiochus IV. On the contrary, there are many indications that Antiochus was tolerant to local cults.[30] The only conclusion that we can draw from I Macc.1.41-51 is that there must have been a religious persecution in this period which was limited to the territory of Judaea (see 7.4.3). Bunge's theory that the Jews outside Judaea were also affected by the persecution[31] seems completely untenable.[32]

As for the background of the information in I Macc.1.41-51, there is much to be said for Lebram's view[33] that the author of I Macc. made an attempt here to put what is mentioned in Dan.11.36-39 in a broad historical framework.[34] At most one can say that the decree in I Macc.1.41-51 and the description in Dan.11.36-39 were influenced by events which were experienced as a more or less total religious persecution at a local level.[35]

7.4.2 *The 'Samaritans' request*

According to Josephus, at this time the 'Samaritans' sent a letter to Antiochus IV (reproduced in *AJ* XII, 258-61) asking him to regard them as non-Jews and to exempt them from taxation. Moreover they asked for their temple on

Mount Gerizim to be allowed to bear the name Zeus Hellenios (or Zeus Xenios[36]). This request was accepted by Antiochus IV (see *AJ* XII, 262-3). The authenticity of the letter and the answer to it have been sufficiently demonstrated by Bickerman,[37] though a later Jewish revision is perhaps not entirely to be excluded.[38]

It is striking that in these passages in Josephus the name 'Samaritan' does not yet appear, nor does it in Sirach 50.26, so presumably it was still unknown at this time. Furthermore, this group was evidently still seen as part of Israel. This seems at least to follow from the fact that here in Josephus, as in II Macc.6.2, it is mentioned in the context of action directed against the Jews.[39]

However, the question is whether the request mentioned above came directly from the 'Samaritans' themselves. On the basis of a closer investigation of a variety of texts,[40] Kippenberg has come to the conclusion that this particular request was in fact made by a colony of Sidonians (cf. also *AJ* XII, 258 and 262), who had settled in Shechem at the time of the Seleucids. In this connection it does not seem coincidental that according to II Macc.6.2 the temple on Gerizim was named after 'Zeus Xenios' (the god of foreigners). Presumably these Sidonians, like the 'Samaritans', were not particularly well disposed to 'Hellenism'. One pointer in this direction is a report in II Macc.5.22f. that Antiochus IV left behind governors 'to suppress the people' both in Jerusalem and on Gerizim. Philip the Phrygian was governor of Jerusalem and Andronicus governor of Gerizim.

The correspondence mentioned by Josephus also seems to indicate that the religious group centred on Gerizim asked to be allowed to celebrate the sabbath undisturbed and that this request was also granted without further ado. This again indicates that there can hardly have been any large-scale religious persecution in the time of Antiochus IV, and confirms the view that what happened was merely an internal Jewish affair (see 7.4.3). The aim of the Samaritan letter was therefore in all probability to seek protection from the king against the all too active moves towards 'Hellenization' which were already being made by a Hellenistic group in Jerusalem, when, with the help of their Seleucid supporters, these were extending their activities even as far as Shechem and its environs.

7.4.3 *The background and character of the religious persecution*

In the preceding section we already noticed that there can be no question of a general religious persecution in the Seleucid empire in the time of Antiochus IV, but that it was principally limited to Judaea. This view has been demonstrated convincingly in a number of studies.[41]

The question now arises as to why Antiochus IV should have embarked on such a persecution in Judaea. In this connection much emphasis is placed on a remark by Tacitus[42] that Antiochus IV strove to do away with Jewish belief and introduce Greek customs. However, it would seem that here Tacitus has incorporated very anti-Jewish sources,[43] so that not too much weight can be put on this remark.

Daniel (11.30) connects the persecution with the disappointment of the king on his Egyptian campaigns. Here the stress falls (see v.30b) on the king's interest in those who 'forsook the holy covenant'. These people are without doubt the supporters of Antiochus IV in Jerusalem. At that time it was certainly very attractive, both politically and financially, for the king to favour this particular group in Jerusalem.

According to this view the Seleucid ruler will have taken a number of measures against the existing cult which in fact restricted the privileges formerly given by Antiochus III (cf.6.2). However, the measures should be attributed not so much to Antiochus IV as to those inclined towards Hellenism in Jerusalem.[44] From the Acra and under the direction of the high priest Menelaus, a number of changes were introduced in the sphere of the cult which angered a large proportion of the population. However, Menelaus and his followers were able to convince the king of their utility.[45] The aim of these changes was to give Jewish worship a more Hellenistic form. One means towards this end was the adoption of the name Zeus Olympius in place of the 'Lord of heaven', which had been usual since Persian times as a designation for God, and to set up a second altar, or perhaps a holy stone, on the existing altar of burnt offering in the temple of Jerusalem. This second altar or stone is referred to by Daniel (11.31; 12.11) as the 'abomination of desolation'.[46] Moreover, the cult was not limited to one place, but altars were erected in several places in Judah (cf. I Macc.1.54).

In connection with this, I Macc.1.47; II Macc.6.21; 7.1 report that the Judaeans were forced to sacrifice pigs. Such sacrifices were rejected among the Syrians, and the Greeks were not in the habit of offering pigs to Zeus as a sacrifice. As Bickerman rightly observes,[47] the sole aim of compelling the Jews to make this sacrifice was to attack the special character of the Jewish religion.

It follows from this that a Seleucid king would never have hit on the idea of introducing pigs as sacrificial animals. This fact is a further indication that almost all the incursions in the sphere of Jewish religion must be attributed to the Hellenists in Jerusalem, though they happened with the consent and even perhaps the support of Seleucid officials and soldiers.

We should not suppose that the persecution in Jerusalem and Judaea was on a large scale. Of course we might get this impression not only from I Macc. but also from II Macc., but the latter is noticeably dependent on the former.[48]

Josephus also suggests something of this kind (*AJ* XII, 253ff.), but his most important source is also I Maccabees.

However, we have seen (1.2.2) that I Maccabees was primarily written with the aim of demonstrating the legitimacy of the Hasmonaean dynasty and thus the attitude of Simon Maccabaeus and his followers to the high priest-king.[49] Since the Maccabees did not belong to the legitimate high-priestly family, the approach of the author of I Maccabees was to show them not only as deliverers of the people but above all as defenders of true religion. The greater the persecution that was described, the greater the prestige of the Hasmonaeans in this sphere. All this must have served as a motivation at least to call them high priests, despite their origin.

As a result of all this, I Maccabees and sources dependent on it like II Maccabees and Josephus cannot be cited as proof of a large-scale religious persecution in Judaea. Rather, we must assume that the persecution was only a limited one.[50]

7.5 *Apocalyptic*

It might be useful at this stage to give some information about the phenomenon of apocalyptic, which was to play an increasingly prominent role in the next period of Israelite history.

The word apocalyptic is connected with a Greek word which means 'unveil'. In theology it is used to denote the thought-patterns and imagery which appear in a number of Jewish writings between about 300 BC and AD 100.[51]

We already find the first literary products of apocalyptic in the Old Testament. Among them may be listed Isa.24-27 (the Isaiah apocalypse); Zech.12-14 and large parts of Daniel.

Opinions vary widely as to the origin of apocalyptic. It is usually seen as an offshoot of prophecy,[52] but wisdom[53] and the cult[54] have also been connected with its origin. Then we also have the view of Plöger[55] that conventicles of pious Jews are to a large degree responsible for the phenomenon. So it is obvious that there can be no question of a common view of the origin of apocalyptic. Presumably a number of influences were at work, since apocalyptic as such cannot be regarded as a homogeneous whole.

The heyday of apocalyptic falls in the period from *c.*165 BC on. A whole series of apocalyptic writings appeared at this time. In addition to Daniel, the most important of them are I Enoch, Jubilees, IV Ezra, the Testaments of the Twelve Patriarchs and (in the New Testament) the Revelation of John.

The most prominent characteristics of apocalyptic can be said to be pseudonymity, numerical symbolism, secret language, a doctrine of angels, references to the coming time of salvation and a division of history into periods.[56] That does not mean that all these characteristics appear in every apocalyptic writing.

Pseudonymity occurs where, in apocalyptic, visions are attributed to great figures from the past like Enoch, Moses, Isaiah and Daniel. By means of these visions these figures then make the secrets of history known to believers.[57]

Numbers always have symbolic value in apocalyptic. Thus the figure four usually serves to indicate totality. Numbers also give a point of reference, since everything is defined by them, like the duration of the world empires and the time that evil will rule over the world.[58]

As to secret language, names from the past are often used to denote contemporary rulers and lands. Thus for example Babylon is used in Revelation (18.2) for Rome. Animals often serve to denote individuals and peoples. The just are described as sheep or lambs (cf. Enoch 90.6-9; Matt.25.31ff.), and the four kingdoms in Dan.7 are described as beasts.

The figure of the angel comes increasingly to the fore in apocalyptic literature. Thus in Daniel there is mention of the angels Gabriel (cf.8.16) and Michael (12.1). These two figures prominent in Daniel belong among the four or seven archangels in other apocalyptic writings (cf. Enoch 9.1; also Tobit 12.15). In Daniel we do not yet have a developed angelology; that comes in the later post-canonical books.

History is divided into periods, as is evident in the account of the four world empires in Dan.7. After these comes the time of salvation (7.13). There is also a marked distinction between 'this (evil) world' and the 'new world to come'.

The 'world to come' will emerge after the downfall of 'this world', in which believers now live and are oppressed. In this expectation, which is expressed in visions, the coming Messiah becomes increasingly significant. This messiah is sometimes described as a national and sometimes as a heavenly figure. Two or three messianic figures are even distinguished in the Qumran community: a messianic king (from the house of David), a messianic priest (from the family of Aaron), and a prophet, who functions as forerunner of the messiah or as an Elijah redivivus.[59]

Apocalyptic movements most often come to the fore in times of oppression and persecution. However, the aim of apocalyptic is to give encouragement by stressing that all powers, even the greatest world empires, will not last and that eventually the kingdom of God, the time of salvation, will dawn. Therefore men are summoned to look closely at the past so as to be able to recognize the signs of the times in their own day. In this way they can face the future with confidence.[60]

7.6 *The literature from this period*

7.6.1 *The Book of Daniel*

By far the most important work from this period is the book of Daniel. It is almost unanimously accepted that the work was written about 167-164 BC.[61] From a literary point of view the book consists of a narrative section (chs.1-6) and an apocalyptic part (chs.7-12). Moreover, part has been transmitted in Hebrew and part in Aramaic.

Despite the complexity of this book, the majority of commentators believe that it is a literary unity.[62] Views differ over the milieu from which Daniel derives. Many scholars[63] think in this connection of the circles of the 'pious' (Hasidaeans or Hasidim). Lebram[64] thinks of priestly circles. His view is based not least on the fact that the cult occupies an important place in the book of Daniel. Presumably we need not distinguish these two views too sharply. The little information we have about the Hasidaeans in the books of Maccabees[65] at least suggests that the cult was very important for them.

The book of Daniel and especially Dan.7-12 must be seen as one of the most important apocalyptic writings. This work marked the beginning of the heyday of apocalyptic (cf.7.5).

Daniel gives us some idea of the tense situation that prevailed in Judaea about 165 BC. It is clear that the author knew the events of this time from personal experience. He depicted Antiochus IV Epiphanes as the great evildoer who was responsible for disaster coming upon city and land.[66] He does not have much respect for the Maccabees. Final deliverance will only come from God. In this respect even the Hasidaeans are only 'a little help' (11.34).

7.6.2 *The rest of the literature from this period*

The most important other writings from this period are a number of apocryphal and pseudepigraphical works.

Most important of the pseudepigrapha is I Enoch (Ethiopian Enoch). Some parts of the book, attributed to the Enoch mentioned in Gen.5.24, certainly come from this time, like the so-called Book of Watchmen or the angelological book (6-36) and the astronomical book (72-82). A number of fragments of Enoch written in Aramaic appear among the scrolls found near the Dead Sea.[67] Like Daniel, I Enoch, too, had a great influence on apocalyptic.[68]

Of the apocryphal books, mention must be made here of III Ezra and Judith. The former in some places recalls the book of Daniel, as in 4.40,58,[69] and may perhaps come from a rather later period than Daniel.[70] This is also true of the book of Judith,[71] which seems above all to have been written under the impact of events from the time of the Maccabees.

Chapter 8

The Maccabaean Struggle

8.1 *Background to the various groups*

8.1.1 *The supporters of Hellenism in Jerusalem*

In the previous chapter we saw how this group tried to make first of all the population of Jerusalem and later also the rest of the country, including Shechem, adopt Hellenistic culture. Their chief aim was to abolish the special status of Judaism.

Even after the events described in 7.2, for a long time the leadership of the group remained – at least in name – in the hands of Menelaus. An end to this came only in *c.*163/2 BC, when he was killed on the orders of Antiochus V.

We can begin by assuming that this group was relatively small.[1] However, its influence and authority was very great, because for the most part it consisted of the important upper stratum of the population, which had a considerable amount of influence and power, above all in the economic sphere (see e.g. 5.3).

All this means that, leaving aside religious conflicts, we certainly need to reckon with social and economic differences between the supporters of Hellenism and the rest of the population. As we have seen, in the meantime Menelaus had voluntarily raised the tribute due to the Seleucid king, which was already high (see 7.2.1). Of course this tax had to be paid by the people, and it was a burden which weighed heaviest on the shoulders of those who had least possessions. Such a development inevitably caused bitterness, and was certainly one of the most important motives for the outbreak of a rebellion. This conclusion must also be drawn from a letter attributed to Demetrius I (I Macc.10.26-45), in which he tries to secure the loyalty of Jonathan (cf.8.5). The letter first (I Macc.10.28-30) promises exemption from many high taxes. This fact is an important indication of the considerable role that economic factors played in the revolt.

8.1.2 *The Maccabees*

The members of the group which played by far the greatest part in the rebellion are known as the Maccabees. This name is taken from the nickname 'the Maccabaean' (presumably 'the hammer') given to Judas, the son of the priest Mattathias, who rapidly became the leader of the revolt. At a later time this family became known as the 'Hasmonaeans', derived from Hasmon, their putative ancestor.[2]

The Maccabaean revolt began not in Jerusalem but in the country (cf. 8.2.1), in Modein, where Mattathias and his family lived. This is an indication that the old conflict between the rich upper class in Jerusalem and the peasant population in the country[3] had again broken out fiercely. In the course of time this conflict steadily increased. We have seen that in the time of Joseph the Tobiad the great landlords preferred to live in Jerusalem. The burden which this group, too, must have represented and the cost of their rich life-style was passed on to the peasant population,[4] who in addition also had to give up part of their harvest for the Seleucid king (cf. I Macc.10.30). It was this group which played an important and often decisive role in the revolt, so it is not surprising that their leaders belonged to the lower priestly class. They were close to the ordinary people, while the powerful priestly families in Jerusalem had allied themselves to the rich aristocracy there.

All this clearly indicates that the Maccabaean revolt must be seen primarily as a peasant war. Bickerman also comes to this conclusion,[5] but in fact he sees the war only as a religious war. Most emphasis is placed on this dimension in the literature (Daniel; I & II Maccabees), but that is because only this aspect was important to later generations and to Daniel. In reality (see above), social and economic factors largely determined the character and course of the revolt.

Of course the significance of religion in all this must not be understimated. The country population was not only among the poorest, but also among the most conservative parts of the people. For them, faithful as they were to Yahwism, the idea of a process of Hellenization was in itself a scandal. However, this attitude does not emerge so much among the Maccabees as among the Hasidaeans, the group whom we shall consider next.

8.1.3 *The Hasidaeans*

The Hasidaeans (Greek) or Hasidim (Hebrew, meaning pious) are a group which played a significant role during the revolt and obviously afterwards. This group is mentioned by name for the first time in I Macc.2.42; 7.13; II Macc.14.6.

In I Macc.2.42 they are mentioned as having joined the Maccabees shortly after the beginning of the revolt, and in 7.13 they are those who wanted to collaborate with the newly nominated high priest Alcimus. According to II Macc.14.6 Alcimus joined forces with the Maccabees. In I Macc.2.42 they are further described as a group of those who 'offered themselves willingly for the law'.

We can deduce from all this that the Hasidaeans took part in the rebellion for only a short time and that their main aim was to live on the basis of the Torah without any hindrance.

This gives the strong impression that even before the rise of the Maccabees the Hasidaeans must already have existed as a kind of party.[6] At the same time we can conclude from this that the Hasidaeans gave a central place to life according to the Mosaic law. As long as freedom of worship was at stake they took the side of the Maccabees, but as soon as this freedom was achieved, they withdrew at least a good deal of their military support.

The influence of this group was very great, both directly and indirectly. As we shall see later, there is a clear relationshp between the Hasidaeans and the Qumran community, the Pharisees and the Essenes. The influence of the group can also be seen in the earliest apocalyptic literature, for example in I Enoch 90.6-15, while the author of Daniel (see 7.6.1) was at least a sympathizer with the Hasidaeans.

8.2 The beginning of the revolt

8.2.1 The emergence of Mattathias

Both in I Maccabees (2.15ff.) and in Josephus (*AJ* XII, 268ff.), we are given an account of the way in which Mattathias rebelled in Modein against the command of Antiochus IV to offer sacrifice there in accordance with the royal command. Mattathias refused to obey the king, and when another Judaean was prepared to do so, he killed him and the king's representative. After this he fled into the hills with his five sons, John, Simon, Eleazar, Judas and Jonathan, along with other fugitives. This event marked the beginning of the revolt.

Troops from Jerusalem, probably for the most part the Seleucid occupying forces which supported Menelaus and his followers, were sent to track down the rebels.[7] One group, evidently Hasidaeans, was massacred on a sabbath because its members refused to offer any resistance on that day.[8] The result of this was that Mattathias and his followers decided from then on even to fight on the sabbath if they were attacked.[9] Another important consequence of this massacre was that the Hasidaeans – or at least many of them - now took the side of the Maccabees in the revolt. This brought considerable reinforcements to the movement.

Mattathias himself was hardly involved in this revolt. He died right at the beginning, which must have been about 166/165 BC.[10]

8.2.2 *The first successes of Judas*

After the death of Mattathias his son Judas became leader of the rebels. It is not clear why he took over this role and not, for example, the oldest son of Mattathias.

Judas mustered and organized his troops and waged a kind of guerrilla war. He soon proved very successful. He defeated an army under the leadership of Apollonius, and killed Apollonius. Seron, according to I Macc.3.13 'the commander of the Syrian army', also suffered a heavy defeat at the hands of the Maccabees. This happened at Beth-horon, about twelve miles north-west of Jerusalem.[11] These successes were due above all to the fact that there were only a few Seleucid troops in the country. Those there were belonged to the auxiliaries stationed in the Acra and elsewhere, who were in no way capable of coping with a guerrilla war in the hills. Moreover, the supporters of Hellenism seem to have underestimated the Maccabaean movement.

While these events were taking place, Antiochus IV was in the East, where he was concentrating all his attention on a war against the Parthians.[12] This shows that he had less interest in events in Judaea than sources like I Maccabees and Josephus suggest.

Only in the autumn of 165 BC did Judas's successes begin to cause some anxiety to the central government. Antiochus IV then gave his chancellor Lysias, his representative in the capital and at the same time the guardian of his son, orders to quash the revolt. Lysias then sent three Syrian generals, Ptolemy, Nicanor and Gorgias, to Judaea. However, they were defeated by Judas near Emmaus.

Immediately after this,[13] Lysias himself went with an army to Judaea. Going through Idumaea he advanced as far as Beth-zur, where he had an encounter with the Maccabees. According to I Macc.4.34f.; II Macc.11.1; *AJ* XII, 314, Lysias was defeated here,[14] but presumably the situation was rather more complicated. Some documents in II Macc.11 rather give the impression that circumstances forced Lysias and the Maccabees to negotiate. Lysias was compelled to return to Antioch by affairs of state (a serious illness of Antiochus IV).

We find the first document in which Lysias reports that he will intervene with the king in favour of Judaea in II Macc.11.17-21. Antiochus IV died in

164 BC, i.e. about the same time,[15] but his son and successor Antiochus V (164-162 BC) responded to the mediation of Lysias by giving the Judaeans full religious freedom. A letter from this king to Lysias to that effect is reproduced in II Macc.11.23-26. In a letter addressed directly to the Judaeans Antiochus V reports that he is granting an amnesty to all rebels who return home and giving the Judaeans permission to live according to their (Mosaic) laws. Otherwise the whole situation remained unchanged (see II Macc.11.27-33). Given the mediating role which is attributed to Menelaus in this letter, it must be authentic, since the author of II Maccabees elsewhere always puts ths high priest in an unfavourable light.

Another factor seems to have determined events after the defeat of Bethzur to a considerable extent, namely the intervention of Rome. At least we get this impression from a letter which is reproduced in II Macc.11.34-38.[16]

8.2.3 *The purification and reconsecration of the temple*

In close conjunction with the events mentioned above, the purification and rededication of the temple took place on 25 Kislev (about 15 December) 164 BC.

We have a letter about this purification of the temple in II Macc.1.10-2.18, addressed to the Jews living in the Diaspora. This is presented as a letter from Judas addressed to Aristobulus, a Jewish governor in Alexandria. At the very least, there is considerable doubt[17] as to whether this letter does in fact come from Judas.[18] However, contacts with Egypt seem possible in this period.[19]

The feast of Hanukkah is still celebrated annually in commemoration of the rededication of the temple. In one respect the inauguration of this feast represents a break with the past. Hitherto every feast was established upon the basis of a divine instruction given in the Old Testament. According to I Macc.4.59; II Macc.10.5-8 and *AJ* XII, 325, the feast of Hanukkah was initiated by Judas and his followers, i.e. on the basis of a human decision. This was common practice among the surrounding peoples, but it was a far-reaching innovation for Israelite tradition and implies that by his action Judas was introducing a Hellenistic custom into Judaism.

Neither Maccabees nor Josephus speaks of the eight-branched candlestick which is customary at this feast. Obviously the custom comes from a later time.

8.2.4 *New successes of Judas*

In 163 BC Judas laid siege to the Acra in Jerusalem. However, the siege was unsuccessful. Judas's guerrillas had neither the expertise nor the means to capture a fortress. Moreover, those besieged in the Acra had called on the

Seleucids for help, and in fact they soon appeared on the scene. Lysias again commanded the Seleucid army. In the meantime he had proclaimed himself regent of the young king Antiochus V and now in fact represented the supreme authority among the Seleucids.

Thereupon Judas had to break off his siege of the Acra. There was an encounter at Beth-zechariah, south of Bethlehem, between the troops of Lysias and those of Judas. Judas was defeated, and one of his brothers, Eleazar, was killed in the fight. Lysias conquered Beth-zur and advanced on Jerusalem, to which Judas had retreated. Now he in turn was besieged by the troops of Lysias.

This should have meant the end of the Maccabees, but as so often in the history of Israel politics on the world stage now proved decisive, even for a conflict on a very small scale. Lysias had to withdraw and the Maccabees again had their hands free. Strangely enough, they had the latest testament of Antiochus IV to thank for this. On his death-bed he had named another general, Philip, rather than Lysias, as regent for his son.

This Philip now went to Antioch to take over power there. On hearing news of this, Lysias wanted to break off the siege of the temple mount and return as quickly as possible to Antioch. Before doing so he made peace with the Judaeans, in fact restoring the situation to what it was before Antiochus' intervention.[20] According to Josephus[21] the Seleucids then took Menelaus with them to Antioch.

On his return to Antioch, Lysias soon managed to eliminate Philip, but his power did not last long. Demetrius I Soter (162-150 BC), who in the meantime had been sent as a hostage to Rome by his father Seleucus IV in place of his brother Antiochus IV (see 7.1), managed to escape from there in 163 BC and shortly afterwards killed Lysias and Antiochus V with the help of the army.

In the meantime Menelaus had been put to death. The new high priest, presumably nominated by Demetrius I, was Alcimus, a priest from the family of Aaron. By 162 BC, now that religious freedom was restored and a legitimate high priest had again been appointed, for many people, including the Hasidaeans, the aim of the struggle had been achieved.

A minor conflict seems to have developed in the meantime. According to Josephus,[22] Onias IV, a son of the former high priest Onias III, fled at this time to Egypt, where he had a temple built in Leontopolis along the lines of that in Jerusalem.[23]

8.3 *The situation after 162 BC*

The consequence of the events described above was that the Hasidaeans immediately detached themselves from the Maccabees. For them the aim of the struggle had been achieved. However, things were quite different for Judas and his followers. Although Judas, as leader of the opposition, must have been involved in the meeting with Lysias, he was clearly not completely satisfied with it. It is not clear precisely what his reasons were. It is possible that he and his followers got less power than they wanted. At all events, from now on the Maccabees clearly directed their struggle towards political power and freedom. Presumably they had already returned to their hiding places in the hill country by 162 BC in expectation of a new chance of success. This was not long in coming.

The new high priest Alcimus had come to Jerusalem with a Seleucid army under the command of Bacchides. There Bacchides, according to I Macc.7.13f., had sixty Hasidaeans killed. Of course this action did not help the reputation of the new high priest. In this situation Judas seems again to have occupied the temple mount in order to prevent Alcimus from exercising his functions as high priest. Thereupon Alcimus appealed for help to Demetrius I.

In response to this request for help, Demetrius I sent an army under the command of Nicanor to Judaea. However, this Seleucid army was defeated at Adasa, in the neighbourhood of Beth-horon, in 161 BC. Nicanor was also killed in this battle. The day of his death was declared a festival under the name of Nicanor's day.[24]

About the same time Judas must have sought to make contact with the Romans. There is an account of this in I Macc.8,[25] in which there is also a document (vv.23-28) with the conditions of the treaty that was made between Judas and Rome.[26] In I Macc.8 it is not said when this treaty was made. Chronologically it comes after the defeat of Nicanor, and there seems little against this.[27] Obviously the treaty was part of Roman policy, the ultimate aim of which was to put Judas in a position dependent on Rome. This process was crowned with success about a century later.[28]

According to II Macc.8.31f., at the same time Demetrius I received a letter from the Romans in which they announced their support for Judas.

Presumably, after these events Demetrius I quickly wanted to restore order in Judaea. To this end he sent an army there under the leadership of Bacchides. Bacchides defeated Judas in the neighbourhood of Jerusalem. Judas died in this action. The high priest Alcimus was restored to his office and for the moment was able to maintain his position with the support of Bacchides.

8.4 *Jonathan as leader of the Maccabees (161-142 BC)*

8.4.1 *The general political situation*

The next period is marked by increasing Roman influence. The Romans were able to develop their power and influence by resorting to the principle of 'divide and rule'. With this aim in view, they now in fact supported anyone and everyone with whom the Seleucids were having difficulties. Their dealings with the Maccabees mentioned in the previous section also fit in with this political policy.

This Roman policy also caused the greatest possible problems for Demetrius I when in 153 a civil war broke out in his kingdom between himself and Alexander Balas. The latter claimed to be a son of Antiochus IV and therefore to have a right to the throne. The situation became impossible for Demetrius I when in 153 the Roman Senate recognized Alexander's rights.[29]

Alexander Balas was able to hold on to the Seleucid kingdom until 145 BC. Thanks to the support of the Egyptian king Ptolemy VI (180-145 BC), Demetrius II (145-138 BC) then managed to regain the Seleucid throne. Alexander Balas fled to Arabia, where he was murdered.[30]

8.4.2 *The political situation in Palestine after the death of Judas*

It is clear that the Seleucids and the Hellenist party again had very firm control of Judaea and Jerusalem after the death of Judas. In order to consolidate this position, fortresses were built in various places in Judaea and Galilee. These included Jericho, Emmaus, Beth-horon, Bethel, Timnah, Pharathon, Tephon,[31] and above all the city of Jerusalem.[32]

For the first eight years after the death of Judas, Jonathan does not seem to have gained any foothold. This is evident, among other things, from the fact that he had to flee into the wilderness and take refuge first in the area of Tekoa and then in Transjordan. The only battle which is reported from this period is an act of vengeance against the Jambrite 'Arabians'[,33] who had killed his brother John.[34]

During this time Jonathan lived in the same kind of conditions as David when he was fleeing from Saul (cf. I Sam.22ff.).[35]

From *c.*156 BC Jonathan resided in Michmash, a place north of Jerusalem, where according to I Macc.9.73 he 'began to rule the people'. He remained there with the approval of Bacchides, with whom he had more or less made peace. I Maccabees 9.23 (see also *AJ* XII,2) also indicates that the Maccabees had singularly little influence in this period.

All this changed in *c.*153 BC, as a result of the great political difficulties in the Seleucid empire.

8.4.3 *The social and economic situation after the death of Judas*

In *c.* 156 BC the high priest Alcimus died. We do not know how the government of Judaea was organized in the subsequent years. According to Josephus (*AJ* XX, 237) there was no high priest in Jerusalem in the years 159-152 BC.[36] It is argued that in fact the 'Teacher of Righteousness' known from the Qumran community (see 9.4.2) was high priest in Jerusalem for seven years.[37] He is said then to have been displaced by Jonathan. On the evidence that we have, this theory is hard to accept.[38]

Of the different groups in the country, hitherto we have heard only of the Hellenistic party, the Maccabees and the Hasidaeans. Although we have only vague information, there must have been other trends. The heyday of apocalyptic in this period (see 7.5) suggests that it derived from certain circles about which we are otherwise completely in the dark. As we shall see in the next chapter, the Sadducees, the Pharisees, the Essenes and the Qumran community now come into view.

As to the economic situation, we hear both in I Macc. (9.24) and Josephus (*AJ* XII,2-3) that there was a severe famine in the land. Both sources also give this as the reason why many people in the country went over to the Hellenist party. However, they do not explain further. It seems likely that many of the ordinary people and the country dwellers had originally taken the Maccabaean side in the hope that the Maccabees would help them to solve their economic problems. However, they gradually came to realize that this was not the Maccabees' most important concern. Obviously an author who was well disposed to the Hasmonaeans like the author of I Maccabees, and Josephus, who is dependent on him, would not bring out such a motivation. The view of Kreissig,[39] that the fortunes of the small farmers will have been improved by the Maccabees, must therefore certainly be ruled out as a general conclusion. I Maccabees 14.12, which he cites in this connection, 'Each man sat under his vine and under his fig tree, and there was none to make them afraid', serves more to glorify Simon the Maccabee than to indicate the actual situation, and can therefore hardly be used as evidence here.

8.4.4 *Jonathan's diplomatic and political successes*

From about 153 BC, Jonathan was able to exploit the difficulties in the Seleucid empire sketched out in 8.5.1 by supporting both Alexander Balas and Demetrius I in turn.

Because Demetrius I gave permission for Jonathan to raise troops in exchange for his help, Jonathan was able to occupy Jerusalem in 152 BC. However, when Alexander Balas sought an agreement with him, Jonathan asked for the high priesthood as the price of his help; thereupon Alexander Balas did in fact bestow this office on him (I Macc.10.18-20; *AJ* XIII, 45). This was again seen by many people as a break with an existing tradition, for while Jonathan was of priestly descent,he could not be regarded as a legitimate descendant of the Zadokites, who were regarded as the legitimate high-priestly family. For these reasons many people regarded the nomination of Jonathan as illegal.

The events described above certainly brought Jonathan personal success, but at the same time they made the internal situation much worse, by simply widening the gulf between different groups.

Not only did Jonathan take the office of high priest; according to I Macc.10.65 he was also appointed by Alexander Balas general and governor of a province, probably Judaea. This must have happened after the death of Demetrius I, when Alexander Balas had built up a good relationship with Ptolemy VI.

In the subsequent period Jonathan succeeded in extending his power considerably by being able to adapt at the right time to the various changes in the political sphere. His support of Alexander Balas gradually brought him into possession of an important part of the coastal plain. When Ptolemy VI again took the side of Demetrius II (145-138 BC) and dropped Alexander Balas, Jonathan managed to occupy the Acra. Soon afterwards Jonathan made an agreement with Demetrius II which confirmed him in all his offices and in addition gave him control over three districts of Samaria and exemption from a number of taxes. We find all this narrated in a letter of Demetrius II, reproduced in I Macc.11.32-37 and *AJ* XIII, 125-8. It is impossible to establish for certain how original this letter is, but there is much to suggest its authenticity.[40]

In a new battle for power in the Seleucid empire between Demetrius II and a certain Trypho, who wanted to put Antiochus VI, the son of Alexander Balas, on the Seleucid throne,[41] Jonathan managed to gain further advantages by supporting one or the other depending on circumstances. Thus in this period he captured the Acra and his brother Simon the stronghold of Beth-zur. At the beginning of 142 BC he was captured by Trypho through treachery and soon afterwards killed by him.

During his rule Jonathan clearly also sought other foreign contacts. According to I Macc.12.3-4 and *AJ* XIII, 163-5, with this in view he sent a delegation to Rome in order to renew friendship with the Romans. However, we have more detailed information about contacts with Sparta. I Maccabees

12.5-18 and *AJ* XIII, 166-70 mention a letter in which Jonathan among other things sought closer contacts with the Spartans. The authenticity of this letter is disputed,[42] and that goes even more for the letter to Onias III quoted in I Macc.12.20-23 (cf. also *AJ* XII, 225-7), which is probably the work of an admirer of the Oniads.[43] All this, however, does not exclude the possibility that there were in fact contacts with Sparta in the time of Jonathan.

8.4.5 *The consequences of Jonathan's policy*

We have seen that Jonathan was able to make very good use of the permanent struggle for power between the various claimants to the Seleucid throne. By making payments and providing soldiers he was in a position to gain increasing privileges. The result of this was not only that Jonathan increased in personal power and influence but also that the territory of Judaea expanded considerably.[44] Therefore we can regard Jonathan as the *de facto* founder of the Hasmonaean empire, the fruits of which Simon and his successors were later able to reap.

Another development was set in motion with Jonathan, totally different from those of the time of Mattathias and Judas. With him there was an assimilation to Hellenism which was unthinkable in the former period. The distinctive feature here is that Jonathan allowed a Seleucid pretender to the throne to bestow the office of high priest on him. In 161 BC Judas and his followers refused to recognize the nomination by the Seleucids of Alcimus, a priest from the family of Aaron, something that the Hasidaeans certainly seemed ready to do.

However, the event mentioned above is very typical of Jonathan and his later successors. Their eyes were fixed only on gaining power. Religious considerations were certainly not predominant for them. On the contrary – as so often in history – they tried to use religion to realize their own aspirations and secure a position of power. Religion played a much more important role in a number of groups which according to Josephus (*AJ* XIII, 171-3) already existed in the time of Jonathan. Since these groups became important later in history, we must now look at them more closely before again taking up the historical thread.

Chapter 9

The Origin and Development of Some Important Groups

9.1 *The Sadducees*

9.1.1 *Sources*

It may be presumed that we have no writings from Sadducean circles. Some works, like Jesus Sirach and I Maccabees, are sometimes attributed to a Sadducean author, but there must be serious doubts as to whether this is the case.[1]

We must therefore derive our information about the Sadducees from those who wrote about them. This means Josephus, the New Testament and rabbinic literature. However, the light that all this sheds on the Sadducees is very fragmentary and often also polemic in perspective. Thus in fact the Talmud only gives a summary of the heresies which were noted among the Sadducees.[2] Of course we should not be surprised at such an account, given that the rabbinic literature has been largely collected and edited from a Pharisaic standpoint (see 9.2.1). As for Josephus, it is well known that he himself was a Pharisee and so his views on the Sadducees are coloured accordingly.[3] Moreover, his account of the Sadducees, as of the Pharisees and Essenes, is aimed at making these groups understandable to Greek and Roman readers. This factor, too, needs to be taken into account in his description. Finally, we also have the New Testament. In it we find only sparse information about the Sadducees, and the main stress is on all their shortcomings.

This verdict on the sources does not of course mean that they do not give us any detailed information about the Sadducees, but it does warn us to approach and interpret the information they contain as objectively as posisble.

9.1.2 *The name*

The etymology of the name Sadducees is disputed. The texts which discuss the group do not give us a clear picture. The logical conclusion, therefore, is that over the course of time different possible explanations were advanced.[4] The most usual explanation is that there is an association with the name of the priest Zadok, who held office in Jerusalem in the time of David and Solomon.[5] Philologically, however, a connection between Zadok and the Sadducees is very uncertain,[6] though that need not mean that the Sadducees did not regard themselves as descendants of Zadok. As we shall see shortly, we also find a similar view in the Qumran community. Thus both groups laid claim to the legitimate priesthood (cf.Ezek.40.46).

The Sadducees were also referred to as Boethusians.[7] The name is derived from the high-priestly family of Boethus which came from Alexandria. This family came to the fore in the time of Herod the Great and was certainly the most powerful of the four families who provided the high priest in the Roman period.[8] The Boethusians were presumably related to the Sadducees.[9] At all events the terms Sadducees and Boethusians are used indistinguishably, and that even gives the impression that they are synonyms.[10]

9.1.3 *Origin and history*

It is impossible to say when the Sadducean party came into being as an organized group or whether it ever existed as such. Apart from this question people are usually inclined to suppose a degree of continuity between the Zadokites of the Persian and Greek period and the Sadducees.[11] In view of what was known in a later period about the important position occupied by the Sadducees in priestly circles (cf. Acts 5.17; *AJ* XX, 199), this too seems very probable.

According to Josephus (*AJ* XIII, 173), the Sadducees, like the Pharisees and Essenes, already existed as a separate group in the time of Jonathan the Maccabee. Certainly from the time of John Hyrcanus (134-104 BC) down to AD 66/70 they played an important role in Jerusalem and Judaea, apart from a period during the brief reign of Salome Alexandra (76-67 BC). It is completely impossible to discover what place they occupied before that. Given their position and views as known from a later period, we may well suppose there to have been some affinity between the Sadducees and the supporters of Hellenism who dominated the city of Jerusalem at the beginning of the second century BC.[12] This does not mean that we should conclude that this last group already consisted of Sadducees.

Ernst Bammel's view is rather different.[13] He believes that one can only speak of a Sadducean party in the first century of our era; it arose as a result of a conflict with the Pharisees. Before that the Sadducees were priestly families brought to Jerusalem by Herod the Great to restrain the influence of the Hasmonaean priest-kings and there presented as legitimate sons of Zadok. The name Sadducee was an honorific name which these priests gave themselves.

9.1.4 *Characteristics*

Clearly the Sadducees were a specific class and indeed an upper stratum of well-to-do members of the society of their time.[14] In Acts 4.1 the Sadducees are mentioned in the same breath as the priests and the captain of the temple, while in Acts 5.17 they are identified as the party of the high priest. This last fact in particular indicates that the high-priestly circles often consisted of Sadducees.[15]

Given what has already been said, it is best to describe the Sadducees as a group of senior clergy and aristocracy, i.e. the classes with possessions. That is evident from their constant concern to preserve political and social stability in order to secure their economic interests. That is also why they constantly favoured a policy of cooperation with foreign rulers, though this does not mean that they were always prepared to collaborate. Given that unrest and turmoil arose all too easily around the temple, they made use of the services of temple police there.

The attitude I have just described implies that the Sadducees were interested in maintaining the *status quo*. As such they can be described as conservatives. Such an attitude was also expressed in their religious views. Here too they did not want any innovations. As is well known, they recognized only the written tradition as holy scripture and in contrast to the Pharisees would have nothing to do with an oral tradition which made new adaptations possible. Moreover they rejected the (Pharisaic) doctrine of the resurrection of the dead and the existence of angels and spirits.[16]

Closely connected with all this is the fact that the Sadducees were very hostile to messianic and apocalyptic movements which brought innovations and in this way threatened the *status quo*. For the same reasons they did not have much time for the message of the prophets.

All this does not imply that there were not different trends within the Sadducean movement. There doubtless were, but in the main the description given here applies to all the Sadducees.

9.2 *The Pharisees*

9.2.1 *Sources*

Our sources for the Pharisees are the same as those for the Sadducees (see 9.1.1), namely Josephus, the New Testament and the rabbinic literature. Although these sources are rather less fragmentary about the Pharisees and often not at all polemic (Josephus and the rabbinic literature), this does not meant that we always have information about the Pharisees at first hand. The works of Josephus were written about AD 75-100 and the New Testament about 50-90, and the regulations and teachings of the Pharisees before AD 70 were only written down by rabbis who lived in the first and second centuries.[17] The influence of the (later) Pharisees on rabbinic literature was enormous. After the fall of Jerusalem in AD 70 they were in fact the only group to survive. It was the Pharisees who guided Judaism through this catastrophe and gave it a new form and hope, especially in the religious sphere. In studying the rabbinic literature this factor must constantly be taken seriously. It is obvious that this applies primarily if we use this literature in order to get a picture of the Pharisees.

9.2.2 *The name*

The name Pharisee is derived from a word which in Hebrew and Aramaic means 'separated'. The question is in what direction this indication points. Most probably the designation is connected with a separation in which not all the people were involved.[18] At all events, the name must have been given them by a third party (opponents). In favour of this is the fact that the Pharisees are described by this name only three times in the Mishnah, and then it is attributed to a Sadducee.[19] The Pharisees themselves used terms which mean 'friend', 'scribe', or 'wise man'. In Jewish literature the preferred description of the Pharisees is 'wise men' or more often 'our wise men'.

9.2.3 *Origin and history*

In fact we know nothing for certain about the origin of the Pharisees. They are often associated with the Hasidaeans or Hasidim who at the beginning of the revolt fought side by side with the Maccabees.[20]

The Pharisees appear on the historical scene for the first time as a more or less independent group, like the Sadducees and Essenes, in the time of Jonathan, if at least this fact in Josephus (*AJ* XIII, 171) rests on accurate information. We have no other information about a still earlier period or about the origin of the Pharisees. Nor do we find any in the rabbinic traditions about the Pharisees. Neusner[21] has pointed out that these traditions go back at most fifty or eighty years to before the destruction of the temple in AD 70.

Presumably from about the beginning of the Christian era the Pharisees banded together in communities.[22] These were made up, for example, of the lower ranks of priests, craftsman, small farmers and merchants. This list already shows that support for the Pharisees, unlike that for the Sadducees, must rather be sought in the middle-class groups. The ordinary people were also fairly sympathetic towards them. Most scribes were also Pharisees, although the two categories should not be identified without further ado.

There were probably always only relatively few Pharisees in the strict sense of the term. Josephus (*AJ* XVII, 42) tells us that they numbered only about six thousand in the time of Herod the Great. However, their influence was usually much greater than one might expect from so small a number.[23] This influence later made itself felt above all through the significance which the school and synagogue acquired in Judaism and especially because the Pharisaic movement after AD 70 was the one dominant force in the existence of Judaism (cf. 9.2.1).

The Pharisees certainly cannot be regarded as a political party, although this does not mean that they had no concern for the political questions of their time.[24] We shall see in due course that in several periods their political influence and their concerns in this sphere were considerable. However, at a later period their main attention seems to have been directed more emphatically to religious matters.[25] Still, it is never possible to see a strict division between politics and religion among the Pharisees, as one would expect in the light of the Jewish and biblical traditions. Political questions were seen in the light of religion. Wellhausen's theory[26] that the Pharisees and Sadducees stood over against each other as the parties of church and state is also very questionable.

9.2.4 *Characteristics*

In contrast to the Sadducees, the Pharisees attached great importance not only to the written Torah but also to oral tradition.[27] In their view this tradition was handed down by word of mouth from generation to generation through Joshua, elders, prophets and teachers until it was set down in writing in the Mishnah.[28] They regarded it as a closer interpretation and further development of the written Torah (cf. Matt.5.21; 15.2).

In addition, they also differed from the Sadducees in believing, unlike them, in the resurrection and in the existence of angels and spirits (cf. Acts 23.8).

Whereas human freedom stood very much in the foreground for the Sadducees (*BJ* II, 164), for the Pharisees the emphasis lay both on divine omnipotence and providence and on human freedom and responsibility (*AJ*

XIII, 173). This is particularly sharply expressed in a remark attributed to R.Akiba in Aboth III.19: 'All is foreseen, but free will is given.' This reproduces a general view in Judaism,[29] although the personal responsibility and free will of the individual were often stressed less in apocalyptic groups than among the Pharisees.

As the centre party the Pharisees had far more divisions than the Sadducees. Thus a Pharisee was among those who founded what would later be the party of the Zealots or a group related to them (see 12.8.1). Another illustration is given by the well-known schools of Shammai and Hillel, founded at the beginning of our era; the views of the former were stricter than those of the latter. However, in later tradition the views of the school of Hillel seem to have gained the upper hand.

9.3 *The Essenes*

9.3.1 *Sources*

If we leave the discoveries in the wilderness of Judah out of account here, we must regard the Jewish authors Josephus and Philo as the earliest and most important sources for the Essenes. Alongside them mention must also be made of Pliny the Elder.[30] Perhaps with the exception of Josephus, these authors did not know the Essenes from their own experience. Thus they have taken the facts about the Essenes from other sources unknown to us. A group in Egypt related to the Essenes, the so-called Therapeutae, may possible have been known personally to Philo.[31]

We know nothing about Essene writings, unless we put those from the library of Qumran in this category.

The Essenes are never mentioned by name in rabbinic literature[32] nor in any of the writings of the New Testament which have come down to us.

9.3.2 *The name*

There is no unanimity over the meaning of the name Essenes.[33] It is often associated with an Aramaic word which means pious,[34] but any connection of this kind is very doubtful.[35] Another theory is that the name Essene is connected with a word that means 'healers'.[36] Reference is then made to the fact that in Philo they are also referred to as Therapeutae. However, this view, too, has not commanded general agreement. So we are in fact completely in the dark here.

9.3.3 *Origin and history*

The question of the origin of the Essenes is also very difficult to answer. The facts that we have about them give us no specific pointers in this direction. Hellenistic Jewish and other writers from antiquity[37] write about them as an existing group without going into detail about their prehistory. Starting from what Josephus tells us,[38] we can only say that the Essenes, like the Sadducees and Pharisees, already formed an existing group in the time of Jonathan.

It is often assumed that the Essenes are the spiritual descendants (from the pacifist side) of the Hasidaeans (see 8.1.3).[39] Among other things, their name would also point in this direction. However, this last theory rests on a very weak foundation,[40] so we must conclude that the question of the origin of the Essenes remains very obscure. The possible identification of the Essenes with the Qumran community will be discussed in the next section of this chapter.

The Essenes were certainly active in the Jewish community down to the end of the second temple in AD 70. This can be established on the basis of the facts that we have. Their numbers were probably always relatively small. Josephus and Philo speak[41] of four thousand in their time. According to Philo the Essenes lived in the villages of Judaea, where most of them worked as small farmers or craftsman. They avoided cities as far as possible because they regarded them as breeding grounds for injustice.[42] However, at another point Philo tells us that they did live in cities.[43] Neither Josephus nor Philo knows anything of Essenes living in the neighbourhood of the Dead Sea. Nor does the classical author Pliny the Elder.[44]

9.3.4 *Characteristics*

Here are some of the most important characteristics of the Essenes as they are described in different sources.

Essenes know no slavery[45] and avoid swearing oaths.[46] They usually wear white clothes and pay careful attention to rites of purification.[47] While they bring gifts to the temple, they reject animal offerings.[48] They observe the sabbath very strictly.[49] All possessions are held in common, and they reject luxury and private possessions.[50] Both Josephus and Philo, and also Pliny the Elder, tell us that the Essenes live celibate lives,[51] though Josephus also mentions a group of Essenes who allowed marriage.[52] Philo also tells us that the Essenes held pacifist views.[53] There were rules for a probationary period and rites of initiation before entry into the community.[54]

A number of these characteristics indicate the priestly character of the group. Some facts, like for example the difference of opinion over marriage, give the impression that the name Essenes is the collective name for a group in which not all were of the same opinion, but had many things in common.

It emerges from all this that the Essenes were a closed community in which there were several shades of opinion but in which abstinence, communal possessions and a sober life-style were the most prominent features. In contrast to the Sadducees and Pharisees we may note that the Essenes had virtually no interest in political matters.

9.4 *The Qumran community*

9.4.1 *Identification*

Very soon after the first discoveries in 1947 in the area of the Dead Sea it became clear that the writings found there must have belonged to a group which had spent a long time in this area. It was more difficult to identify the group in question. Most scholars think that the Qumran community consisted of Essenes or a group closely related to them.[55] There are also some who think the group was made up of Sadducees,[56] Pharisees,[57] or Zealots.[58] Very recently it has even been argued that the nucleus of the Qumran community was a group of conservative Judaeans who returned from Babylon to Palestine shortly after 165 BC.[59]

All these views show that the identification of the Qumran community is by no means a straightforward matter. The affinity with the Essenes is in fact their most striking feature, but that does not mean that we should immediately identify the group with the Essenes. Moreover, the community seems to have consisted above all of priests who presented themselves as 'sons of Zadok'. It seems best to see the group as largely consisting of priestly families (perhaps of a lower class) and in many respects showing great affinity to the Essenes.[60]

9.4.2 *Origin and history*

From archaeological evidence it has been established that the central buildings of the community settlement in the area of the Dead Sea were at Hirbet Qumran (about twenty miles north of Engedi). On the basis of the archaeological and literary material that has been discovered it can be assumed that the community lived there from about 150/140 BC – AD 68.[61] The settlement seems to have been abandoned from about 31 BC to about the beginning of our era as the result of an earthquake.[62] The living quarters of the community were again destroyed during the struggle against the Romans in AD 68.

One much-disputed question is the identity of the 'Teacher of Righteousness' who is mentioned in many of the community writings. Various attempts have been made to identify him with a particular figure, as for instance with Onias III, the high priest who succeeded Alcimus in about 159 BC (see 8.5.3), and with Jesus,[63] but without any convincing results. We could be more certain about his identity if we knew who was meant by his opponent, 'the godless priest' or 'the man of lies'.[64] There are also a great many different views about the identity of the latter. He has been directly identified with Jonathan, Simon, Alexander Jannaeus and Hyrcanus II.[65] Most recently there seems to be a consensus in favour of Jonathan, but there is considerably uncertainty all round. It is also a real possibility that the 'godless priest' could represent a number of figures.[66]

Thus the figure of 'the Teacher of Righteousness' remains anonymous.[67] His influence on the community was certainly very great, as is evident among other things from CH I,11; 1 QpHab XI.4-8 and 1QH V, 23-25. It is impossible to establish whether this teacher was also the founder of the community. There are often allusions to the fact that the 'Teacher of Righteousness' and his followers went into captivity to the 'land of Damascus' or 'the land of the north',[68] where they entered into a 'new covenant'. Some scholars[69] think that 'Damascus' here must be taken literally; others[70] think of Qumran, while yet others[71] suppose that this is an allusion to the Judaeans who were taken into captivity in Babylon in the time of Nebuchadnezzar.

CD I, 6ff. describes how the Qumran community came into being in the 'time of wrath', viz., in the three hundred and ninetieth year after the fall of Jerusalem in 586 BC (cf. Ex.4.5). Although this figure looks very symbolic, the end of this period (the beginning of the second century BC) can certainly be seen as the time when the community came into being.[72] Archaeological evidence also points in this direction. Excavations have indicated that Qumran was built and lived in very close to about 140 BC.[73] If the community settled here about this time, the group must certainly have came into being some decades earlier.

In about 100 BC the settlement seems to have been expanded considerably. Presumably as a result of an earthquake (see above), there was a time when it was uninhabited, but soon after the death of Herod the Great the group returned and rebuilt everything. This phase of the settlement finally came to an end when in about AD 68 the Romans destroyed the settlement and the whole complex of buildings belonging to it.

9.4.3 *Library*

Since 1947 a large number of Hebrew, Aramaic and Greek manuscripts or fragments of manuscripts have been found around Ḥirbet Qumran.[74]. It is almost universally accepted that all these writings formed the library of the Qumran community.[75] The manuscripts from a much later period which were found at Ḥirbet Mird (about six miles south-west of Qumran) and Wadi Murabbaʿatʿ[76] (about twelve miles south of Qumran) cannot be included with them. The manucripts found in the valleys of Nahal Tseʿelim, Nahal Ḥever and Nahal Mismar, even more to the south, are yet further removed; for the most part they come from the period of AD 132-135. The same is true of the manucript finds from the citadel of Masada, the fortress known from the fight against Rome in AD 66-73.

Clearly the documents in the library of Qumran must have been written before AD 68. The earliest of them can be dated to the second century BC. Among the manuscripts that have been discovered there are biblical manuscripts, apocrypha, pseudepigrapha, pesharim (Bible commentaries), Targums and rules of the Order. To identify these manuscripts found in eleven caves of Qumran a particular system of abbreviations is used, the first two characters indicating the place where the manuscript was discovered. Thus 1Q denotes Qumran Cave 1. The following characters then give the content (p = pesher, commentary; ap = apocryphon and tg = targum) and the name of the manuscript in question, e.g. 1QpHab, 1QapGen, and 1Qtg Job. If a large number of manuscripts of the same book are found, this is indicated by a small superior letter. Thus 1QIs[a] is the first Isaiah scroll from Cave 1 and 1QIs[b] the second. If a manuscript cannot be identified, the indication of where it was found is followed by a figure in Arabic numerals, e.g. 4Q180.

The significance of these manuscript discoveries is enormous. In the first place they provide us with insight into and knowledge of the customs, the history and the faith of the Qumran comunity itself. Furthermore, they are important for studying Hebrew from the third century BC to the second century AD and for the history of the text of the Old Testament. Finally, the great importance of the literature for understanding the background to the New Testament needs to be stressed.

9.4.4 *Characteristics*

It is clear that the priests of the Qumran community were rivals of the priests from the Jerusalem temple. Whoever may be meant by the 'godless priest', he was certainly high priest in Jerusalem. The community regarded worship in Jerusalem as illegitimate, since the priests there did not observe the rules, at least as Qumran understood them.

The rules of the Order are the best source for the views of the community. The most important of these are 1QS 'Community Rule' (*serek* = rule) and

CD (= Covenant of Damascus), the 'Damascus Document'.[77] The first of these comes from about 90 BC and the second from about 30 BC. In addition, mention might also be made of the Temple Scroll (11Q Temple),[78] which can be roughly dated to the first century BC.[79] 1QM, the 'War Scroll', also provides useful information.

From the evidence at our disposal it looks as if the Qumran community regarded itself as the true Israel. This view means that the community made polemical attacks not only on the priests in Jerusalem but also on the Pharisees and Sadducees, who are referred to as Ephraim or Nineveh and Manasseh or No-Amon respectively.[80] The community even called itself Judah or Jerusalem (cf. CD VI.5).

The leadership of the community lay with a council consisting of twelve people who represented the tribes of Israel and three priests (see 1QS VIII, 1f.). Each group within the community, which had to consist of at least ten people, was led by an 'overseer'.

In order to be admitted to the community someone first had to undergo a probationary period of three years. After giving an oath he could then enter the community (cf. CD XV, 5-7). Very strict rules were observed within the community. Anyone who dishonoured the name of the LORD was cast out of the community, and the same went for those who rebelled against the rules of the community (cf. 1QS VI, 27-VII,2; 1QS VII, 17).

Great stress was laid on purity and ritual washings (see CD X, 10-13; XII, 12-14). Communal meals were also held regularly.

In contrast to worship in Jerusalem people in Qumran observed the solar calendar of fifty-two weeks known to us from I Enoch and Jubilees, according to which feasts fell on the same day of the week every year (cf.1QpH XI, 4-8).

These brief notes about the views held in Qumran must suffice here.[81] More detailed information can be found in numerous specialist studies on this material.[82]

Chapter 10

The Period of the Hasmonaean Priest-Rulers

10.1 *Simon (143/42-135/34 BC)*

10.1.1 *The international situation*

In 8.5.4 we saw that from about 145 BC Trypho made attempts to remove Demetrius II from the Seleucid throne and replace him with Antiochus VI, a son of Alexander Balas.

However, Trypho's real intentions soon emerged. In 142 BC he had his charge, the young king Antiochus VI, killed and put the crown on his own head.[1] But his reign did not last long. He was only able to hold power from 142 to 138 BC. In 138 he was driven from the throne by Antiochus VII Sidetes (138-128 BC), a brother of Demetrius II. The latter had been taken prisoner in the same year by the Parthian king Mithridates I (*c.* 171-138 BC), when he was trying to regain territory lost to the Parthians. Antiochus VII later made a similar attempt, but had just as little success.[2]

So we can see that the Seleucid empire was collapsing on all sides. Both the Parthians and the Maccabees were able to strengthen their position at Seleucid expense. In the long run the Seleucids lost all control over the territories of the Parthians and Judaea and its wider surroundings. However, it must be emphatically stressed that the Maccabees and Parthians did not gain this position and their independence by virtue of their own might. They owed their success to Rome, which had every interest in weakening the Seleucid empire. Moreover, the independence of Parthia and Judaea was only temporary, and only lasted as long as the Romans wanted it to.

10.1.2 *Freedom from taxation*

After the capture of Jonathan by Trypho (8.5.4), the leadership of the Maccabaean rebels came into the hands of Simon, the last survivor of the five brothers. In the dispute between Demetrius II and Trypho, Simon soon took the side of the former. However, he made it a condition that Demetrius II should give the people complete exemption from taxation. Demetrius had little option but to consent to this demand (cf. I Macc. 13.36-40; *AJ* XIII, 213). This happened in 143/2 BC. From that moment the Seleucid calendar was also abolished in Judaea. All documents and treaties were now dated according to the years of Simon (cf. I Macc.13.41; 14.27; *AJ* XIII, 214). This last practice was a formal confirmation of the independence that had been gained.[3]

The granting of freedom from taxes was an important milestone in the history of Judaea. In I Macc.13.41f. and *AJ* XIII, 213, this event is regarded as the end of oppression, and it clearly indicates that economic motives played a large role in the Maccabaean struggle.

An important factor in the Seleucid system of taxation was so-called state leasing, which was imposed by the aristocracy on the small farmers and the country population.[4] The disappearance of this state leasing was an enormous relief for the oppressed country-dwellers.

Rostovtzeff's view[5] that the Hasmonaeans took over the Seleucid system of taxation unchanged has been rejected out of hand by Kippenberg.[6] The Hasmonaeans made certain of income by raising a tithe, which was a very old custom,[7] a tax on the produce of the country and a levy consisting of one tenth of what had been sown.[8]

The abolition of the Seleucid system of taxation meant that the economic aim of the rebellion had been achieved. The Maccabees who had had so great a part in it now began to reap its fruits.

10.1.3 *Simon nominated high priest, general and leader*

In I Macc.14.28 (cf. also 14.41-43) we are told that a so-called 'great assembly' was summoned, composed of priests, leaders of the people and elders of the land. It is uncertain precisely what is meant by 'great assembly' here.[9] Clearly this is meant to be the same sort of gathering as those mentioned in I Kings 8.65 (cf. II Chron.7.8); Neh.5.7. In I Macc.14 it is said that this gathering praised Simon and his brothers greatly for all that they had done and resolved on, and also that Simon was to possess the hereditary title of high priest, leader and general (I Macc.14.25-49). Only one reservation is made. Simon and his descendants are to hold this title 'until a true prophet shall appear' (I Macc.14.41). This last reservation is seen as a compromise between the Maccabees and their following and those who found it difficult to accept that the 'Maccabees' should have a high-priestly function and, moreover, a hereditary one. Moreover, the concession had no political value.

In particular, the nomination of Simon as hereditary high priest was a great break with existing religious tradition. Until 152 BC, when Jonathan was nominated high priest by Alexander Balas (see 8.5.4), only the Zadokites were regarded as legitimate high priests. Although there is no specific mention of the fact, we can assume that at that time many people found it difficult to accept the nomination of Jonathan. It is understandable that a hereditary high priesthood involving Simon was now even more difficult to accept.

Be this as it may, the nomination of Simon as hereditary high priest, general and leader was endorsed by the decree of the 'great assembly'. According to I Macc.14.27, 48f., the words of this decree, given in I Macc.14.27-45, were engraved on copper plates which were set up in the sanctuary.

10.1.4 *Simon's relations with foreign powers*

Soon after the death of Jonathan, Simon sought contacts with Rome. His aim was to strengthen his position as an independent ruler, so good relations with Rome were very important. Therefore he sent a delegation led by Numenius there (I Macc.14.24). According to I Macc.15.15, 22f., the result of this mission[10] was that the Roman consul Lucius sent a letter to the kings of the surrounding countries in which the Romans guaranteed the independence of Judaea. The text of this letter is given in I Macc.15.16-21. Its authenticity is disputed. Josephus mentions a similar document, but dates it much later, in the time of Hyrcanus II (*AJ* XIV, 145-8). Presumably, however, it must be put in the time of Simon and therefore dated about 139 BC.[11]

Meanwhile, Antiochus VII Sidetes, the brother of Demetrius II, had come to power in the Seleucid empire (see 10.1.1). This king, who still had to deal with Trypho, began by confirming all the privileges which he had granted to Simon. According to I Macc.15.1-9, on this occasion Antiochus also granted Simon the right to mint his own coins. Josephus (*AJ* XII, 223-4) also relates the concessions that the Seleucid king made at the time.

This right to mint coins comprised the making of coins which were valid only in a particular city or district, in this case Jerusalem (I Macc.15.6). It is almost certain that Simon never made use of the privilege,[12] although against that it is argued that Simon indeed made use of his rights, but that his coins bore the name of Jerusalem rather than his own name.[13]

The attitude of Antiochus VII to Simon changed once he had driven out Trypho. He then felt strong enough to advance on Simon. He asked Simon to return the cities of Gadara (Gezer), from which Simon had driven out the pagan population in 142 BC,[14] Joppa (Jaffa) and the Acra in Jerusalem. Moreover, he asked for taxes from all the cities and places outside Judaea, or in lieu of that for a tribute of about a thousand talents of silver (I Macc.15.25-31). When Simon seemed only ready to pay a mere hundred talents for Gadara and Joppa, Antiochus VII sent his general Cendebaeus to Judaea. Simon, who was himself too old, put his sons Judas and John at the head of the army which went to meet Cendebaeus. Cendebaeus was killed, and the city of Ashdod, from which the Seleucids had fled, was burned (I Macc.16.8-10; *AJ* XIII, 226f.). During the lifetime of Simon, Antiochus VII did not make any further attempt to gain control of Judaea.

10.1.5 *The end of Simon*

Ptolemy, a son-in-law of Simon from Idumaea, who was district commander of Jericho, made an attempt to seize power from the Hasmonaeans. To this end he invited Simon and his sons Mattathias and Judas to a feast in Dok, the fortress he had built near Jericho. When they arrived, Ptolemy had them put to death. At the same time he had also sent men to the city of Gadara to murder John there. However, this last attack failed because John was warned in time. John immediately rushed to Jerusalem and was able to seize the city before Ptolemy arrived. So in fact Ptolemy's *coup d'état* had already failed.

Simon's violent end shows once again how turbulent and full of unrest the time of the Maccabees must have been. All those in the first generation of Maccabees lost their lives through violence. It is clear that the population in this period shared in the violence and unrest. That was also true of Simon's time. The report in I Macc.14.12 that in the time of Simon 'Each man sat under his vine and under his fig-tree, and there was none to make them afraid' says more about the exaggerated sympathy of the author of I Maccabees for Simon than about the real situation.

I Maccabees ends with the account of Simon's death (I Macc.16.11-22). For the rest of the history of the Hasmonaeans for the most part we only have the works of Josephus. The work mentioned in I Macc.16.24 about the history of John Hyrcanus I has not survived.

10.2 *John Hyrcanus I (135/34-104 BC)*

10.2.1 *The beginning of his reign*

On the basis of the honorific titles granted by the 'great assembly' (see 10.1.3), the third and last surviving son of Simon, Johanan, better known under his Greek (!) name John, was named his lawful successor, with the title John Hyrcanus.

John Hyrcanus first of all had to deal with Ptolemy, which he did quickly and successfully. After that, right at the beginning of his rule he had to cope with an invasion by Antiochus VII. Antiochus ravaged the whole land of Judaea[15] and besieged Hyrcanus in his capital, Jerusalem.[16] According to Josephus (*AJ* XIII,236) this took place in the first year of the rule of Hyrcanus (134 BC), but that is by no means certain.[17]

Lack of food in the beleaguered city forced Hyrcanus to come to terms with Antiochus VII. Among other things Hyrcanus had to pay five hundred talents of silver, break down the walls of Jerusalem, take part in a Seleucid campaign against the Parthians, and again recognize Seleucid sovereignty over Judaea.[18] The extreme moderation of these conditions seems above all to be due to the fact that Antiochus VII was also forced to break off the siege of Jerusalem as a result of an intervention by the Roman Senate.[19]

In fact at this time Hyrcanus seems to have had secret contacts with Phraates II, the king of Parthia.[20] In this period the Parthians also freed Demetrius II, the brother of Antiochus VII (see 10.1.1), to provide the latter with a rival. Antiochus VII died in 128 BC in battle against the Parthians, after which Demetrius II again ascended the Seleucid throne.

The campaign against the Parthians mentioned above was a failure. As a result of this, and through internal conflicts in the Seleucid empire, John Hyrcanus I was in a position to make Judaea independent again and to emerge as sovereign ruler. From 129 BC Hyrcanus no longer needed to bother about the Seleucids and could devote his full attention to Judaea and the surrounding area.

Moreover, the events described here show once again that Judaea could be independent only while the Seleucid empire was in difficulties, because it was occupied with internal problems or conflicts with foreign enemies. Rome was always behind the latter, either openly or in a disguised way.

10.2.2 *Conquests of John Hyrcanus I*

The rule of John Hyrcanus I was marked by a series of conquests in the area around Judaea. First Hyrcanus invaded Transjordan, where after a siege of six months he conquered the important city of Medeba on the Via Regis.[21] Medeba is also well known and mentioned often in the Old Testament (see e.g. Num.21.30; Josh.13.9). Scythopolis, the old Beth-shean, also seems to have been occupied in the time of John Hyrcanus.[22] This place west of the Jordan was an important crossroads.

Great emphasis must be placed here on two of John Hyrcanus' conquests, because they made an important mark on later history. First, Hyrcanus conquered Idumaea with its district capital Marisa.[23] He compelled the Idumaeans to be circumcised and to observe Jewish laws, as he did the inhabitants of other conquered areas. As a consequence of this the Idumaeans later thought of themselves as Jews (*BJ* IV, 270-84). So the Idumaean Herod the Great could claim to be a Jew, though we know that the Jews themselves, above all the leading circles in Jerusalem, regarded him as inferior (cf. *AJ* XIV, 403).

Even more decisive was the conquest and the subjection of the 'Samaritans' and the destruction of their temple on Mount Gerizim.[24] This event in particular made a great impression and created an unbridgeable gulf between Judaeans and 'Samaritans'. The traces of this are at least still perceptible down to the first century AD.[25] We do not know precisely when this event happened. On the basis of *AJ* XIII, 254 it is often assumed that it took place in the first years of Hyrcanus' government, namely in 128 BC.[26] Others tend to think more in terms of about 108 BC.[27] In the latter case the destruction of Shechem would then have taken place about the same time as that of Samaria.

As a result of all these conquests John Hyrcanus secured a kingdom which in broad outline was similar to that of Solomon. The degree to which in all this John Hyrcanus was purely pursuing political aims emerges from the fact that in his campaigns he did not employ a Judaean army, but made use of foreign mercenaries (*AJ* XIII, 249). Thanks to these troops and the weakness of the Seleucid empire he was able to achieve territorial expansions.

10.2.3 *Foreign contacts*

Like his predecessors, John Hyrcanus was concerned for good relations with Rome. Josephus mentions at least two resolutions which were passed about Judaea by the Roman senate in the time of the Hasmonaeans. The first (*AJ* XIII, 259-66) confirmed the treaty of friendship between Judaea and Rome and the second (*AJ* XIV, 247-255) was on the same lines.[28] However, both documents are concerned with the return of the fortresses of Joppa (Jaffa) and Gadara (Gezer) to John Hyrcanus. At that time both fortresses were in the possession of Antiochus. It is not clear which king is meant here. Both Antiochus VII Sidetes and Antiochus IX Cyzicenus are possibilities. With the former these documents would have to be dated about 132 BC and with the latter about 105 BC. The exact dating of the two documents mentioned by Josephus in this connection is, however, largely uncertain.[29]

John Hyrcanus wanted good relations not only with the Romans but also with the Ptolemaic court in Egypt.[30] He was also able to achieve this, probably above all because there were numerous Jews living in Egypt who had close contact with the court (cf. *AJ* XIII, 284-287). However, little is known about contacts between John Hyrcanus and these Judaeans. There is, though, a letter in II Macc.1.1-9 from the Judaeans in Judaea and Jerusalem addressed to the Jews in Egypt dating from 124 BC, calling for the celebration of the Feast of Tabernacles in the month of Chislev.[31]

Thanks among other things to these contacts with Rome and Egypt and also to the weak position of the Seleucids, in the time of John Hyrcanus Judaea was completely independent of the Seleucid empire.

10.2.4 *The domestic policy of John Hyrcanus*

In 10.1.4 we saw that Simon probably did not mint any coins. According to many scholars,[32] John Hyrcanus did. In fact a great many coins have been found on which the name Johanan appears, but they may well connected with Hyrcanus II (76-67 and 63-40 BC). On the basis of the information given by the finds of coins it is most probable that Alexander Jannaeus (103-76 BC) was the first Hasmonaean to have coins minted.[33]

John Hyrcanus' strong position in the political and military sphere, which, like David and Solomon at one time, he largely owed to his foreign mercenary troops,[34] could not relieve him of having to cope with enormous problems at home. One of the reasons for them was doubtless his plundering of the tomb of David, which is mentioned by Josephus (*AJ* XIII, 249). John Hyrcanus needed the proceeds of the robbery, three thousand talents of silver, to pay his foreign mercenaries. It is understandable that such tomb-robbing and plundering caused great offence in many quarters. Such action doubtless recalled the way in which the Hellenists and the Seleucids had acted in former times. One can also see many parallels in other respects between the early Hellenists and the Hasmonaeans. The latter had a government which can be increasingly described as Hellenistic. The hiring of pagan soldiers also fits into this context; it must have been a thorn in the flesh particularly for the 'pious' in Judaea.

According to Josephus (*AJ* XIII, 288-92), in the course of time a break developed between John Hyrcanus and the Pharisees. The latter wanted John Hyrcanus to surrender the office of high priest. Because of all this John Hyrcanus is said to have turned away from the Pharisees and made a closer alliance with the Sadducees (*AJ* XIII, 293-8).

We find a parallel story about this event in the Babylonian Talmud,[35] but Hyrcanus' son Alexander Jannaeus is mentioned here in place of John. However, the reading by Josephus is the correct one.[36]

10.3 *Some important literature from about 150-100* BC

As the title of this section indicates, here I shall limit myself to discussing a few of the most important works, restricting myself further to those which were written in Palestine. One exception to this is the Letter of Aristeas, which was written in Egypt.

The final redaction of I and II Maccabees, to which we have already devoted a good deal of attention in 1.2.2, must have taken place about 100 BC.

In addition to these important apocryphal or deutero-canonical works, mention needs to be made of the pseudepigraphical Jubilees. One name used for this book in the early church was the 'Little Genesis', because its content largely runs parallel to that of the first book of the Bible. The name Jubilees is taken from the division of the history narrated in this work into jubilee-year periods of forty-nine years (cf. Lev.25.8-13). The book as a whole has only come down to us in Ethiopic,[37] but among other evidence a number of Hebrew fragments found in the Qumran caves[38] indicate that it must go back to a Hebrew original.

A special feature of this book is that, like Enoch, it uses the traditional solar calendar,[39] which after the Babylonian captivity was gradually replaced in Palestine by the lunar calendar.[39] This last feature already shows that the book comes from a group which attached great importance to preserving old traditions. Therefore the author must have come from anti-Hellenist circles.

It is impossible to date the book exactly, but the final redaction must have taken place in roughly the period I have given above.[40]

Another important work from this period is the Letter of Aristeas. In form and content this work is not a letter but a narrative. The greater part of it is the account, or rather the legend, of the origin of the Greek translation of the Pentateuch. Above all through the action of Ptolemy II Philadelphus mentioned in 4.2.2, seventy-two translators, chosen from the twelve tribes of Israel, are said to have completed the work in Alexandria in seventy-two days. The whole Greek translation of the Old Testament was later called the Septuagint after the number of seventy(-two) translators mentioned here.

The legend of the origin of the Septuagint which appears here in the Letter of Aristeas cannot go back to a historical event. The language and background of the work show that it can only have been written about 100 BC. Its aim is rather to stress the legitimate character of the Greek translation by showing the miraculous way in which it came into being.

Chapter 11

The Reigns of the Hasmonaean Priest-Kings

11.1 *Aristobulus I (104-103 BC)*

It had been the aim of John Hyrcanus I that his oldest son Aristobulus I should succeed him as high priest after his death and his widow take over the government of the country. However, Aristobulus had his mother and his brothers, other than Antigonus, whom he named his co-regent, put in prison. His mother died of hunger there, and shortly afterwards Antigonus was put to death on Aristobulus' orders. In this way Aristobulus himself took all power.

According to Josephus (*AJ* XIII, 301; *BJ* I, 70), Aristobulus was the first of the Hasmonaeans to take the title king. Strabo,[1] however, attributes this to Alexander Jannaeus. We should probably regard Josephus as the more reliable tradition. At all events there are no compelling reasons why he should have given this information unless there were some historical background.[2] In addition, it is striking that Strabo nowhere mentions Aristobulus I and therefore possibly knew nothing of his very short reign.

We do not know whether there was opposition to Aristobulus' taking the title of king. It is, however, certain that from the return from exile up to this time a majority in Judaea was against the restoring the monarchy.[3]

Aristobulus was regarded as a friend of the Hellenists (cf. *AJ* XIII, 318). The fact that he used a Greek name in place of his Hebrew name Judas already points in this direction, though of course all the Hasmonaeans did the same thing.[4] It is probably also above all because of this leaning towards Hellenism that Josephus (*AJ* XIII, 319) attributes a friendly and modest character to him. However, his activities (see above) hardly bear this out.

The most important event during the short reign of Aristobulus was his conquest of the greater part of Ituraea. The inhabitants of this area were forcibly circumcised.[5] The northern part of Galilee also belonged to the territory of Ituraea at this period,[6] and this was the part that Aristobulus I conquered. Otherwise, it can hardly be assumed that compulsory circumcision was imposed on the whole population of northern Galilee. Descendants of the old population of Israel must still have been living there. They, or at least some of them, may well have neglected the practice of circumcision. Aristobulus corrected this when he conquered them.

In 103 BC Aristobulus I suddenly died.

11.2 *Alexander Jannaeus (103-76 BC)*

11.2.1 *The beginning of his reign*

After the death of Aristobulus I, his brothers were freed from their captivity by his widow. This widow, who bore the name Alexandra Salome, married Alexander Jannaeus and appointed him king and high priest. Alexander was the third son of John Hyrcanus I and thus a brother of Aristobulus. The fact that Alexander Jannaeus married his brother's widow shows that he had little respect for Mosaic legislation, according to which a high priest was not allowed to marry a widow (cf. Lev.21.14). Moreover Alexander Jannaeus showed himself to be an unworthy high priest in every respect. He was concerned only with military conquests and with extending his own power.

Thus throughout his reign of twenty-seven years Alexander Jannaeus was constantly involved in wars, while constantly causing new conflicts in the domestic sphere. All this began very soon after his accession.

11.2.2 *The general political and social situation*

The successes which Alexander Jannaeus achieved in the military sphere are very closely connected with particular developments which took place on an international level.

First of all there was the situation in Egypt. At this time Cleopatra III was on the throne; she was nicknamed 'the red'. She did not much care for Egyptian nationalism and therefore had her son Ptolemy IX, who was very popular with the Egyptians, sent away in about 107 BC to Cyprus as military governor. For the same reason she also supported Alexander Jannaeus in his attempt to take control of Ptolemais and a number of other places (see 11.2.3) when Ptolemy IX came to their help.

Then there was the political and social situation in Rome. Political differences there led to a civil war around 88 BC. Thanks to the encouragement of the consul Sulla, the *optimates*, who supported a traditional policy under the direction of the Senate, were at that time able to get the better of the *populares*, who wanted to rule by means of a popular assembly. The result of this civil war, which was preceded by two decades of disturbances, was that in Rome people were far more concerned with domestic matters than with foreign affairs.

In this troubled situation, Mithridates VI, king of Pontus, with some help from Ptolemy IX, who was still on Cyprus, succeeded in conquering almost the whole of Asia Minor, the Greek islands and part of Greece. In 84 BC Sulla made peace with Mithridates on conditions which very much favoured the latter. Sulla was forced to do this because the growing influence of the *populares* in Rome forced him to return rapidly to the city. In 83 BC Sulla succeeded in regaining power in Rome.

The situation I have just outlined shows that almost throughout the reign of Alexander Jannaeus Rome had its hands full with the conflicts in its own land and the war with Mithridates. Above all because of this, Alexander Jannaeus was in a position to pursue his extensive expansionist policy.

11.2.3 *The first conquests of Alexander Jannaeus*

Very soon after becoming ruler in 103 BC, Alexander Jannaeus made an attempt to seize the important coastal city of Ptolemais (Acco). The inhabitants of Ptolemais called on Ptolemy IX for help, and shortly afterwards he landed south of Carmel with an army. Alexander then had to break off the siege of Ptolemais. There was a battle by the Jordan in Galilee between Ptolemy IX and Alexander Jannaeus, in which Alexander was defeated.

At that moment Cleopatra III, on whom Alexander Jannaeus had called for help, intervened. Ptolemy IX was defeated and forced to go back to Cyprus. Through the mediation of Hananiah, the Egyptian-Jewish commander of the Egyptian army, Cleopatra made a treaty with Alexander Jannaeus, which again left his hands free.[7]

Directly after that Alexander Jannaeus undertook a campaign in Transjordan, where he conquered Gadara and other places. He was also able to capture the city of Gaza by treachery, whereupon he had it plundered and razed to the ground. A short time beforehand Gaza had called on Aretas II, the king of the Nabataeans, for help, but it came too late.[8]

From this time on (*c.* 95 BC), Alexander Jannaeus had the whole of the coastal plain with the exception of Ashkelon under his control.[9] After that he had to turn all his attention to domestic problems. The matters which concerned him here were to take him eight years to deal with.

11.2.4 *Domestic conflicts*

In chapter 9 we looked at a number of important Judaean groups, some of which begin to come to the fore especially in the period described here. In

Judaea at this point we have the conservative group of the old priestly élite which may be said to have included not only the Hasmonaeans but also the Sadducees (cf.9.1), and the popular party of the Pharisees which in this period was certainly to be regarded as progressive (cf.9.2).

It was especially at this time that the Pharisees adopted an increasingly critical attitude to the Hasmonaeans. The break which had come about in the meantime between John Hyrcanus I and the Pharisees (see 10.2.4) increased enormously in the time of Alexander Jannaeus. The Pharisees were deeply offended by Alexander, since though he was high priest he was married to his brother's widow, which was forbidden by law (see 11.2.1). Moreover they were scandalized by the fact that a cruel warrior like Alexander Jannaeus should hold this sacred office.

The extent of the influence of the Pharisees and the unpopularity of Alexander Jannaeus is evident from an incident during the Feast of Tabernacles in *c.* 90 BC. When Alexander Jannaeus on this occasion deliberately went against the prescribed ritual by pouring holy water on the ground instead of on the altar, the people pelted him with the lemons which they had with them for the feast.[10] According to Josephus (*AJ* XIII, 373), the king thereupon had six thousand people executed.

Some years later Alexander Jannaeus was defeated in a campaign against . Obodas I, king of the Nabataeans (*c.* 93-85 BC). When Alexander fled back to Jerusalem, open rebellion broke out against him. The civil war that ensued lasted six years. Fifty thousand Judaeans were killed in this war. Evidently the struggle did not go very well for the opponents of Alexander Jannaeus, since in *c.* 88 BC the rebels called in the help of the Seleucids.[11] Thereupon Demetrius III (95-87 BC) invaded the territory of Alexander Jannaeus with an army. To begin with, Demetrius had great successes and was also able to inflict a heavy defeat on Alexander Jannaeus at Shechem.

At that point many Judaeans again had a sense of national solidarity. In the last resort they preferred a bad Hasmonaean ruler to Seleucid domination. So a large number of Alexander Jannaeus' opponents again took his side. As a result of the changed circumstances Demetrius III was forced to leave the country again. Soon after that, Alexander Jannaeus succeeded in eliminating the other rebels and their leaders. After the struggle was over he had about eight hundred rebels crucified in Jerusalem.[12] Many of his opponents also went into exile. Alexander Jannaeus then largely had peace in his country, but not outside the frontiers of his kingdom.

This civil war and the campaign of Demetrius III are presumably also echoed in the writings of Qumran, at least if the Demetrius mentioned in 4QpNah2 is indeed Demetrius III.[13] In that case there would be an allusion to these events in 4QpNah 1-12. and the designation 'those who seek smooth things' in 4QpNah 3 could simply be the Pharisees. This passage would then show that the relationship between the Qumran community and the Pharisees was not particularly good at this time. However, this should not lead us to conclude that people in the community had a positive attitude towards Alexander Jannaeus. The way in which the crucifixion of his opponents (presumably for the most part Pharisees) by Alexander Jannaeus is condemned in 4QpNah 8 speaks volumes in this respect.

11.2.5 *The struggle against the Nabataeans*

Alexander Jannaeus' position in foreign affairs was also weakened by the civil war. This became clear when the Seleucid king Antiochus XII Dionysus (87-84 BC) was involved in a dispute with Aretas III (*c.*85-62 BC), the king of the Nabataeans. In his campaign against Aretas III, Antiochus XII went straight through Judaean territory, but Alexander Jannaeus hardly dared to defy him openly.

When a short time later Antiochus XII was killed in a battle against Aretas III, the rule of the latter extended far into Syria in the north and as far as Egypt in the south.[14] After this conquest Aretas III attacked Judaea. It soon became clear just how dangerous the situation was for Alexander Jannaeus. Aretas III advanced quickly and defeated Alexander at Adida, a place about four miles north-east of Lydda, controlling the route from Joppa to Jerusalem.[15] However, Alexander succeeded in making an agreement with Aretas III, the result of which was that the latter again withdrew from Judaea.[16] Thus the victory of Aretas seems to have been less decisive than appeared at first sight.

After these events Alexander Jannaeus controlled Judaea, Samaria and Galilee, part of Transjordan and the Philistine coastal region. In order to take possession of the whole of the territory east of Jordan he invaded Transjordan, where in *c.* 83-80 BC he succeeded in conquering a number of predominantly Greek cities.[17] Most of them were part of the Decapolis, which became particularly famous at a later stage.[18]

The inhabitants of these cities went over to Judaism, but not without putting up some resistance; only the people of Pella refused. For that reason their city was destroyed.[19] After this campaign Alexander Jannaeus returned home, where he was again enthusiastically greeted by many people because of the successes he had achieved.

11.2.6 *The end of Alexander Jannaeus*

Shortly before his death Alexander Jannaeus again went on the warpath in Transjordan. He died during the siege of the fortress of Ragaba[20] in 76 BC.

Shortly before his death, according to Josephus (*AJ* XIII, 400ff.), he had advised his wife Salome Alexandra to make peace with the Pharisees again. Alexander clearly saw that otherwise the situation in the country would be untenable.

After Alexander's death his corpse was brought to Jerusalem and there buried with the pomp and splendour befitting a king and high priest.[21] He had been king for twenty-seven years. In this period he had waged numerous wars and exercised a real rule of terror on at least part of his subjects, like the Pharisees. It goes without saying that all this had great and often catastrophic consequences for the country and the population.

11.3 *The political and economic consequences of the reign of Alexander Jannaeus*

In the previous section we saw that Alexander Jannaeus was involved for much of his reign in wars and that this resulted in a considerable expansion of his territory. All this happened especially in the years 103-95 and 83-76 BC.[22] Obviously these wars inflicted an enormous amount of suffering and damage. So they also led to the downfall of many cultural centres. In the so-called Hellenistic cities Greek culture was often eradicated root and branch. This was especially true of the coastal cities which flourished at that time, and the Hellenistic cities east of the Jordan.

In order to safeguard his kingdom, Alexander arranged for new fortresses to be build or already existing fortresses to be extended and strengthened. Among the latter can be included a fortress in the neighbourhood of Engedi.[23] The new fortresses certainly included Machaerus, in Transjordan east of the Dead Sea,[24] and Alexandrium in the area of the Jordan north of Jericho.[25] The well-known fortress of Masada is also regarded as the work of Alexander Jannaeus, though it is more probable that it was an initiative of Herod the Great.[26]

It is also evident that the civil war described in 11.2.4 inflicted great suffering on the land. Thousands died or fled the country. A situation of this kind was obviously not conducive to prosperity in the country. Great poverty and bereavement in many families was the sorry consequence, not to mention the vast destruction that was inflicted in the process.

However, the activity of Alexander Jannaeus must also have had its positive side for various aspects of the economy of the country. It was no coincidence that his first and prime aim was to capture the coastal cities. The possession of these cities meant that Judaea controlled connections with the sea, a situation which was particularly favourable for trade, and this must again have favoured the development of agriculture.

Minting coins was also important for trade. Quite apart from the question whether Alexander Jannaeus was the first Hasmonaean to have his own coins minted (see 10.2.4), it is clear that in his time the minting of individual coins increased. It is no coincidence that an anchor is engraved on some of them:[27] this indicates trade connections overseas. We do not know whether this trade had already developed to any degree in the time of Alexander Jannaeus. Given the constant conflicts in which he was involved, we must assume that it developed only after his death.

These coins are also instructive in another respect. A large number of them bear the title 'Alexander the king' (in either Hebrew or Greek). However, coins have also been found which were reminted; these now bear the title 'Jonathan (= Jannai) the high priest and the community of the Jews'. Some scholars see the new inscription as the result of a concession that Alexander Jannaeus had to make to the Pharisees after the civil war (11.2.4).[28] It has also been suggested that the coins come from opponents of Alexander in this war.[29] If all this is true, these coins would come from the last period of Alexander Jannaeus' reign. However, we cannot be certain about that.

11.4 *Messianism*

In the coming period of the history of Israel the expectation of the messianic time and of the messiah, which has a background in the Old Testament,[30] was to have an increasingly prominent place. It is for that reason that we must now pay some attention to this phenomenon.

Messianic expectations are directed towards the (coming) period of salvation in which God achieves his final goal with the people and the world and in which he makes use of particular figures like an anointed or Messiah. In the period described here messianic expectations were strongly determined not only by tradition but often also by the circumstances of the time. In no case can we speak of a uniform structure. Thus for a long time it has been inappropriate to speak in terms of *a* messiah.

The Book of Jubilees is one of the works that can be put in this context.[31] In addition, a book like the Psalms of Solomon (17.21-25) mentions a political messiah who will purify the city of Jerusalem of Gentiles (17.32-38). Israel will not only have independence but also extend to the ends of the earth. Sometimes in messianic expectation we also find more than one Messiah, as in the Qumran writings (see 7.5) and in the 'Testaments of the Twelve Patriarchs'.[32]

The majority of messianic expectations in this and later periods have a common feature. All are permeated by the notion that God will deliver his people and free them from whatever situation they are in. In this connection there is also a clear difference from the apocalyptic mentioned in 7.5. The apocalyptists were very pessimistic about the survival of the existing world. By contrast, in messianic expectation the hope was that the time of salvation would be realized in this world. So it is no coincidence that messianic expectations played a role in liberation movements like those of the Zealots and Bar Kochba ('Son of the star'). It is also precisely for these reasons that messianic movements flourished most in situations of need and times of oppression. Least of all should we be surprised that such movements found many supporters, especially in Galilee. The messianic expectation was the only hope of a human existence for the impoverished country population.

Chapter 12

The Downfall of the Hasmonaean Dynasty

12.1 *The international situation*

In this period international politics were increasingly dominated by Rome. Despite problems in Spain and Italy, where among other things a slave rebellion broke out in 74 BC, and another confrontation with Mithridates the king of Pontus (see 11.2.2), the Romans succeeded in putting things in order within a few years and even in considerably strengthening their position of power in Asia. The person who came in the fore here was the Roman general Pompey. He undertook a successful campaign in the East, where in about 66 BC he inflicted a decisive defeat on Mithridates.[1] A conflict with Armenia was also brought to a satisfactory conclusion. Tigranes, the king of Armenia, made peace with Rome. He remained in possession of his empire on condition that he restrained the increasing Parthian aggression from the East. The result was that Armenia became a kind of vassal state of Rome and at the same time functioned as a buffer between Rome and the Parthians. Sulla (see 11.2.2) had signed a treaty with the Parthians in 84 BC in which it was determined that the Euphrates should be the frontier between Rome and the Parthian empire;[2] this treaty was endorsed and renewed by Pompey.[3]

After dealing with these matters Pompey turned his attention to Syria, the former Seleucid realm. In 65 BC he sent Scaurus to Damascus to restore order there. The following year (64 BC), Syria became a new province of the Roman empire,[4] which soon included the greater part of Palestine. The high priest still had some authority, but he was under the strict control of the governor of Syria (cf. also Luke 2.2).

The Romans had never had so strong a position in the East. The Seleucid power had finally vanished from the political scene. The Roman empire extended as far as the Euphrates. Within this territory there were still some miniature states which were vassals of Rome, but almost everywhere else was under direct Roman supervision of Rome. It is clear that from now on the

Romans began to be extremely interested in Judaean affairs. The unpleasant fraternal dispute between the Hasmonaeans Aristobulus and Hyrcanus gave them good reason for this.

12.2 *Salome Alexandra (76–67 BC)*

In accord with the wishes of Alexander Jannaeus, his widow Salome Alexandra took over the rule of Judaea after his death. Of course she could not be high priest. She nominated her oldest son, whom the tradition portrays as a weak man, to this post.

Whatever may be the truth in the tradition in Josephus and the rabbis[5] that shortly before his death Alexander Jannaeus advised his wife to be certain to secure the favour of the Pharisees, the Pharisees certainly had great influence during her reign. Josephus says that during her reign they in fact had all the power in their hands.[6] According to a rabbinic tradition,[7] Simeon ben Shetah, a brother of Salome Alexandra,[8] was their most important leader in this period.

A change also seems to have taken place in the composition of the *gerousia* (see 3.4.2) under Salome Alexandra, which favoured the Pharisees. Hitherto it had been made up of the heads of the leading families in Judaea and priests who were related to the high priest or had a very important function in the priestly hierarchy. Over the course of time these two groups had come to consist mainly of Sadducees. However, Salome Alexandra introduced a change by giving a third group, the scribes, a place in the *gerousia*. In this way the Pharisees, too, from then on had a voice in the assembly, since many of them were scribes.[9]

Under the influence of the Pharisees, many of those who had been imprisoned during the reign of Alexander Jannaeus were freed and countless fugitives returned to the country. However, when the Pharisees began to take vengeance on their former opponents, the fervent supporters of Alexander Jannaeus, opposition developed. A delegation of Sadducees supported by Salome Alexandra's younger son Aristobulus (see below) seems to have prevailed on her to keep them in check. That avoided civil war for the time being.[10]

All in all, the rule of Salome Alexandra may be said to have been a fairly peaceful time. In foreign affairs we are told of an expedition by Aristobulus against Damascus on behalf of the queen. However, this campaign came to grief.[11] The threat of an invasion by Tigranes, king of Armenia, against Judaea was warded off when in 69 BC Tigranes was defeated by the Romans under the command of Lucullus.[12]

For the moment there was also peace and quiet at home, but trouble was brewing. The ambitious Aristobulus wanted to take over power. To this end he secured the support of former friends of his father, who formed a group of rich and powerful figures.[13] Above all through their help he succeeded in occupying twenty-two important fortresses in Judaea shortly before his mother's death.[14] The Pharisees in particular looked askance at this development. They saw their newly secured position threatened by Aristobulus, through whose activity the Sadducees were again coming to the fore.

12.3 *Aristobulus II (67-63 BC)*

After the death of Salome Alexandra it was already clear that Aristobulus had the strongest position. The legitimate successor of the dead queen was, however, Hyrcanus II, who already held office as high priest. A conflict between him, supported by the Pharisees, and Aristobulus II, supported by Sadducees, was therefore understandably soon in coming. There was a battle between the two sides near Jericho, which went completely against Hyrcanus II. He fled to the Acra in Jerusalem, but even there he soon had to yield to his brother. Aristobulus and Hyrcanus then made an agreement under which Hyrcanus handed over power to Aristobulus. However, this treaty allowed Hyrcanus his possessions and income.

In the account of this event it is not very clear whether Aristobulus was now king and high priest. In *AJ* XIV, 41,97 and *AJ* XX, 243f., Josephus says that Aristobulus was also high priest, but in *AJ* XIV, 6 and *BJ* I, 121 he says only that Aristobulus was king. However, taking *AJ* XIV, 7 into consideration, and given the fact that Hyrcanus nowhere gives the impression of being an ambitious figure (he is portrayed as a peace-loving character), it seems most probable that Aristobulus was given both offices under the treaty.[15]

At this moment, however, Antipater, the father of Herod the Great, appeared on the political scene. Antipater was the son of a rich Idumaean, also called Antipater, who had been nominated *strategos* (a kind of governor) by Alexander Jannaeus. This son, who perhaps held the office which was formerly his father's, tried to exploit the fraternal dispute between the two Hasmonaeans. He realized that he would get more influence and power under a government led by Hyrcanus than under that of the powerful and energetic Aristobulus. Antipater succeeded in persuading Hyrcanus to make a treaty with Aretas III (*c.*85-62 BC), the king of the Nabataeans. In it Hyrcanus promised Aretas III the land conquered by Alexander Jannaeus from the Nabataeans, while in turn Aretas III was to support Hyrcanus in the battle against Aristobulus.

Along with supporters of Hyrcanus, Aretas was able to defeat Aristobulus. After that, Aretas laid siege to Aristobulus in the temple of Jerusalem, where he had fled with his troops.[16] In this situation both Hyrcanus and Aristobulus turned to the Romans for help.[17]

12.4 *The intervention of Rome*

While the events described here were taking place in Judaea, the Roman general Pompey was busy with his successful campaign in Asia (66-62 BC); one of his generals, Scaurus, had captured Damascus for him in 65 BC (see 12.1). Soon after that he turned his attention to Judaea. At about that time delegations came from both Aristobulus and Hyrcanus to ask for his help. Both offered him gifts. On this occasion the Romans opted for Aristobulus. Presumably they did so because Hyrcanus had Aretas III as his ally, and the Romans did not want the Nabataeans on any account to gain too much influence in Judaea. Moreover, Scaurus commanded Aretas to retreat from Judaea, which he immediately did, because he dared not risk a war with Rome. On his retreat Aretas was attacked by Aristobulus, who inflicted heavy losses on the Nabataeans.[18]

In 63 BC Pompey himself arrived in Damascus. There not only delegations from Aristobulus and Hyrcanus but also representatives of the people of Judaea came to him. These last asked Pompey to abolish the Hasmonaean dynasty because they wanted to be ruled by priests.[19] Josephus also tells us that on this occasion Aristobulus offered Pompey a golden vine which was worth five hundred talents.[20] According to Strabo[21] this so-called *terpole*[22] came from Alexander Jannaeus and was later put in the temple of Jupiter Capitolinus in Rome.

At the time of this meeting Pompey did not make any decision, but promised that he would sort things out in Judaea as soon as he had dealt with the Nabataeans.[23] Aristobulus was least happy with the delay. He probably was all too well aware that after dealing with the Nabataeans the Romans would take the side of the weak Hyrcanus. So he established himself in the fortress of Alexandrium to make his position secure. This action aroused the wrath of Pompey, who immediately invaded Judaea. Aristobulus quickly surrendered, but most of his supporters refused. Pompey then went back to Jerusalem and besieged the city.[24] Hyrcanus and his followers opened the gates to the Romans, who were then able to occupy the city and the royal palace. However, a group of the supporters of Aristobulus, who had already been taken prisoner, occupied the temple. Only after a siege of three months did the temple fall into the hands of the Romans.[25] To the dismay of the pious, on this occasion Pompey entered the Holy of Holies.[26]

Pompey led Aristobulus and numerous Judaean prisoners through Rome in the triumphal procession by which he celebrated his return. When they were later freed, the latter formed the beginning of a great Jewish community there.[27]

12.5 *The reorganization of the Judaean state*

The intervention of Rome in fact meant the end of the Hasmonaean dynasty and of Judaean independence, which had lasted about eighty years. The fact that Pompey again established Hyrcanus as high priest did not do anything to change this. Judaea lost all the territory won by Alexander Jannaeus and a good deal of that conquered by Simon and Jonathan. This included all the coastal cities from Raphia to Dor and all the non-Jewish cities east of the Jordan.[28] All that was left of the former Hasmonaean kingdom was Judaea, Galilee, Idumaea and Peraea. Moreover, Jerusalem and Judaea had to pay tribute to Rome. In this way the same sort of situation came into being as formerly under Ptolemaic and Seleucid rule.

Presumably the founding of the federation of ten cities, called the Decapolis in the New Testament, also dates from this time.[29] All these cities were subordinate to the newly-established Roman province of Syria.

It is clear that the Romans found Hyrcanus a willing tool. Moreover, the *de facto* power came into the hands of Antipater, whose policy was particularly favourable to Rome.

At the beginning of the Maccabaean struggle Judas and his followers could not foresee that this would ultimately be the result of their calling on the Romans for help. A long period of Roman domination now began. This domination would in future hit the Jewish state harder than the Seleucids had ever done.[30]

12.6 *Hyrcanus II (63-40 BC)*

12.6.1 *The position of Hyrcanus*

The renomination of Hyrcanus II as high priest by the Romans gave the state of Judaea still an appearance of independence. Hyrcanus himself had hardly any influence on the course of events in Judaea. He had to pay tax to the Romans, and moreover was very strictly controlled by the Roman governor of Syria. Presumably as high priest Hyrcanus was allowed to levy a temple tax. Such a privilege would fit in with the tolerant attitude which the Romans always had towards Jewish reliigon.

Hyrcanus' position was somewhat strengthened when after the death of Pompey in 48 BC he and Antipater took the side of Julius Caesar, Pompey's opponent in the second Roman civil war. They supported Caesar with Jewish auxiliaries on his campaign in Egypt. As a reward, in 47 BC Hyrcanus received the title 'ethnarch of the Jews', which gave him a kind of political status. Perhaps this also meant that Hyrcanus was now seen as a representative of all the Jews, both those in Judaea and those in the Diaspora.[31] However, this cannot have meant much, since the central figure in Jewish politics was and remained Antipater.

12.6.2 *The role of Antipater*

In the previous section we saw (12.3) that Antipater's father had been appointed *strategos* of Idumaea by Alexander Jannaeus when he conquered the region. Now the roles were completely reversed. Antipater gave his sons Phasael and Herod (later Herod the Great) the task of governing Jerusalem and Galilee respectively.[32] The corner-stone of Antipater's policy was to maintain good relations with Rome and to keep himself and his sons in the public eye. Here he was almost completely successful. Above all his younger son Herod came into the limelight.

In 47 BC Herod made quite a reputation for himself by launching a fierce attack on a certain Ezechias (Hezekiah) who with his followers was waging a guerrilla war in the north of Galilee. Herod had him and his men put to death after a mock trial. This arrogant attitude brought Herod into conflict with the Sanhedrin, which called him to account for his action. Herod did not go there in the customary penitential dress but in purple, surrounded by an armed bodyguard. He was almost condemned by the Sanhedrin, but at the decisive moment Hyrcanus had the session of the Sanhedrin interrupted, probably on the orders of the Roman authorities, and advised Herod to leave Jerusalem.[33]

Herod thereupon wanted to attack Jerusalem, but he was restrained by Antipater and Phasael. Antipater rightly understood that a new civil war would do no good to his own position and that of his sons.[34] During his conflict with the Sanhedrin, Herod's position was considerably strengthened by his nomination as *strategos* of Coele-Syria, and probably also of Samaria, by Sextus Caesar.[35]

Antipater himself did not live long after these events. In 43 BC he was murdered by a certain Malichus, who was attempting to win more influence in Judaea at Antipater's expense. Soon afterwards this Malichus was killed on Herod's orders by assassins in the region of Tyre.

12.6.3 *Political and economic developments*

The first years after the conquest of Jerusalem by Pompey seem to have been relatively peaceful. After that the situation deteriorated considerably. This was particularly the case in the years after the death of Antipater.

The changed situation was closely connected with the fact that Cassius and Brutus, who wanted to restore the old republican traditions in Rome, were defeated in 42 BC at Philippi in Macedonia by the troops of the triumvirate of Octavian, Antony and Lepidus.[36] From this moment on the government of the Eastern provinces of the Roman empire fell into the hands of Antony. Soon after that (*c.*41 BC) a Jewish delegation appeared before Antony to complain about Phasael and Herod. Herod himself was able to neutralize these accusations by going straight to Antony. A new attempt by a Jewish delegation that same year to complain about the two Idumaeans also had no success. Phasael and Herod were even nominated tetrarchs of Judaea by Antony.[37] We do not know precisely what this function involved (see 14.2.1).

The period of Antony's government was a bad time for Palestine. Antony's ostentatious life-style demanded a good deal of money and to provide this his subjects had to endure very heavy taxes. Since the coming of the Romans these had not been particularly light anyway,[38] but now they were quite intolerable. The tumultous times which now dawned must certainly be seen in this light.

In 40 BC the Parthians began a large-scale invasion of the ancient Near East. On this occasion Antigonus, a son of Aristobulus II who was captured in 63 BC, offered them his services in exchange for their help in setting him on the Jewish throne. The invasion succeeded. Antigonus got a good deal of support, above all in Judaea and Galilee, presumably also because of the bad economic situation there.[39] The Parthians took Phasael and Hyrcanus II prisoner by a trick, and Herod was forced to flee. The ears of Hyrcanus II were cut off, thus making it impossible for him to be high priest (cf. Lev.21.17). He died later in Parthian captivity. Phasael committed suicide.

After these events Antigonus was installed king by the Parthians.[40] Dio Cassius[41] reports the accession of Antigonus, but wrongly calls him Aristobulus instead of Antigonus.

12.7 *Antigonus (40-37 BC)*

During his brief reign Antigonus also had coins minted. These coins had the usual inscription 'King Antigonus' (in Greek) on one side and 'Mattathias the high priest and the community of the Judaeans' on the other.[42]

In the meantime Antigonus was little more than a vassal of the Parthians and virtually completely dependent on them for his throne. This situation could not last long, because Rome would soon put things in order. In this connection Antigonus' most important opponent was Herod.

As early as 40 BC Herod was nominated king of Judah by the Roman Senate with the approval of Antony and Octavian; this was almost at the very moment that Antigonus took over the throne. So Herod had first to conquer his kingdom with the help of the Romans.

In 39 BC Herod was able to seize Joppa and the fortress of Masada, but a subsequent siege of Jerusalem failed because he did not have enough Roman help.[43]

When the Parthians were defeated by the Roman general Ventidius in 38 BC, Antigonus' power soon faded. In the same year Herod was able to conquer the whole of Palestine apart from Jerusalem with the aid of Ventidius' successor Sosius. Only the onset of winter prevented him from actually capturing Jerusalem.[44] He only managed that in the spring of 37 BC.

Jerusalem did not hold out long. It was soon occupied by the Romans, who fought side by side with Herod's troops. A fearful blood-bath followed. Antigonus was taken prisoner and beheaded in Antioch by the wishes of Herod and on the orders of Antony.[45]

Herod, who in the meantime had married Mariamne, a granddaughter of Hyrcanus II, now had control of his kingdom. Before we look more closely at him, we must first pay some attention to a group that was to be very influential in Palestine in the days to come, the Zealots.

12.8 The Zealots

12.8.1 The rise of the Zealots

According to Josephus,[46] in AD 6 a fourth philosophy arose alongside the Sadducees, Pharisees and Essenes. Judas, surnamed 'the Galilean',[47] is named as the founder of this group, along with the Pharisee Zadok. It is strange that this 'fourth philosophy' is not named by Josephus in *AJ* XVIII, 23ff.; *BJ* IV, 121ff., when the Sadducees, Pharisees and Essenes are. According to Hengel,[48] this may be because this group still had no name when it was founded, or Josephus did not think the designation 'Zealots' appropriate for the movement. It is certainly impossible to demonstrate that Josephus here identifies the 'fourth philosophy' with the Zealots.[49] Moreover Josephus uses the designation Zealots almost solely for a group which played an important role in the First Jewish War against Rome under the leadership of the priest Eleazar.[50]

This information in Josephus, our main and indeed almost our only source of information in this period, gives the impression that only during the First Jewish War did the Zealots come into the limelight as a group. However, we must remember that he is extremely tendentious, above all in his view of revolts against the Roman authorities. Especially in the *Jewish War* he is constantly concerned to praise the Romans, the victors in the First Jewish War. This attitude is presumably to be explained by the fact that during this war Josephus had problems with particular groups of rebels and himself went over to the Romans at that time. Josephus often calls rebels against Rome robbers, a terminology which, as we know, is also used in the New Testament.[51]

Apart from the two terms mentioned above we also find the designation *sicarii*, men armed with a *sica*, dagger. By these Josephus understands the followers of Judas the Galilean and his descendants.

It is generally thought that the groups above mentioned by Josephus are in fact the Zealots and that the Sicarii formed an extreme wing of them.[52] This group as a whole would then be identical with the 'fourth philosophy' founded by Judas the Galilaean, which therefore came into being about AD 6.

However, not everyone puts the beginning of this movement at this time. Kohler[53] sees its origins in the time of the Maccabees, and Klausner[54] suggests the Hasmonaean period. Driver[55] and Roth[56] identify the Zealots with the Qumran community. However, this last view has found hardly any following.

Alongside these views which put the origin of the Zealot movement around AD 6 or even earlier, in a very instructive article[57] Menken has defended the view that only from 66 BC onwards can we speak of a party of Zealots.[58] Earlier rebel movements would then have been connected with other groups, e.g. the followers of Judas the Galilaean and his successors with Sicarii.[59] On the basis of Josephus' terminology it is indeed hard to come to any other conclusion. The extremely sparse information in the other sources, like the New Testament and the rabbinic literature, do not give us any support here. One thing is evident: if there were in fact different groups, it must be said that, broadly speaking, these strove for the same goal. So in the long run the term Zealots can certainly be a collective name for a movement which, while it may have combined different groups, on the whole was governed by the same aims (see 12.8.3). This movement became stronger in the course of time and then finally disappeared from the scene after the first Jewish War.

12.8.2 *Terminology*

The word 'Zealot' denotes someone who has 'zeal for the honour and glory of God'. Here the great examples are the priest Phinehas (cf. Num.25.6-13) and the prophet Elijah (cf. I Kings 19.10,14). Phinehas is recalled in I Macc.2.26 and Sirach 45.23 and Elijah in Sirach 48.1-11. According to Hengel,[60] this zeal was an important characteristic of Jewish piety between the Maccabean period and AD 70 (or AD 135).

It follows from this that at the time which we are considering, the term 'Zealot' was understood as an honorific title. It is therefore conceivable that

Josephus does not like using this term of the rebels.[61] However, it is certain that many Zealots fought for the cause of their God with heart and soul. They wanted to acknowledge only him as their Lord; therefore they staked all on the liberation of Israel from the Roman oppressors; they were ready to give their lives for this and to realize the kingdom of God on earth by force of arms.[62] And that brings us to the aims of the Zealots.

12.8.3 *Aims*

The most important aim of the Zealot movement was, as I have said, the liberation of Israel. This idea of freedom was indissolubly connected with the feeling that God is king of Israel. As we shall see, the Zealot opposition was fiercest when this freedom was most threatened and attacked. A special characteristic of the Zealots was that they were prepared to die as martyrs rather than to bow to foreign rulers.[63] In particular the events at the fall of Masada in AD 73 are a vivid illustration of this.

What I have just said at least indicates that the activity of the Zealot movement was not governed by social factors.[64] As so often in the Bible, for the Zealots, faith, social concern and politics went hand in hand, as we shall see again in a later chapter.

Chapter 13

The Reign of Herod the Great
(37-4 BC)[1]

13.1 *The situation in the Roman empire in c.37-4* BC

13.1.1 *The rivalry between Antony and Octavian*

Antony (see also 12.6.3) began to behave more and more like a Hellenistic prince in the eastern part of the empire. His close relationship with Cleopatra of Egypt was a major factor here. This relationship was sealed by marriage in 36 BC. Antony's way of behaving was greatly disapproved of both by Octavian and in Italy generally. His marriage with Cleopatra was at the same time a repudiation of his wife Octavia, a sister of Octavian. A request by Antony for troops to fight against the Parthians was rejected in Rome.

An open conflict between Antony and Octavian was not long in coming. Pressure from Antony to drive Octavian out of Rome did not find any support. But when Octavian called on the Romans to send a punitive expedition against Antony his summons did find a response in Italy. The conflict between the two rivals was resolved at the battle of Actium in 31 BC.[2] Antony was defeated and had to flee with Cleopatra to Egypt, where they both committed suicide. Egypt became part of the Roman empire.[3] It goes without saying that all this considerably strengthened Octavian's position.

13.1.2 *Octavian as sole ruler*

After the death of Antony, Octavian soon took all power into his own hands. The Roman senate bestowed on him the title Augustus, the exalted one. This name, by which he is also known in Luke 2.1, had previously been reserved for gods. He was also given the honorific title *princeps civitatis*, 'the first of the citizens'. This term became the designation of the form of state which began under Augustus: the principate, the monarchical form of state in which the emperor was the first of the Roman citizens.[4] When Lepidus, who had previously formed a triumvirate with Octavian and Antony, died in 12 BC, Augustus was to all intents and purposes the undisputed ruler of the Roman empire.

The territorial expansion in the time of Augustus was enormous. For example, great tracts of territory in North Africa and Central Europe were conquered. However, in the East Augustus did not annex any more territory. In the last years of his rule his policy was above all concerned with consolidation.[5] It is because of this that his rule is usually described as a period of peace in the empire.

One of Augustus' most faithful servants in carrying out his policy was Herod the Great. In the rest of this chapter we shall be mainly concerned with him.[6]

13.2 *Herod's position*

13.2.1 *Characteristics*

Only in *AJ* XVIII, 130, 133, 136 does Josephus call Herod 'the Great'. Nor is this title found elsewhere in Josephus. Presumably the designation 'the Great' is used to distinguish him from his sons, who were also called Herod. Herod was not a 'great' man in the sense that he was an admirable ruler. His rule was characterized by the greatest possible cruelty, of which a number of examples are given in both Jewish and Christian literature, although that is not always very objective.[7] As we shall see, he did not even spare his own children. In this light even the well-known story of the massacre of the children in Bethlehem (Matt.2.16) is certainly credible.[8]

Herod's attitude is closely connected with his awareness that his rule over Judaea rested purely on oppression. The whole of his domestic policy was directed towards the preservation of his own life and rule. As far as that was concerned he mistrusted everything and everyone.

So as a statesman, Herod can be described as merciless. This is already evident, as we saw in the previous chapter (12.6.2), from his action against the rebels in Galilee and his attitude towards the 'Sanhedrin'.[9] His policy towards Judaism might be described as tolerant. Although under the influence of his court historian Nicolaus of Damascus[10] he favoured Hellenism, he presented himself to the Jewish community as a Jew. The coins minted on his orders have no image on them. Nor were statues placed on important buildings in Jerusalem. As far as possible he respected the views of the Pharisees, who were important in his time (but cf. also 13.5).

It would be wrong to judge Herod purely in negative terms. There were also positive features to his government.[11]For example, when the country was visited about 25 BC by a severe famine, Herod used all the gold and silver from his palace to buy corn in Egypt in order to provide the hungry population with food.[12]

Herod's foreign policy was quite different from his domestic policy. It was entirely based on the principle of maintaining his friendship with Rome, in all circumstances and at any price. Here he completely succeeded, although often he could hardly complain about his luck.

13.2.2 *Relations with Rome*

The vassal kings set up by Rome in certain areas were usually chosen from princes. Herod was an exception to this. Hereditary monarchies were not tolerated by the Romans. In specific instances investigations were made as to whether a son could follow his father.[13]

Herod's power was in many respects limited. A Roman vassal was not allowed to make treaties with other peoples or wage wars on his own. In time of war his duty was to help Rome with troops. Thus we know that in a campaign by Aelius Gallus in 25-24 BC against the Sabaeans in Arabia (which proved a failure), five hundred Jewish auxiliaries were also involved.[14]

Vassals were given limited rights to mint coins, to have their own army (a small one) and to raise taxes. They also had unlimited power of life and death over their subjects.[15]

The greatest crisis in Herod's relations with Rome came in 32-31 BC at the time of the civil war between Antony and Octavian (cf.13.1), from which the latter emerged as victor. As a protégé of Antony Herod risked being put in a dangerous position. However, luck was with him in that he had not been involved in this civil war; at the time Cleopatra had sent him, against his will, to fight against the Nabataeans. After the victory at Actium Herod resolved to pay a personal visit to Octavian, who at that time was on Rhodes. Without disguising his former friendship with Antony, Herod now offered Octavian his services. Octavian accepted them, and in addition gave Herod Cleopatra's possessions in Palestine.[16] When further extended in Samaria and Transjordan, Herod's kingdom soon became the same size as it was in the time of Alexander Jannaeus.[17] According to Josephus,[18] Octavian trusted Herod to such a degree that he ordered the procurators of Syria to use Herod as their advisor in all matters. However, this piece of information is extremely dubious.[19]

13.3 *Building works*

13.3.1 *In Jerusalem*

Without question Herod made a great impression with the many imposing buildings that were erected on his initiative. One of his most important projects was the rebuilding and expansion of the temple in Jerusalem. Work went on here for years even after the death of Herod. Only in AD 64, in the time of Agrippa, was it completely finished. This means that the temple only stood for six years after being completed. Not only tens of thousands of laity but also thousands of priests worked on the project. Priests had to do the work in places to which non-priests had no access. So here, too, Herod had to cope with religious sensibilities.

The splendour and size of this temple seem to have been proverbial. We have detailed descriptions of its extent and arrangement in Josephus[20] and in the Talmud.[21] The two descriptions largely agree.

In the temple an inscription was put up prohibiting foreigners (non-Jews) from entering the inner court: it stated that the penalty for transgressing this command was death.[22] According to Bickerman,[23] Zerubbabel had already put up a notice to this effect in the temple in 200 BC (see also 6.2.2).

As in the time of the temple of Solomon (see I Kings 7.1), even this temple in all its glory did not compare with the palace which Herod had built for himself in Jerusalem. The palace was built on a high hill in the west of the city and dominated the whole panorama of Jerusalem. The palace had three gates on the north side, Phasael, Hippicus and Mariamne. According to Geva,[24] Hippicus was on the site of the former 'gates of David'.

The citadel of Antonia, well known from the New Testament, and situated on the north-western corner of the temple mount, was another of Herod's buildings from this time. This citadel was particularly important from a military point of view. Herod also had an amphitheatre built in the immediate environs of Jerusalem.[25]

13.3.2 *Buildings outside Jerusalem*

Outside Jerusalem and Judaea, as I have already said, Herod behaved as a non-Jew. So in various non-Jewish cities he had temples built, mostly in honour of the Roman emperor.[26] He did so, for example, in Samaria and Caesarea. These two cities are to be seen largely as Herod's creation. He almost completely rebuilt the city of Samaria and renamed it Sebaste[27] in honour of Augustus. In about 22 BC he began to built a completely new port, which he called Caesarea.[28] Another city refounded by Herod was Antipatris.

It was presumably on the site of the city of Aphek, mentioned e.g in Josh.12.18.[29] These three places are typical non-Jewish cities. According to Broshi[30] the number of this sort of city increased from twelve to twenty-five in Herod's reign.

Excavations have also shown that in Jericho Herod built a great winter palace with a large garden, reservoirs and swimming baths on the remains of a Hasmonaean winter residence.[31]

Another important enterprise was the building, rebuilding or extension of a number of fortresses. Thus he strengthened the fortresses of Alexandrium, north of Jericho, Hyrcania in the wilderness of Judah about seven miles south-east of Jerusalem, Machaerus in the extreme south of Peraea, and Masada in the wilderness of Engedi (cf. I Sam.24.1), on the west coast of the Dead Sea, all of which had been built by the Hasmonaeans. He also rebuilt Anthedon, on the coast near Gaza,[32] which he called Agrippium[33] or Agrippias.[34] Two new fortresses were named Herodium in his own honour.[35] One was near the village of Tekoa, about six miles south of Jerusalem,[36] and the other in the hills facing Nabataean territory. However, the exact site of this last fortress is not known. A new fortress was also built at Jericho, which was called Cyprus after Herod's mother.[37]

13.4 *The social and economic situation*

13.4.1 *Taxation*

It is almost certain that Herod largely took over the system of taxation which existed in the time of the Hasmonaeans (cf. 10.1.2).[38] The burden of taxation became enormous under Herod's rule. He needed an vast amount of money; even more than the Hasmonaeans. The countless building works in his day (see 13.3) and the state which he developed must have swallowed up very great sums of money.[39] The only way in which he could get it was by raising taxes. That these taxes were unacceptably high is evident, for example, from the fact that directly after his death the Judaeans asked his successor Archelaus to reduce the high taxation;[40] this situation recalls events after the death of Solomon.[41]

We do not know precisely how high these taxes were. Nor do we have any information about how they were raised. However, it is certain that one way was to make rich aristocrats[42] who from the start had been supporters of Herod responsible for them;[43] another way particularly favoured was the use of a system of publicans which is known from the New Testament. In one form or another this institution goes back to the system of tax farmers which existed in the Ptolemaic period.[44] The publicans also had a contract from the authority for collecting direct taxes.

In one instance we know that Herod granted a remission of a third[45] of the taxes, but this was to stave off the threat of a rebellion. All this shows how heavy the taxes must have been.

We do not know whether or not Herod had a census in his kingdom in connection with the raising of taxes. According to Schalit,[46] he must have done something of the sort, probably in 20 and 14 BC. One of Schalit's arguments is that something of the kind is also reported of another client king, namely Archelaus of Cappadocia.[47] A considerable objection to this is that, for example, Josephus says nothing about such a census.[48] The census reported in Luke 2.1-2 could just as well have taken place in the time of Herod.[49]

13.4.2 *Poverty and riches*

Avigad[50] has established on the basis of archaeological investigations that there were great riches in Jerusalem in the time of Herod. Excavations in the suburbs of the city where the well-to-do then lived show this clearly. The houses there have reservoirs and splendid mosaic floors, which is certainly evidence of the great wealth and prosperity of the well-to-do citizens of Jerusalem in this period. Such an observation should not surprise us, given what was said in 13.4.2 about Herod's supporters.

However, these riches were limited to a particular small group of the population. Alongside that there was very great poverty in the country. The heavy taxation was a burden not so much for the rich supporters of Herod mentioned in 13.4.1 as for the country and peasant population. The fact that rebels against Roman (Herodian) authority could count on much support from this population[51] itself points clearly in this direction. Above all, Galilee constantly came to the foreground at that time. In this context we might recall the activites of Ezechias (Hezekiah) and his supporters in the time before Herod became king (see 12.6.2).

However, not all the well-to-do escaped Herod's demands for money. At all events, Josephus[52] describes how, shortly after the occupation of Jerusalem in 37 BC, Herod robbed the well-to-do to get money. Above all the former supporters of Antigonus, who were especially to be found in Judaea and Galilee, were the losers here. And Herod needed a good deal of money, not only to maintain his army and his famous capital but also to be able to give large gifts to his friends. We know, for instance, that at the beginning of his reign he gave large gifts to Antony and his staff.[53]

One advantage for the country was that for a great deal of Herod's rule (from *c.*31 to 4 BC) there was relative peace. Such a situation meant that the farmers could work without being troubled by war and violence. Given the severe burden of taxation this at least was a relief.

13.5 *Herod's religious policy*

We saw earlier (13.2.1) that Herod was very cautious over Judaism and Jewish customs and that he presented himself to Jews as a Jew. However, later traditions suggest that people did not respect him very highly in religious matters.[54] There were reasons enough for offence here. We may recall his contemptuous attitude towards the Sanhedrin (see 12.6.2). Another great source of offence was the golden eagle[55] which he had fixed to the gate of the temple. Herod would not have it removed, and when towards the end of his reign it was taken away as a result of a conspiracy led by the scribes Judas and Matthias, these suffered terrible punishment.[56]

Herod also nominated and deposed high priests at will. For high priests he chose people who were well disposed towards him and took little notice of existing traditions. This way of carrying on did not do much for the respect of this old institution. It can also be assumed that Herod's action widened the gulf between the people and the priests. Even apart from this, the reputation of the priests continued to sink in an uninterrupted decline.

Although in religious matters Herod took account of the views of the Pharisees, Josephus[57] says that he clashed with them when they refused to give an oath of allegiance to him and the emperor. This refusal clearly had a religious background.[58] It would have put too much emphasis on their obedience to a foreign (and indeed pagan) ruler. It is striking that in this case Herod did not have the Pharisees killed, as he did other offenders, but let them off or simply imposed a fine.

One reason for Herod's accommodating attitude to the Pharisees was doubtless that this group had great influence among the people. In addition, another factor may have played a role. This group gradually transferred its concern from political matters more towards the religious sphere. Such a shift cannot have ben displeasing to Herod. Politically he had nothing to fear from them. Another reason for his tolerant attitude towards the Pharisees may well have been that at the siege of Jerusalem in 37 BC the gates of the city were opened on the urgent advice of two Pharisees, Shemaiah and Pollio.[59] However, they did this not so much out of sympathy for Herod as from a sense that he was a divine instrument for punishing the apostasy of the people.[60]

It is clear that not all the Pharisees kept religion and politics apart. One striking figure here was, as we shall see in the next chapter, the Pharisee Zadok.

13.6 *Herod's action against his family*

Herod regarded the Hasmonaeans as a constant threat to his throne. That is evident from the fact that during his government he had all the members of this family put to death.

This might seem to be contradicted by Josephus' report[61] that in 40 BC Herod urged Antony to make Aristobulus, a grandson of Hyrcanus II, king over Judaea. However, this information in Josephus presumably comes from Nicolaus of Damascus, Herod's court historian, or from Herod's own memoirs, and was simply aimed at presenting Herod's attitude towards the Hasmonaeans in as favourable a light as possible.[62]

Herod's marriage to the Hasmonaean Mariamne, a sister of this Aristobulus, was an attempt to give his rule a kind of legitimacy. Clearly this marriage caused great problems and conflicts at court. The first came very soon.

At the beginning of his reign Herod had nominated a certain Ananel, an unknown figure, high priest. This was not to the taste of Alexandra, the mother of Mariamne, who wanted this office for her son Aristobulus (see above). With the help of Cleopatra, Alexandra got her way. However, when Aristobulus seemed to be enjoying great popularity among the people as high priest, in 35 BC Herod had him drowned by his underlings during a game in a bath.[63]

After this, executions followed in rapid succession. In 29 BC Mariamne was executed, as was her mother Alexandra a year later on grounds of treachery and conspiracy; here Salome, Herod's sister, played a malicious part.

In about 23 BC Herod sent Mariamne's two sons, Alexander and Aristobulus, to Rome to be brought up. After about five years they returned to Jerusalem, whereupon Herod arranged a wedding for them. Alexander took as wife Glaphyra, a daughter of Archelaus, king of Cappadocia, and Aristobulus married Berenice, a daughter of Salome, Herod's sister.

New intrigues in which again Salome and also Antipater, the son of Herod's first wife Doris, were involved, led to accusations against Alexander and Aristobulus. Despite attempts at reconciliation by Archelaus of Cappadocia and even Augustus, the two sons were executed on the orders of Herod. This happened in Sebaste, about thirty years after Herod's marriage there to Mariamne, their mother.[64]

Antipater also suffered the same fate in 4 BC, only a few days before Herod himself died.

This lack of compassion was characteristic of Herod's whole life. Obviously he could only maintain his authority over family and people by harsh and cruel action.

13.7 *Herod's end*

Herod died in 4 BC[65] after a terrible illness. It is unclear from the text in Josephus what this was,[66] since it is difficult to interpret what it is saying.[67] A funeral procession with great pomp and ceremony bore his body to the Herodium south of Jerusalem, which he had built, and there he was buried.

The direction of this funeral was in the hands of his son Archelaus, whom Herod had named as his heir shortly before his death. This last act was typical of Herod's character. His insecurity led him to nominate one heir after another. However, his testamentary disposition had no value until the emperor had given it his approval. In the following chapter we shall see how this raised some problems. First, though, we must pay some attention to the group which was closely allied to the dynasty of Herod.

13.8 *The Herodians*

In the New Testament[68] there is only one mention of the Herodians. These Herodians must be regarded as sympathizers with the Herodian dynasty and as favourable to Rome. It is not altogether clear whether this group already existed at the time of Herod the Great. In one passage,[69] Josephus speaks of 'followers of Herod'. According to Schalit,[70] this reference is certainly to a group which is known in the New Testament as that of the Herodians. Every strong personality, according to Schalit, manages to surround itself with such a group of followers. This conception seems to be closer than that which sees the Herodians as servants of Herod Antipas.[71]

In no way can the Herodians be regarded as non-Jews. Were that the case it would be inconceivable that the Pharisees could be paired with them, as happens in the New Testament passages where they are mentioned.[72]

It seems best to regard the Herodians as supporters of the dynasty of Herod. This group would then have been more or less active during both the time of Herod the Great and that of his sons.

The fact that in Luke 20.20, the parallel to Matt.22.16; Mark 12.13, the Herodians are not mentioned, need not be an argument against their historicity.

13.9 *Literature from the first century* BC

In an account of the most important literature from the first century BC originating in Palestine, a work like Jubilees, which appeared about 100 BC, must be regarded as a borderline case. However, this work has already been discussed in 10.3.

Some parts of the book of Enoch, which has already been discussed in 7.6.2, also come from this period. These include the 'Book of Admonitions' in chs.91-105, with the exception of the 'Ten Weeks' Apocalypse' which is included in 91.12-17 and 93.[73]

The Psalms of Solomon are another important work from this period.[74] These are eighteen psalms which have been preserved partly in Greek and partly in Syriac, but which very probably go back to a Hebrew original. In various respects they show agreements with the apocryphal psalms found at Qumran.[75]

In addition to these pseudepigraphical works there is also the apocryphal I Baruch. The author of the book purports to be Baruch, the secretary and friend of the prophet Jeremiah. The dating already shows that this is historically impossible.[76] There are some indications (see e.g. Baruch 1.1-14) that this work had a place in the liturgy of 9 Ab, when the destruction of the temple was recalled.

In addition to these literary works mentioned above we should also pay some attention to the Damascus Document, various fragments of which were found in the caves of Qumran (see 9.4.4). A good deal of this writing was in fact already known from two mediaeval manuscripts which were discovered in 1896.[77] The final redaction of the Damascus Document presumably took place in the first century BC, though a rather earlier dating of this work, or part of it, cannot be ruled out.[78]

The 'covenant' which is mentioned in the document is with a holy remnant. This holy remnant forms the true Israel, who observe the rules of the 'covenant' (cf. CD VI, 1ff.). The element of choice also plays an important role in the Damascus document. If this work was not written in the Qumran community, at all events it has many features which resemble the views of the community.[79]

Chapter 14

The Period from the Death of Herod the Great to Agrippa I (*c.* 4 BC to AD 41)

14.1 *Events after the death of Herod*

14.1.1 *Rebellions*

Immediately after the death of Herod a rebellion broke out in Jerusalem. This rebellion was a consequence of the execution of Judas and Matthias shortly before Herod's death (see 13.5). Their sympathizers now asked for Herod's advisors to be punished. Archelaus, who had been appointed by Herod as his successor, sent troops to put down the rebellion. This action failed in the first instance, after which Archelaus sent new troops who made a bloody end to the revolt.[1]

After the departure of Archelaus to Rome (cf.14.1.2), new unrest broke out in Judaea which was checked by Varus, the governor of Syria. Having restored order he returned to Antioch, but left behind in Jerusalem a legion under the command of Sabinus to keep the peace there. However, this peace did not last long. When Sabinus oppressed the people violently, new unrest broke out, This happened just about Pentecost, when there were many pilgrims in the city.[2] In Jerusalem even some of Herod's soldiers joined the rebels.[3] Revolts also broke out outside Judaea, in Galilee, under the leadership of Judas, a son of Ezechias (see 12.6.2), and in Peraea under Simon, a former slave of Herod.

As a consequence of these events Varus again returned to Palestine. Using forces including auxiliaries from the Nabataean king Aretas IV (*c.* 9 BC – AD 40),[4] he succeeded in defeating the rebels. After the revolt two thousand of them were crucified.[5]

All this shows that the period directly after the death of Herod certainly cannot be called a peaceful time.[6]

14.1.2 *Herod's testament*

While most of the events described above were taking place, the majority of Herod's family was in Rome in order to clear up the matter of Herod's testament. Three sons of Herod were present: Archelaus, the successor to the throne whom he had nominated; Herod Antipas, to whom he had assigned Galilee and Peraea; and Philip. These three argued for their interests in the presence of Augustus, who had to endorse the testament. Herod Antipas, supported by most of Herod's family, moreover pressed Herod to nominate him successor to the throne in place of Archelaus, in accordance with an earlier testament.

Meanwhile two further delegations came from Palestine to Rome. There was a Jewish one which asked that none of the family of Herod should be made king, but that the government should be entrusted to a high priest, and one from the Greek cities of Gadara, Hippus and Gaza, who asked to be incorporated into the Roman province of Syria.

After some heart-searching Augustus decided to endorse Herod's testament. The three cities with Greek names were incorporated into Syria: Archelaus got Judaea, Samaria and Idumaea; Herod Antipas got Galilee and Peraea; and Philip got Auranitis, Trachonitis and presumably Ituraea.[7] None of them was allowed to call himself king. Archelaus became ethnarch and the two others tetrarch (see 14.2.1).[8]

14.2 *The government of Palestine after the death of Herod*

14.2.1 *Judaea and Samaria*

As we have seen, Archelaus became ethnarch of this part of the country. The title ethnarch is higher than that of tetrach, 'ruler of four', but lower than that of king, and was often given to a vassal.[9] Matthew (2.22),however, calls Archelaus king. Josephus also does this once (*AJ* XVIII, 93), but wrongly so. Of all the sons of Herod he most resembled his father in cruelty.[10]

The rule of Archelaus lasted only from 4 BC to AD 6. Complaints made by a delegation from Judaea and Samaria were taken seriously by Augustus. Archelaus was dismissed and sent to Gaul.[11] It is possible that Augustus' decision was also influenced by the way in which Archelaus' style of government threatened the peace and security of the important trade route from Syria to Egypt.[12]

The territory of Archelaus was now part of the Roman province of Syria and governed by a procurator.

The removal of Archelaus brought a decisive change in the existing situation.

Despite everything, both Herod and Archelaus, unlike the Roman procurators, had taken account of Jewish religion because of their knowledge of affairs in this area. The subsequent procurators Coponius (6-9), Marcus Ambibulus (9-12), Annius Rufus (12-15), Valerius Gratus (15-26), Pontius Pilatus (26-36), Marcellus (36-37) and Marullus (37-41) made mistake after mistake in this respect. There was also a constant threat of unrest, which sometimes could be defused by the spiritual leaders in Jerusalem but sometimes in fact erupted, albeit on a limited scale. The situation in Jerusalem was particularly tense at the time of the great feasts.

One of the greatest difficulties arose at the beginning of Roman rule. A census had to be taken when a country was incorporated into the Roman empire. This census took place in 6 or 7 BC under the direction of Quirinius, the legate of Syria.[13] A census of this kind included a registration of land as well as a kind of head count. The head count in particular provoked great religious objections (cf. II Sam.24.1ff.). The high priest of the time, Joazar, had the greatest difficulty in persuading the people to accept this census. Despite his efforts, a minority of the population rebelled. This group, which consisted of Zealots or a group related to them (cf.12.8.1), was led by Judas the Galilean. The revolt, in which Judas presumably lost his life, was put down by the Romans. However, the embers of rebellion continued to glow until there was a great conflagration in 66.

The best-known procurator of the period described in this chapter is Pilate.[14] In his time conflicts flared up. More than once he hurt Jewish religious sensibilities, among other things by putting up shields with the emperor's portrait on them in his palace in Jerusalem. The Jews, who saw this as a beginning of the imperial cult, protested to Tiberius, Augustus' successor. He gave Pilate orders to take back the shields to the residence in Caesarea.[15]

In some respects the Judaeans still enjoyed a degree of freedom. For example, Jews were exempt from military service in the Roman army. Relations with the Sanhedrin even seem to have improved compared with the period of Herod and Archelaus. It had much more power in domestic matters (cf. Matt.5.22). In the liturgical sphere, the Sanhedrin also made its influence felt in the Diaspora. The leadership of the Sanhedrin rested with the high priest, who as such was also regarded by the Romans as the representative of the domestic government. The Sanhedrin was also responsible for raising the direct taxes which had to be paid to the emperor (see 14.3.1).

14.2.2 *The territory of Philip (4 BC-AD 33/34)*

The areas assigned by Augustus (see 14.1.2) to Philip lay in the north and east of the country,[16] and were almost all inhabited by non-Jews. These were areas which had originally never been part of Old Testament Judah or Israel, and were only added to it at a later period.

Philip was regarded as the least important of Herod's heirs. He was certainly the most attractive. His behaviour was moderate, and he did not undertake great political activities in an ambitious way.[17] Like his father he seems to have been very interested in building work. Thus among other things he rebuilt and extended the old city of Panias at the source of the Jordan; to distinguish it from the well-known coastal place of the same name it was called Caesarea Philippi (cf. e.g. Matt.16.13). After Philip's death this kingdom was first added to Syria, and afterwards, in 37, was given to Agrippa I as his kingdom.

14.2.3 *The territory of Herod Antipas (4 BC-AD 39)*

Herod Antipas[18] had inherited a more important area from Herod than Philip (see 14.2.2). His tetrarchy is also important because it was principally the sphere in which John the Baptist (Peraea) and Jesus (Galilee) worked. Peraea was on the other side of the Jordan and was divided from Galilee, the other part of Antipas' kingdom, by the Decapolis and Samaria.

Herod Antipas most resembled his father in his behaviour, but he was less skilful. The judgment that Jesus passes on him is very unfavourable, in Luke 13.32 calling him 'that fox'.

Antipas was just as involved in building as his father and brothers. One of the most important places to be built on his initiative was the city of Tiberias, named after the emperor Tiberius (14-37), with whom Antipas was in great favour.

Herod Antipas was first married to a daughter of the Nabataean king Aretas IV. When he rejected this wife and married Herodias, the former wife of his brother Philip, he came into conflict with the Nabataeans, who inflicted a heavy defeat on him.[19] According to Josephus (*AJ* XVIII, 116ff.), some Jews saw this defeat as a divine punishment for the killing of John the Baptist. The authenticity of this passage is sometimes disputed, but most scholars regard it as genuine.[20] If it is, it is a supplement to what the Gospels tell us about John the Baptist in this connection. According to Matt.14.3-12 par., John was beheaded at the instigation of Herodias after Salome's dance.

After the death of Tiberius in 37 the power of Herod Antipas soon declined. Moreover, as a result of the intrigues of Herod Agrippa he fell into disfavour with Caligula, who in 39 banished him to Gaul.

14.3 *Social and economic conditions*

14.3.1 *Taxation*

Taxation fell into two categories: direct taxation and tolls. The Sanhedrin, under the supervision of the Roman procurator, was responsible for raising direct taxes. These taxes included a tax on the produce of the land[21] (*tributum soli*) and a poll tax (*tributum capitis*). The *tributum soli* had been paid to Rome since 63 BC. The *tributum capitis*, which provoked most opposition, had only to be paid after the annexation in AD 6 (see 12.2.1). The poll tax is the tax discussed in the question put to Jesus whether people should or should not pay tax to Caesar.[22] It was a particularly heavy burden on the population of Syria and Judaea, especially in about 17.[23]

Although the system of tolls, like most of the taxes mentioned above, already existed in one form or another in an earlier period,[24] we will not go further here into the figure of the person responsible for collecting it, the publican, since a good deal of attention is paid to him in the Gospels. Tolls included import and export taxes and also money for roads, ports and markets.[25] The raising of these taxes was farmed out by the Romans to entrepreneurs, who were usually rich men.[26] The real work of the tax farmers consisted in raising taxes through subordinates and other personnel. The tax-collectors mentioned in the New Testament are probably always the latter, except in the case of Zacchaeus (Luke 19.1-10). Thus Levi mentioned in Mark 2.14 is probably an ordinary publican. These belonged to a socially unprotected group and were usually very badly paid. It was almost inevitable that in such a situation there should be corruption.[27] So these people were often despised, not so much by the poor and the day-workers, since they usually did not have to pay any tolls, but by the well-to-do, who had to make use of their services. That Jesus is called a friend of publicans (Matt.11.19) implies that he was against such social arrogance.

14.3.2 *Landowners and leaseholders*

In a number of the parables of Jesus (see e.g. Matt.20.1-15; Mark 12.1-11) the characters are clearly large landowners. On the basis of the Mishnah and archaeological evidence Applebaum argues that land ownership increased markedly in the first century of our era. Whole villages often came to be owned by one landowner.[28]

The reason for this was that an increasing number of farmers were forced to sell their land as a result of sickness, drought and above all high taxation. These farmers and their sons then became day-workers. The new owners, the great landowners, themselves lived in the cities (often in Jerusalem) or went on travels (cf. Luke 16.1-8). They included many relatives of the high-priestly families and merchants. They usually left the supervision of their possessions to stewards. The real work was done by day-workers, slaves and leaseholders.[29]

It need hardly be argued that all this had a considerable influence on the social and economic situation in the country. In Judaea and Samaria and above all in Galilee agriculture was always the main mode of existence. The impoverishment of the farmers resulted in an enormous exodus from the country. Galilee was particularly affected by this because most of the villages were there. It has therefore been supposed that the designation 'Galileans' in Josephus usually means 'village dwellers'.[30]

In addition to the great landowners and the decreasing number of farmers there were also various kinds of leaseholders in the country. Some had to pay a fixed part of the harvest (often a half or a third) to the owner, while others paid a fixed sum in the form of 'money';[31] yet others cultivated a piece of ground and then later paid half of the harvest as their lease.[32]

The cost of the lease to be paid itself meant that these leaseholders had a hard life. In addition to their lease they also had to pay taxes (see 14.3.1). How difficult their existence often was is evident from a number of the parables of Jesus.[33]

14.3.3 *The position of the poor*

First mentioned in this category, which also included most leaseholders, come the day-workers. These were people who served a master for a fixed time, amounting to at least a day. As well as day-workers we hear of labourers, those who had a more fixed contract of service. In the period with which we are concerned here the situation of these two groups was far from rosy. Such men were often out of work, with all the consequences that followed. In the parable of the workers in the vineyard there seem to have been plenty of people standing around the market without work, for example at the eleventh hour (Matt.20.6f.). The circumstances of slaves were even more difficult. People could find themselves slaves if they were not in a position to pay their debts. Here the parable of the merciless servant is instructive. It suggests that there were two ways of paying a debt. The first was for the debtor to be sold, along with his wife, children and possessions (Matt.18.25); the second was for the debtor to be thrown into prison until his family had paid the debt.

Even in the time of Jesus many of his fellow-countrymen were slaves.[34] In addition there were also slaves of foreign origin, but it is not clear whether these were in the majority.[35] The fact that between 67 and 70 Simon bar Giora commanded the freeing of all (Jewish) slaves (*BJ* V, 108), suggests otherwise.

It is clear from the New Testament that in this period there were also a great many beggars in the country. As elsewhere, their position was very bad (see e.g. Luke 16.20).

14.3.4 *Competition and trade*

According to information given in Jewish literature there were more than forty different groups of craftsmen in Palestine at this period.[36] Many of them were connected with agriculture. Priests and scribes also practised a craft alongside their office (cf. e.g. Acts 18.3).

The craft was a profession which was often handed down from father to son. Sometimes there were families which had a particular skill at a craft (cf. m.Joma, III, XI) and kept it carefully within the family as a professional secret. Despite the very large difference in types of craft, the numbers of those involved was few in comparison to the many people involved in agricultural work.

From ancient times trade was carried on only by Phoenicians and later above all by Canaanites.[37] Hence the word Canaanite ultimately became synonymous with 'merchant'.[38] Gradually Judaeans and the inhabitants of Galilee and Samaria increasingly became involved in trade (cf. e.g. I Macc.14.5). In the time of Jesus it must have flourished.[39]

The development of trade was brought about by a variety of factors. The situation of Palestine on the important trade routes from Egypt to Mesopotamia[40] involved transit operations. In addition there was trade with Greek cities and above all with the Judaeans in the Diaspora. We should also remember the pilgrimages to Jerusalem, which doubtless encouraged trade. The markets in various cities were also important for the increase in trade. Archaeological investigations have demonstrated the important role played by the market in Jerusalem.[41] Alongside the products of the crafts, agricultural products were also very important objects of trade. Of course the tolls (see 14.3.1) which had to be paid were a disincentive.

14.4 *The religious situation*

14.4.1 *The temple*

The focal point of religious life at this time was still temple worship in Jerusalem. The temple was of great significance not only for Judaea and a wide area around,[42] but also for the Diaspora. This is clear, for example, from the temple tax of half a shekel a year paid by the Jews in the Diaspora,[43] and from their participation in pilgrimages. According to Safrai[44] tens of thousands of people came to Jerusalem for the three great festivals, from Judaea, Galilee and the Diaspora.

The daily sacrifice, which was offered morning and evening, was one of the most important cultic activities in the temple. We know very little about the temple liturgy[45] apart from the fact that sacrifices were offered regularly. It seems certain that the Psalms,[46] and also the blessing from Num.6.24-26, had a function in it.[47]

The temple had a key position not only in religious matters, but also in finance and the economy. Like all sanctuaries in antiquity,[48] it also functioned as a financial institution.[49] The many sacrificial animals that were needed, the payment of the temple tax and other gifts, the fact that the temple acted as a kind of bank, gave it a prominent position. The result of this was that the primary purpose of the temple as a 'house of God' often fell right into the background. Jesus' action against the money-changers and merchants in the temple forecourt (Mark 11.15-17) must be seen in this light.

14.4.2 *The synagogue*

There is a large literature on the question when and where the synagogue came into being.[50] Its origin must definitely be sought in the Diaspora, and in all probability in Babylon[51] or in Egypt.[52] The most probable time seems to be the third or second century BC.

In Palestine, the institution of the synagogue only developed fully after the destruction of the temple in AD 70 (see 17.3.3). According to the Gospels there were already synagogues in Palestine in the time of Jesus. Matthew and Mark mention synagogues only in Galilee, but Luke (4.44) also mentions synagogues in Judaea. Here some manuscripts have 'Galilee' instead of 'Judaea'[53] (see also 17.3.3).

Most investigations begin by stating that the reading of scripture and prayer were already the most important parts of the synagogue liturgy at a very early stage.[54] We find an earlier example of the later synagogue practice in Neh.8.1-8,[55] where we are told that Ezra read the Torah (which is what we must understand the text to refer to)[56] aloud to the people on New Year's Day.

It is hard to establish precisely on what days and on what occasions scripture reading (and exposition) had a fixed place in the synagogue liturgy. Originally, perhaps, it happened only on special occasions and feast days and later became a regular part of celebrating the sabbath. It was evidently common practice in the time of Philo.[57]

14.4.3 *The Sanhedrin*

The Sanhedrin can be seen as being in some sense a continuation of the Great Assembly and the *gerousia* (see 3.4.2). The name Sanhedrin came to be used from about 63 BC.[58] During the reign of Herod the Great it had hardly any influence. After the country was taken over by Rome the situation improved somewhat. One of the most important tasks of the Sanhedrin was to expound and apply the traditional law, and pronounce on secular and religious cases. It was also able to exercise some authority in Judaea in the political sphere. However, no important decision could be taken on any matter without the approval of the Roman procurator.

It is evident from the information in the New Testament and Josephus[59] that in the time of Jesus not only the senior priests but also scribes and elders had a place in it. The former were Sadducees, and the majority of the latter were Pharisees. We have no precise information about the numerical relationship between Sadducees and Pharisees there. However, in view of the fact that the high priest functioned as president and that the senior priests are always mentioned first, we must assume that at all events the Sadducees had the greatest power in the Sanhedrin. As we shall see in 14.5.3, this is also clear from the trial of Jesus.

14.4.4 *Spiritual leaders*

Having looked at the Sadducees and Pharisees in 9.1 and 9.2, we must now pay special attention to the priests and scribes.

As in ancient times, the high priest was the head of the priesthood. After the time of Herod the Great he was no longer the political leader of the people. However, he remained president of the Sanhedrin. This function, and the fact that the high priest was always chosen from one of the leading aristocratic families in Jerusalem, meant that he still had some influence in the political sphere. As had been customary from Persian times, the high priest was nominated by the foreign power in control, in this period the Romans. The best known high priest in the time of Jesus was Joseph surnamed Caiaphas,[60] who held this office from about 18 to 36.

The high priest was supported in the cult by priests who from Persian times had been divided up into twenty-four courses.[61] Each of these courses served in the temple for one week (from sabbath to sabbath). Thus Zachariah belonged to the course of Abijah (Luke 1.5; cf. I Chron.24.10). Each of the courses was in turn divided into 'father's houses', each of which did service in the temple on a particular day.[62] The leadership of these courses and 'fathers' houses' was in the hands of some prominent families in Jerusalem.[63] Members of these priestly families benefitted specially from the offerings brought to the temple. The priests of a lower grade usually lived in the country and had to earn a living, generally by engaging in a craft.

The main task of the priests was to offer sacrifices in the temple. They were helped here by Levites, who evidently also served as singers and musicians in the temple.[64]

One important group at this time was that of the *sop͑rim*. The *soper* (originally scribe) was the man of the book, the scholar whose task it was to expound and study the message of God. We already hear of scribes in an earlier period (cf. Neh.8.2; Sirach 38.24-39.14), but only in the first century of our era; they come into prominence especially after the fall of Jerusalem in 70.[65]

In the time of Jesus the scribes still formed a group distinct from the Pharisees, though there was a great affinity between the two. Many scribes were also Pharisees, but not all of them. After AD 70 they and the Pharisees formed the group of rabbis.

In the period before 70 attention must be paid above all to the 'schools' of Shammai and Hillel. After 70 that of Hillel had a dominant position.[66] Shammai is usually thought to have been more conservative and Hillel more progressive. Hillel came from Babylon to Jerusalem as an adult, while Shammai spent his whole life in Judaea. Otherwise very little is known about them and their work. Many of their supposed views come from accounts by their followers from the time after 70 and it is far from certain that these are always authentic.[67] In Pirqe Aboth (m.Aboth I,II) Shammai and Hillel are the fifth and most famous pair of those who handed down oral teaching from the time of Moses to their own day.

14.4.5 *Religious life*

We know very little about the religious life of ordinary people. They were only very passively involved in temple worship. All the sacrificial actions were performed by priests, and the same was true of other ritual actions. Ordinary people were not even allowed to enter the sanctuary proper. Institutional and ritual elements were completely predominant. The rise of the scribes shows that there was a concern for another kind of religion in which a more personal involvement and concern for the spoken word were to the fore. In the New Testament we can also see this quite clearly from the appearance of Jesus.

It is often assumed that the observation of the regulations of the oral and written tradition was at the centre of many people's lives.[68] However, it cannot be demonstrated that this was true of many of the ordinary people, because most of the evidence comes from a later time. At all events, we should be doubtful whether there was a generally accepted orthodoxy at this period.[69]

The three great feasts in which pilgrims came to Jerusalem were like great meetings. However, here, too, only a small part of the population actually had any part to play. Most of them were not in a position to make that sort of journey.

14.5 *The ministry of Jesus*

14.5.1 *Chronology*

Roughly speaking, it may be said that Jesus was born and lived during the reigns of the Roman emperors Augustus (BC 27 = AD 14) and Tiberius (14-37).

We may sure that the beginning of the Christian era does not coincide chronologically with the birth of Jesus. This is because of a mistake of four years in the calculations made by the monk Dionysius Exiguus in the sixth century.

It is impossible to tell precisely from the Gospels when Jesus was born. Matthew (2.1) says 'in the days of King Herod', which would mean not later than 4 BC, the year in which Herod died. Luke (2.2) connects the birth with a census in the time of Quirinius, the legate of Syria. In that case Jesus would have been born in AD 6 or 7, when Judaea and Samaria came under the direct rule of Rome (see 14.2.1). Attempts have also been made to fix the birth year of Jesus with the help of astronomy in connection with the star mentioned in Matt.2.2. This has led to the birth year of Jesus being put at 7 BC.[70] So the evidence is not unanimous. That in Matt.2.1 agrees most with the corrected calculations of Dionysius Exiguus (see above), according to which Jesus must have been born in about 4 BC.

The same problems arise over the length of Jesus' ministry. The Synoptic Gospels mention one passover, which gives the impression that Jesus spent only one year going around preaching. By contrast, the Gospel of John mentions a passover three or four times,[71] and that suggests a longer period. Given that the evangelists have no more than a selection of the many stories which were in circulation about Jesus,[72] it is conceivable that the Synoptics were only interested in the one passover in Jerusalem which was so important in connection with the death and resurrection of Jesus. Consequently, a three-year activity on the part of Jesus seems more likely.[73] According to the tradition of the evangelists, Jesus spent most of this time in Galilee, particularly in the broader surroundings of Nazareth, 'his father's home'.[74]

We are also uncertain of the year and date of Jesus' crucifixion. He died on the day before the feast of the Passover (cf. Mark 15.4). According to Lev.23.6

the Passover had to be celebrated on 15 Nisan. It is usually assumed that Jesus was crucified and buried in April of the year 30 or 33.[75]

14.5.2 *Jesus and the various trends of his time*

The New Testament evidence suggests that Jesus most often engaged in discussion with the Pharisees and that he also agreed with them in his polemic against the Sadducees,[76] as for instance over the question of the resurrection.[77]

At the time of Jesus the Sadducees formed a small but powerful aristocracy (cf. also 9.1) who also occupied key positions in political matters. They do not seem to have had much contact with ordinary people and we do not know that they had any sympathy with the poor (cf.9.1.4). It is clear that here, too, Jesus was closer to the Pharisees, who enjoyed much respect and sympathy from the ordinary people.

All this does not alter the fact that more than once Jesus was critical of the Pharisees (see e.g. Matt.23.3-4, 27-28). However, it is striking that much of his criticism of the Pharisees also emerges in one way or another in the Talmud, which is certainly of Pharisaic origin. There is an instance in b.Sota 22b, where seven types of inauthentic Pharisee are criticized.[78] Jesus seems to have clashed with the Pharisees, for example, on the matter of divorce (Mark 10.2-12) and healing a lame man on a sabbath (Mark 3.1-6), though it is uncertain whether this was a clash with *all* Pharisees. It is striking that in none of the three Synoptic Gospels are the Pharisees mentioned in connection with the trial of Jesus (cf. 14.5.3).[79]

It has been stressed that both Jesus and John the Baptist must have had close connections with the Qumran community (see also 9.4).[80] However, there are also obvious differences between Jesus and the community of Qumran, and the same is true of John the Baptist. Moreover, any agreements with this group are primarily indirect.[81]

Jesus' relationship to the Zealots is problematical. Some scholars have constantly stressed that he had close relations with this group.[82] Others reject such a view out of hand.[83] It is in fact hard to imagine how Jesus could have been a supporter of violent resistance against the Romans, which is what the Zealots stood for. Different sayings of Jesus show that he believed that violence was not the way to realize the kingdom of God.[84] This does not rule out the possibility that many people in his day nevertheless regarded Jesus as a Zealot. Above all his Galilean background may have suggested such a view.

14.5.3 *The trial of Jesus*

As I have just said, nowhere in the Synoptic Gospels are the Pharisees connected with the trial of Jesus.[85] They are in the Gospel of John. There we read, for example, 'Pharisees' in 18.3,12 where Matthew has 'elders of the people' (26.47) and Mark 'scribes and elders' (14.43), while Luke has 'leaders of the temple and elders' (22.52). The fact that John has 'Pharisees' here presumably indicates a later interpretation which is again connected with the fact that this Gospel came into being later than the Synoptics.[86]

All this gives the impression that the Pharisees did not play a very active role in the trial of Jesus and were more sympathetic to him than is often assumed. The often protective attitude of the Pharisees to the first Christians also points in this direction.[87] When apostles are imprisoned by the Sadducean high priest, the Pharisee Gamaliel secures their freedom (cf. Acts 5.17-42). Josephus also reports[88] that when James the brother of Jesus was killed in 62 on the orders of a Sadducean high priest, the Pharisees complained to Agrippa II with the result that the high priest was deposed.

In addition to all this it is pointed out that in Mark 14.33-64 par. there can be no question of a trial along Pharisaic lines.[89] This could suggest that we should imagine the trial to have been a legal process implemented by the Sadducees, though we have no knowledge of such legal procedures.

Another question which has never been satisfactorily resolved relates to the authority of the Sanhedrin in matters involving the death penalty. It is often assumed that they did not have authority to impose this penalty,[90] but that is far from certain.[91] At all events it is a fact that Jesus was finally condemned to death by Pilate and executed by the Romans. So Dequeker[92] is right in saying that 'the responsibility of Pilate for the execution of Jesus was greater than the Gospels suggest; for understandable reasons, since they were written for a Roman public'.[93]

Closely connected with this is the question whether Jesus was condemned on political grounds. This view has in fact been put forward by some scholars.[94] I have already said (cf.14.5.2) that Jesus can hardly have been a Zealot. However, it is quite conceivable that the Roman authorities and the Sadducees, who were sympathetic to them, saw it as such, given his Galilean background, above all because in recent decades Galilee had been regarded as a cradle of rebel movements.

14.5.4 *The preaching of Jesus*

Between the activity of Jesus and the writing of the Gospels lies the preaching of the community which drew on traditions about him.[95] Despite this, we can certainly demonstrate some of the main features of the preaching of Jesus in the Gospels.

It is clear that Jesus did not develop any systematic teaching. His proclamation must primarily be understood as a message of salvation. Salvation is indissolubly bound up with an announcement of judgment. The proclamation of salvation and judgment indicates that the kingdom of God is near. Jesus' attitude towards the Old Testament must also be seen in this light. The coming of God's kingdom means the fulfilment, the complete establishment of Torah and prophets. Jesus himself shows that all this is being realized in his actions. This is evident among other things from his social concern with the masses 'because they were like sheep without a shepherd' (Mark 6.34), and with 'tax-collectors and sinners'.

Jesus' remarks in Luke 6.20f. (cf. Luke 6.24-26) are particularly important in this connection,[96] as are his words to John the Baptist in Matt.1.4-6 (cf. Isa.35.5f.; 61.1) and the parables. When Jesus speaks here about the poor he always means poor in the literal sense. For him the coming of the kingdom of God opens up new perspectives (Matt.11.4-6). It is significant that Jesus was called the 'hope of the poor'.[97] This aspect comes clearly to the fore in the earliest traditions about him.[98]

The preaching of Jesus about the coming kingdom of God does not offer any mirage, but a reality which is brought about in his own life and work. The central notion of a judgment on the actions of men and women in the preaching of Jesus is also to be explained in this light (cf. Matt.5.16). For this reason Jesus also calls his disciples and followers to follow him. The words with which he ends the parable of the good Samaritan are typical: 'Go and do likewise' (Luke 10.37). Of course the parables have a very important place in Jesus' proclamation of the coming kingdom of God. Anyone who takes them seriously will also understand their meaning.[99]

Finally, Koester[100] is right in stressing that Jesus' ethics are above all eschatological and not interim. The coming kingdom of God is a real event and puts Jesus' followers in a new situation. The Samaritan in the parable (Luke 10.29-37) does no more than what is needed in this situation, in the context of God's rule.

Chapter 15

The Period from Agrippa I to the Beginning of the First Jewish War (AD 41-66)

15.1 *The general political situation*

After the death of Augustus, during the period described in this chapter the Roman empire was governed by the emperors Tiberius (14-37), Caligula (37-41), Claudius (41-54) and Nero (54-68). None of these figures had the diplomacy and supremacy of Augustus. One result of this was that they had more difficulty in keeping in check the opposition to the sole rule of the emperor.

Tiberius, mentioned in the New Testament only in Luke 3.1, was far from popular in the Senate or among the people, although he courted the good will of the former, especially at the beginning of his reign. His greatest mistake in government was probably his supreme trust in Sejanus, the commander of the imperial bodyguard. In 31 Sejanus was imprisoned and killed when he began to take on imperial airs. Military successes in the time of Tiberius were repeated in Gaul, Germany and Armenia. However, these successes were mostly due to Germanicus, a nephew of the emperor.

Gaius, a son of Germanicus, better known by his nickname Caligula, 'little boots', succeeded Tiberius as emperor in 37. He achieved nothing in either the political or the military sphere. Soon after his accession his mind was impaired by an illness which made him take the most crazy decisions. One of them was to seek to be worshipped as a deity during his life. We shall see (15.2.1) that this also threatened to have consequences for the temple in Jerusalem.

The 'best emperor after Augustus'[1] was Claudius. During his reign the people of Gaul obtained the right to become senators.[2] Claudius made his mark above all in the legal sphere by beginning to set up an efficient administrative apparatus.[3]

Claudius was succeeded by Nero, who was notorious for his cruelty. He neglected both his administrative duties and foreign policy. There were countless conspiracies against him, the last of which (in 68) succeeded. Before he could be imprisoned, Nero committed suicide. During his reign there was the famous burning of Rome (in 64). Nero was suspected of being responsible. To shift suspicion he accused the Christians in Rome. This led to the first persecution of Christians there.[4]

15.2 *The reign of Agrippa I*

15.2.1 *Agrippa's relations with Rome*

Agrippa[5] (in Acts 12.1-23 called Herod), who was a grandson of Herod the Great and Mariamne, was friendly with Caligula. On being appointed emperor in 37, one of Caligula's first acts was to give Agrippa Philip's tetrarchy (see 14.2.2). When two years later Antipas was banished, Agrippa also got his territory (see 14.2.3). He also seems to have had a hand in the repudiation of Herod Antipas.[6]

At about the same time Caligula, wanting to be worshipped as a deity (cf.15.1) gave orders for a statue of himself to be put in the temple at Jerusalem. In 40/41 the Syrian governor Petronius went to Palestine to carry out the commission. However, when he arrived he did not go ahead with it because he saw that to carry it out would lead to a revolution. Thanks among other things to Agrippa's skilful policy and the fact that Caligula was murdered in 41, a conflict was avoided.[7]

After these events Agrippa again played an important role in Rome on the accession of Claudius. In gratitude Claudius appointed him king over the whole area which had previously been ruled by his grandfather Herod the Great.[8]

15.2.2 *Agrippa I as king of all Palestine (41-44)*

This decision by Claudius again detached Judaea and Samaria from the Roman province of Syria, so that it was no longer under the direct rule of Rome. In the meantime, Pilate's bad administration[9] had given way to the administrations of Marcellus (36-37) and Marullus (37-41), of whom we know little more than their names.

In contrast to Herod the Great, Agrippa seems to have found more sympathy among the leading groups in the land. It is not impossible that this was because, as the grandson of Mariamne, he was regarded as a more or less legitimate descendant of the Hasmonaean dynasty.[10] He also had the right approach. In Jerusalem he presented himself as a pious Jew who observed the law.[11]

It is evident that Agrippa only did this to keep his subjects in Jerusalem happy. Outside Jerusalem he acted as a patron of Hellenistic culture. He had statues of his daughters put up in Caesarea (*AJ* XIX, 357) and organized games there (*AJ* XIX, 343). The coins which he had minted also show his ambivalent attitude. Those minted in Jerusalem have no image, but those from other cities bear his image or that of the emperor.[12] His upbringing in Rome doubtless contributed to this attitude.

In his domestic policy Agrippa seems to have made some attempts to be rather less dependent on Rome. He wanted to build a new wall on the north side of Jerusalem. However, he could not finish the work because Rome prevented him.[13] He also held a conference in Tiberias with five Roman client-kings, clearly with the aim of producing a more independent policy. This conference also failed because Rome again intervened (*AJ* XIX, 338ff.).

Agrippa had rather more success in another sphere. Through his interventions at court he managed to persuade Claudius to grant important privileges to the Jews in Alexandria (*AJ* XIX, 279ff.), which were later extended to all the Jews in the Roman empire (*AJ* XIX, 288ff.). In the New Testament Agrippa is described as a persecutor of the first Christians. According to Acts 12.1-19 James, one of the sons of Zebedee (Mark 1.19), was killed on his orders and Peter almost suffered the same fate.

His reign lasted only a short time. He died in Caesarea in 44. According to Josephus (*AJ* XIX, 356), news of his death was received with joy in Sebaste (Samaria) and Caesarea. Evidently Agrippa I was less popular in non-Jewish circles than among the Jews, from whom we hear of no such expressions of delight (cf. also Acts 12.21-23).

15.3 *The whole of Palestine under direct Roman rule*

15.3.1 *The Roman procurators from 41-66*

After the death of Agrippa I, Claudius made the whole of Palestine a Roman province. This measure suggests that Agrippa did not have the full confidence of the Roman authorities, probably as a result of his attempts to carry on a more independent policy (see 15.2.2).

The first procurator to be nominated by Claudius was Cuspius Fadus (44-46). During his rule a prophet named Theudas appeared (cf. Acts 5.36) who persuaded many followers to go with him to the Jordan. Fadus scented danger and attacked the group with his cavalry, which resulted in a fearful bloodbath.

Fadus' successor was Tiberius Julius Alexander (46-48). He came from Alexandria and was a nephew of the famous philosopher Philo. In his time the land was afflicted by a famine (*AJ* XX, 10; cf. also Acts 11.27-29), and James and Simon, the sons of Judas the Galilean (see 12.8.1), were crucified (cf. *AJ* XX, 102). Like his predecessors, Alexander remained only a short time as procurator in Palestine. In 70 we find him back at the siege of Jerusalem, where he was an advisor to the Roman commander.[14]

After Alexander, Ventidius Cumanus became procurator (48-52). Under him unrest in the land increased, a situation which was largely due to the thoughtless action of Cumanus himself. The worst incident cost Cumanus his post. About 52 a conflict broke out between Galilaeans and Samaritans when a Galilean was murdered in Samaria. When Cumanus failed to do anything about this, conflict spread, and inhabitants of Jerusalem also became involved. Two 'Zealots', Eleazar and Alexander, then undertook a punitive expedition into Samaritan territory with a group of followers. The conflict was finally resolved by Claudius, who declared the Samaritans guilty and punished them. This action on the part of Claudius was largely due to the mediation of the man who was later to be King Agrippa II. Cumanus was relieved of his office and exiled.[15]

Antonius Felix (52-60) was nominated the new procurator. This Felix is the procurator mentioned in the New Testament, who held Paul in Caesarea as his personal prisoner.

The period of Felix's government was marked by an ongoing and increasing disquiet among the population. There were also constant attempts at rebellion.[16] Felix dealt with it not only very cruelly but also very untactically. The result was that the opposition to Rome steadily increased. All in all Felix was a very bad governor.[17] Acts 24.26 also gives some indication of his corrupt attitude.

In 60 Felix was removed from his post by Nero and replaced by Porcius Festus (60-62). Paul appealed to his Roman citizenship (Acts 25.11f.), so Festus sent him to Rome to answer there to the emperor.

Festus can be seen as a moderate and cautious governor. This is evident from his attitude to Paul and also his intervention in a conflict between Agrippa II and the priests in Jerusalem. These priests had had a wall built which deprived Agrippa of a view of the temple. Agrippa wanted to have the wall pulled down. Festus agreed with him, but at the same time he allowed the priests to send a delegation to Rome to put the question to Nero. Nero then decided in favour of the priests.[18]

The procurators Albinus (62-64) and Gessius Florus (64-66) who followed Festus are best known for their venality and greed. Under Albinus any prisoner could get his freedom for money, and Florus plundered whole cities and villages. The First Jewish War broke out under his rule, in 66.

15.3.2 *Agrippa II (c.49–92)*

Agrippa II was only seventeen years old on the death of his father Agrippa I in 44. According to Josephus,[19] Claudius' intention was that he should succeed his father on the latter's death, but Claudius' counsellors advised him against this (see also 15.3.1).

Like almost all the members of the household of Herod, Agrippa too was brought up in Rome. Even after the death of Agrippa I he remained there for some time. This period saw his mediation on behalf of the Jews in their conflict with the Samaritans (see 15.3.1).

In 49 Agrippa II was appointed king of Chalcis, a small kingdom in the Lebanon (*AJ* XX, 104). Here he was at the same time entrusted with the oversight of the temple in Jerusalem and was given the right to nominate the high priest there. Agrippa made much use of this right.

About 53, the territory of Agrippa was extended by the former tetrarchy of Philip (see 14.2.2), to which Abilene was added. Later Nero gave him another four cities with the surrounding territory, namely Abila and Julias[20] in Peraea and Tiberias and Tarichaea in Galilee.[21] This probably happened in about 54/55,[22] though the year 61 has also been suggested.[23] Freyne[24] conjectures that this assignation of territory was a personal gift of Nero and had nothing to do with the political strategy of Rome. This also seems most likely.

The private life of Agrippa II was looked on very unfavourably. Above all the fact that his sister Berenice often lived with him was a great cause of scandal.[25]

In the sphere of foreign policy Agrippa showed himself at all points a faithful vassal of Rome. Almost all the coins that he had struck bore the name and image of the Roman emperors ruling in his time.[26] In Acts we hear that he very soon made his mark on the new procurator Festus. Rome also supported him in the war against the Parthians.[27]

He managed to establish a good relationship with the Judaeans in domestic affairs. Rabbinic sources even say that he made serious enquiries about the law to the well known Rabbi Eleazar ben Hyrcanus.[28] However, we have seen that he also came into conflict with priests in connection with the building of a wall (15.3.1).

Agrippa II did everything possible to prevent the outbreak of the First Jewish War with Rome in 66. However, once it started he was completely on the side of the Romans. After that he seems to have acquired even more territory.[29]

In the further course of history we hear virtually nothing more about him.

He probably died in about 92, but we cannot be sure. Of course the whole chronology of his life is very uncertain and disputed.[30]

15.4 *The social and economic situation between 41 and 66*

The economic situation[31] got steadily worse in the period after 44. This was also largely due to the bad administration of most procurators, whose régimes were based on greed and corruption. Such a policy aroused opposition and therefore provoked disturbances. Obviously the attitudes of the higher authorities were reflected at a lower level. Thus, for example, far more tax was collected than was needed, because too much of it disappeared in the hands of intermediaries. All this fed anti-Roman feelings, especially among the groups which were already fiercely opposed to paying tax to the Roman emperor. Such groups saw their popular following steadily increase in this period.

Of the main areas in Palestine – Judaea, Samaria, Galilee and Peraea – Judaea and its capital Jerusalem were still by far the most important places in this period. The main priestly families lived there, the most prominent people and the rich landowners. The city owed this position to the fact that it was the most important religious centre and had a flourishing economic life. Other important cities in Judaea were Jericho, Jaffa (Joppa) and Jabneh.

Samaria had a special position. Geographically it formed a kind of bridge-head between Judaea and Galilee. The religion of the inhabitants of Samaria was not centred on Jerusalem. The Samaritans had a temple of their own as a religious centre. This temple was on Mount Gerizim, near Shechem. It is evident from the New Testament (cf.e.g. John 4.9) and other sources (see 15.3.1) that the relationship between Jews and Samaritans was particularly bad. However, Samaritans fought alongside Judaeans in the later struggle against the Romans.

The centre of Peraea was Gadora.[32] This area was relatively sparsely populated. Most people lived in the cities in the east and north, but these were typically Hellenistic places.

Despite the difficulties outlined in 14.3.2, Galilee seems still to have been a relatively prosperous place in the last decades before the First Jewish War. The main cities there were Sepphoris and Tiberias. The former seems even to have been friendly to Rome. Tiberias, which with its immediate surroundings belonged to Agrippa II (15.3.2), had the character of a Greek polis, though many Judaeans must have lived there at that time. Another important place in Galilee was Gabara, where Johanan ben Zakkai (see 16.3.3) lived and worked in the last years before 66.

We already noted earlier that there were important developments in Galilee.

Jesus spent a lot of time here and it was also the cradle of the anti-Roman movement. John of Gischala, one of the defenders at the siege of Jerusalem in 66-70, also came from there.

15.5 *The first Christian church*

15.5.1 *The community in Jerusalem*

The book of Acts (2.41) describes the origin of the first Christian church in Jerusalem. We have only very scanty information about the activities of this earliest community. The author of Acts (Luke) did not have the aim of writing 'history'. The first chapters of his book simply seek to stress that 'there is no salvation other than in Jesus Christ'.[33] It is clear that John, James and Peter were important figures in this community.[34]

In Acts 2.44f.; 4.32-37 (cf. also 5.1-11) we are told that the solidarity of the community was also expressed for a while in the common possession of goods, though the authenticity of the content of this passage is disputed.[35] However, it seems quite likely that the community should have taken such a step in this period,[36] not least because many instances of this kind of life-style can be demonstrated in antiquity.[37]

There is much to suggest that the community remained faithful to Jewish belief and therefore was also usually seen as a group within Judaism. Its members took part in temple worship (cf.Acts 3.1) and presumably also observed the other regulations that went with Jewish worship. Moreover, for some time the Roman authorities regarded the Christians as a stream within Judaism.[38]

Baptism and the eucharist (I Cor.11.23) must already have been celebrated in the Jerusalem community, but for want of further information we cannot say when and in what form.[39]

We may assume that in the first period the 'twelve disciples' formed the nucleus of the Jerusalem community. Despite the fact that we know very little about the earliest community in Jerusalem, it must be accepted that it was of very great significance. From it groups of people came into being everywhere who felt themselves to be united in belief in the risen Lord.

15.5.2 *The Greek-speakers in the Jerusalem community*

We have already noted often in previous chapters that in the course of time Jerusalem had become an important city. One of the consequences of this was that Greek speakers had also settled in the city, while the use of Greek also came into vogue in some Jewish circles. Evidently some of these people also joined the earliest community, and their presence there led to a conflict (cf. Acts 6.1).[40] Luke describes how in this situation seven men were appointed deacons from the group of Greek speakers (cf. Acts 6.3). We get the impression that the term deacon in this period was used primarily as a name for missionaries (cf. Acts 8.4ff.). One of these seven deacons, Stephen, was killed during a brief persecution (cf. Acts 7.57f.). Evidently this persecution was directed only against the Greek-speaking part of the community in Jerusalem, since figures like John, James and Peter continued with their work there undisturbed. The Greek-speaking members of the community, on the other hand, were driven out of Jerusalem.

The result of this was that Christian communities became established in other places. In Acts (7.14ff.) there is an emphatic reference in this connection to the activity of the deacon Philip, who preached the gospel of Christ in the city of Samaria. Others went, for example, to Antioch (Acts 11.19ff.), where later the name 'Christians' was used for the followers of Jesus.

15.5.3 *The death of James*

For a long time the leadership of the earliest community was in the hands of Peter, one of the apostles, and James, the brother of Jesus. James eventually came to have the most prominent place.[41] In the year 62, when after the departure of Festus (see 15.3.1) there was a short period without a procurator, this important leader of the community in Jerusalem was killed. We are told about this by Josephus in *AJ* XX, 200ff. According to his account James was summoned before the Sanhedrin on the orders of the high priest Annas II and then stoned on a charge of having broken the law. This action aroused opposition among moderate Jews and the Pharisees. They laid charges against Annas II to Agrippa II and the newly arrived procurator Albinus, and Annas was deposed by Agrippa II as high priest.

It is clear that there can be no question here of a normal trial. Rather, we get the impression that this was a brief witch-hunt in which other members of the community in Jerusalem were also taken prisoner.

15.5.4 *Flight to Pella?*

Eusebius describes in his Church History (III,5,3) how the Christians in Jerusalem fled to Pella in Transjordan in 66 BC, shortly before the Romans laid siege to the city. For a long time this report was almost universally regarded as accurate, and still is by some scholars.[42] However, in recent times it has been increasingly challenged.[43] Among other things, scholars point out the great distance between Pella and Jerusalem (about sixty miles), involving a journey through a region controlled by the Romans, and that in 66 Pella was plundered by Jewish partisans, which certainly would not have encouraged the Jewish Christians to settle there. It therefore seems most likely that the members of the earliest community in Jerusalem shared the fate of their fellow-citizens in the siege and after its capture by Titus in 70. All this does not exclude the possibility that individual members of the Jerusalem community like Johanan ben Zakkai (see 16.4.3) could have fled before or during the siege.

Chapter 16

The First Jewish War (66-74)

16.1 *The beginning of the struggle*

16.1.1 *Causes*

It is clear that the corrupt and bad government of various Roman procurators (see 15.2.2; 15.3.1) and the hatred of many Judaeans towards the Roman occupying forces was one of the immediate occasions for the outbreak of the struggle. In addition, social, economic, nationalistic and religious motives also played a part. No single one of these, however, can be said to have been the decisive cause of the war.[1] Social and economic factors (see 16.1.3) must be supposed to have been particularly to the fore, though the events between 66 and 74 certainly cannot be described as the culmination of a class struggle.[2] Still less can the hostility between Jewish and Greek communities be regarded as the fundamental cause of the dispute with Rome.[3] Rather, we must say that a combination of all these factors eventually led to the outbreak of hostilities. In this connection we must also be very cautious about the information in Josephus, since he describes the events very subjectively in what is in effect an apologia for his own position.[4]

A combination of events sparked off the war, beginning in Caesarea. This city had a mixed population of Jews and Greeks. When Greek inhabitants built on a piece of ground next to a synagogue, as a result of which the synagogue was partly blocked off, a conflict arose between the two population groups. The dispute was even referred to Nero, who in 61 decided in favour of the Greeks (cf. *AJ* XX, 184). After that, unrest continued in Caesarea, and in 66 this led to street fighting in the city.

At the same time the procurator Florus gave orders for seventeen talents to be taken from the temple treasury. This sort of thing had happened before, but not seemed provocative; now part of the population mocked Florus by holding a street collection for him. This made Florus so angry that he gave his soldiers orders to punish the population. However, the opposition to him was so great that he had to retreat to Caesarea, leaving behind only one cohort in Jerusalem and making the leaders of the city responsible for law and order (*BJ* II, 318ff.). They failed to keep it.

These events were the last straw for groups like the Sicarii and Zealots (but see 12.8.1), who had increased in number over the years,[5] and they began to fight against the Romans.[6] The majority of the population of Judaea and Galilee soon joined them, along with the Idumeaeans and in 67 also the Samaritans.

16.1.2 *Peace initiatives*

Not everyone was happy with this course of events. Agrippa II, who at this time was staying in Alexandria, rushed back to Jerusalem to mediate there. His attempt failed, above all because he had so little support from Florus.

Agrippa II was not the only one to try to settle the conflict. The high priest and the Sadducees, along with the Pharisees, who were satisfied that there were no hindrances to worship, and the supporters of the dynasty of Herod, did everything possible to restore peace. At a later stage the Pharisees do seem to have taken part in the struggle, though they were always only moderately enthusiastic about it.[7] However, for our information we are almost entirely dependent on Josephus,[8] who himself was a Pharisee and wanted to present the Pharisees to his readers, who were Romans, in as favourable a light as possible. Nothing is known about the attitude of the Essenes, but we may assume that in view of their character (cf.9.3.4) they kept out of the hostilities.[9]

In the meantime the Zealots had already conquered various fortresses, including Masada, and under the leadership of Eleazar, a son of the high priest, they occupied the temple and put an end to the offering of the daily sacrifice to the emperor.

In this situation, the groups who had tried to mediate in the conflict called for help from Agrippa II. He sent three thousand troops to eliminate the Zealots and their supporters. This attack failed completely and war with Rome became inevitable.

16.1.3 *The first successes*

Directly after this abortive intervention on the part of Agrippa II, the palaces of Agrippa, Berenice and the high priest were set on fire by the Zealots. The city archive was also burned to ashes. This last action was connected with the social and economic aims of the Zealots and their supporters – which were to achieve a redistribution of land[10] and do away with the discontent over the excessive disparity between the wealth of Jerusalem and the poverty of the rest of the country.[11] A few days later the fortress Antonia was captured, and soon afterwards the whole city was liberated from the Romans.[12]

Vigorous fighting also broke out in the rest of the country. There were particularly bloody scenes in cities with a mixed Jewish and Gentile population. Depending on which party was in the majority, the rest were often cruelly butchered.

After a long period of preparation the Roman governor of Syria, Cestius Gallus, began an expedition to Palestine in the autumn of 66. He advanced on Jerusalem, but soon afterwards had to retreat again. On his withdrawal the greater part of his army was annihilated in a pass near Beth-horon.[13]

The main result of this victory was that many people now joined the anti-Roman group. The first coins dated according to the years of the war must derive from this time.[14]

16.2 *The battle in Galilee*

16.2.1 *Preparations*

After the defeat of Gallus, measures were rapidly taken to offer resistance to the new campaign by the Romans which was a foregone conclusion. In the meantime the leading priests in Jerusalem realized that thy would lose their positions of importance if they did not come out against Rome. Many of them did precisely that. The Sanhedrin was now entrusted with executive power, while a popular assembly, which had had no significance under the client kings, was now reorganized as the supreme authority.[15] To begin with its leadership lay primarily with the upper class of priests and Pharisees.

This popular assembly entrusted Flavius Josephus, later to become a historian, with command of the troops in Galilee. Without doubt this was a very responsible and important post, because the first great attack of the Romans could certainly be expected there.

One of Josephus' first tasks was to strengthen the cities in Galilee. Those involved were Jotapata,[16] Taricheae, Tiberias, Sepphoris and Gischala.[17] According to his own account, Josephus was able to mobilize 100,000 men and train them for battle (*BJ* II, 572ff.). Given the short time that he had, this figure seems exaggerated, to say the least. Moreover we get the impression that initially Josephus tried to keep his hands free, *vis-à-vis* both Rome and Agrippa II.

The Zealots, and above all their leader John of Gischala, probably had good reasons for suspecting Josephus of entering into negotiations with the Romans than preparing for a decisive battle. This mistrust even led to armed opposition to Josephus, who on his own account (*BJ* II, 614ff.; *Vita* 84ff.) only just escaped an atttempt on his life.[18]

Josephus says that there was further opposition in Galilee between the country population and the larger cities. The inhabitants of the countryside, who according to Freyne[19] are usually described in Josephus' *Vita* as 'Galileans', were more nationalistic than those of the cities, who were usually more well disposed to Rome.

All these factors were of great influence in preparing for the coming fight against the Romans. The differences which have been mentioned suggest that the preparation cannot have been very good.

16.2.2 *The Roman advance in Galilee*

Nero was in Greece when the war broke out in Palestine. He sent his general Vespasian to restore order there.[20] In 67, as soon as the weather allowed, he set out. There had already been some fighting before that, and the important city of Sepphoris had fallen into his hands.

With an army consisting of three legions supplemented by auxiliaries from, among others, Agrippa II and the Nabataean king Malchus II, Vespasian advanced into Galilee. At that moment, according to Josephus,[21] many of the Jewish troops took flight. Josephus himself retreated to Tiberias, while the main part of his army fled to the fortress of Jotapata. Shortly afterwards, Josephus also went there to take personal charge of its defence.

According to a detailed account in *BJ* III, 145ff., Jotapata was besieged by Vespasian for forty-seven days. Finally it fell into Roman hands through treachery. All the inhabitants were killed or taken into slavery, while the city itself and all its defences was razed to the ground. This happened in about June or July of 67. With the fall of Jotapata the Romans had regained one of the most important fortresses in Galilee. Josephus himself took refuge with about forty of his fellow-fighters in a cave. Josephus claims to have escaped with his life by a miracle and as a result of his forecast that Vespasian would become emperor (*BJ* III, 340ff.).[22] However, his account gives us the strong impression that he is simply disguising his treacherous defection to the enemy.

After the fall of Jotapata Tiberias pressed on with hardly a blow being struck against him and soon the Romans had also conquered Tarichaea, the fortress of Gamala in Gaulanitis, and Mount Tabor. By the end of 67 the Romans had the whole of Galilee under their control again. John of Gischala then fled with his supporters to Jerusalem.

16.3 *The course of the war in 68-69*

16.3.1 *The situation in Jerusalem*

After the rapid advance of Vespasian in Galilee there were bloody clashes in Jerusalem. The Zealots blamed the fiasco of the loss of Galilee on the old leaders and were also aggrieved that these were so ready to enter into negotiations with the Romans. So they did not rest until these leaders were eliminated. Leadership in Jerusalem now fell into the hands of the Zealots. However, they needed a helping hand from the Idumaeans to succeed in their coup.

A short time later, however, in the summer of 69, new difficulties arose. At that time another Zealot leader, Simon bar Giora, arrived; he and his followers had been driven out of Idumaea by Vespasian (see 16.3.2). Moreover, yet a third group of Zealots were active. This last group consisted of Jerusalem Zealots who had split from John of Gischala's party under the leadership of the priest Eleazar ben Simeon. This split took place shortly after the Idumaeans had left Jerusalem.

These three groups had vigorous disputes, although Josephus' account (*BJ* IV, 573f.) is highly coloured. However, between the disputes people were busy fortifying the city. The building of the most northerly or third wall, begun in the time of Agrippa I, was continued.[23] The minting of coins also continued in Jerusalem, during this time.[24] On the other hand we hear[25] that large stores of grain in the city were burned, an action which soon caused great problems for the defenders during the siege.

When the Roman troops were approaching Jerusalem, the city was in fact divided into three fortresses: Simon bar Giora held the upper city and a good deal of the lower city, John of Gischala the temple mount and Eleazar the inner forecourt of the temple. In this situation Titus prepared to encircle the city.

16.3.2 *Vespasian's further advances in 68-69*

According to Josephus,[26] to begin with Vespasian left Jerusalem alone, until the parties fighting there had exhausted one another. He first turned his attention to Peraea and it was not long before the whole of this area was in his hands. After that, Antipatris, Lydda, Jabneh (Jamnia) and the territory of Idumaea were conquered. Next he advanced through Samaria to Shechem, where the Samaritans who had begun the battle against Rome in 67 were defeated.[27] Jericho was also captured. By then the Romans had reconquered most of the country.[28]

At that moment, just as Vespasian was making preparations for an attack on

Jerusalem from Caesarea, where he had his headquarters, the news reached him that Nero had died on 9 June 68. From then on Vespasian had other things to worry about than Palestine, so he decided for the moment to suspend all activites.

However, he must later have regretted this, when Simon bar Giora made use of this *de facto* ceasefire to plunder the south of Judaea with a group of his followers and even attacked the city of Hebron.[29] Thereupon Vespasian launched another campaign against Judaea, Hebron being among the other places to be destroyed. Apart from Jerusalem and the fortresses of Herodium, Masada and Machaerus, Vespasian at that time had the whole of Palestine again under Roman rule.

Before he could begin an attack on Jerusalem, Vespasian was proclaimed emperor by the armies in the eastern part of the Roman empire, on 1 July 69. Directly after that he left Palestine and travelled through Antioch and Alexandria to Rome. His son Titus then took command of the Roman troops in Palestine.

16.4 *The flight of Johanan ben Zakkai*

The flight of Johanan ben Zakkai[30] from Jerusalem must have taken place in this period. There are various detailed accounts of this flight in the rabbinic literature.[31] All the versions agree that Johanan ben Zakkai left Jerusalem during the First Jewish War and received permission from Vespasian to settle in Jabneh.

The question is precisely when Johanan ben Zakkai left Jerusalem. Momigliano[32] assumes that we must read Titus for Vespasian in the rabbinic literature mentioned above and that the flight took place in 70. However, it seems to me more probable that we should put it in the period when Jerusalem was troubled by new internal disputes (see 16.3.1), about the time when the Idumaeans also left the city. It is known that a number of people fled at that time.[33] In that case Johanan ben Zakkai will have left Jerusalem in the early summer of 69. This dating comes close to that of Doeve,[34] who wants to put this flight between 15 May and 25 June 69.

At all events, the flight of Johanan ben Zakkai must be seen as one of the most important events of the First Jewish War. As we shall see in the next chapter, this simple event was of crucial significance for the later development of Judaism.

16.5 *The siege and fall of Jerusalem*

In early 70 Titus began the siege of Jerusalem. His followers included Josephus and the former procurator Tiberius Julius Alexander (see 15.3.1). Titus had in all four legions and auxiliaries for this siege.[35] The beginning of the siege fell some weeks before the Passover. At that very moment the various groups in Jerusalem were still engaged in a life-and-death struggle. When Eleazar opened the gates of the temple forecourt for those who came to celebrate the Passover, his group was attacked and overcome by that of John of Gischala.[36] From that moment on there were just two rival groups in the city.

The Romans began by attacking the northernmost wall. In military terms this side was always the most vulnerable part of the city to defend.[37] Only then did John and Simon stop their mutual dispute. Despite that, three weeks later the Romans had the whole of the inner city in their hands (*BJ* V, 299f.; 331ff.).

Meanwhile a pressing lack of food in the city made itself felt. That of course was disastrous to the morale of the defenders.

The focal point of the dispute now shifted to the temple mount with the citadel of Antonia and the upper city. When the defenders succeeded in destroying the entrenchments which the Romans threw up against the wall, Titus had a stone wall put round the whole city. This was done in three days.[38] Shortly after that the Romans were able to capture the citadel of Antonia in a night attack; it was then completely destroyed.[39]

A great blow to the morale of the besieged was the day when the offering of the daily morning and evening sacrifice had to be stopped.[40] From that day on the temple was only a fortress. At the cost of very severe losses Titus succeeded in gradually getting it into his hands. According to Josephus,[41] Titus wanted to spare the temple. This does not sound very plausible, since such an action would go against the usual military practices of the time.[42] Be this as it may, the temple went up in flames. This event is still recalled in the synagogue on 9 Ab (about August).

The fall of the temple did not, however, mean that the battle was over. John of Gischala and his supporters succeeded in escaping to the upper city and continued the fight from there. After the fall of the temple, according to Josephus there were negotiations between Titus and the besieged.[43] Titus offered them their lives, but they also wanted free passage to the wilderness, which Titus refused.

The struggle did not last much longer, not least because the besieged were exhausted through lack of food. Consequently the Romans soon succeeded in rapidly storming the upper city as well. That settled things, and after a siege of five months the Romans were again in full possession of Jerusalem.[44] Traces of the destruction which was inflicted at the time of the fight for the city and temple have come to light from various archaeological investigations over the course of time.[45]

After the fall of Jerusalem, 700 young men were taken to Rome to participate in the triumphal procession of Titus; others were put to work in mines in

Egypt or sold as slaves. To begin with, John and Simon managed to remain hidden in underground passages with some followers, but they were soon captured and also taken to Rome for Titus' triumph. After that, according to Josephus[46] Simon was put to death, while John spent the rest of his life in prison.

The city was almost completely destroyed. Only some few remnants still recalled the Jerusalem of the time of the second temple.

16.6 *The battle for the last fortresses (70-74)*

At the time of Titus' triumphal procession in Rome, which included not only a large number of prisoners but also the seven-branched golden candlestick and the table of the showbread from the temple, the fortresses of Herodium, Masada and Machaerus had not yet been captured. Titus delegated this task to Sextus Lucilius Bassus, who in 71 was nominated procurator of Judaea by Vespasian.

Herodium was probably conquered without too much difficulty as early as 71.[47] The siege of Machaerus took rather longer. However, here, too, the fighting did not last long because the defenders surrendered on the promise of free passage.[48] Archaeological investigations have confirmed the devastation that Bassus did there in 72.[49]

A short time after this Bassus died, and it was now the task of his successor Flavius Silva to conquer the last surviving fortress of Masada. He began on it in the early part of 73.

The leadership of the occupation of Masada was in the hands of Eleazar, a grandson of Judas the Galilean (see 12.8.1). Eleazar and his followers had been in Masada since 66 and they had not been idle. They had made the casemates as habitable as possible for their families,[50] and seen to good supplies of food and water to withstand a long siege. By contrast, the Romans had the greatest problems in providing food and water, because these had to be brought over a long distance. Moreover they had to conquer the citadel early in the season, since from May onwards the heat was almost unbearable.[51]

Silva began to build a wall of almost 4000 yards, further strengthened with a number of towers from which shots could be fired at the fortress.[52] The Romans succeeded in making a breach in the casemate wall by an earth wall. The defenders succeeded in making good the breach with wood, but the Romans were able to undo their work rapidly by setting fire to it. The fall of Masada was then only a matter of time.

Before things got that far, according to Josephus there was a drama in the fortress.[53] When the Romans entered Masada the besieged and their families seemed to have committed suicide.[54] Eleazar's call for this seems to be based on Deut.6.5.[55] According to Josephus (*BJ* VII, 406), the action even aroused the amazement of the Romans. Only two women and five children escaped.

As a result of excavations, in a small cave close to the top of the rock of Masada, twenty-five skeletons have been found which in Yadin's view[56] come from the last defenders of Masada. It is not completely clear in what year Masada fell, but the usual assumption is that it was in 73.[57] However, on the basis of two newly-discovered inscriptions,[58] the year 74 seems more likely.[59]

16.7 *Consequences*

Apart from the great devastation and the loss of countless human lives, the defeat by Rome also had major consequences in the field of religion, politics, and social and economic life. The significance of these consequences for the further history and development of Judaism cannot be put too highly,[60] though Noth goes too far[61] in talking of the end of the history of Israel.[62]

The devastation of the temple meant that the religious and national centre had been lost. This had consequences for both the mother country and the Diaspora. From now on there were no longer any pilgrimages to Jerusalem at the great festivals. However, the former significance of the temple as the centre of religious life must certainly not be overestimated. The existence of a community like that of Qumran shows that for a long time there had been those who did not regard the temple in that way.

Another consequence of the loss of the temple was that sacrifices were no longer offered.[63] However, it can legitimately be asked whether they could not have been offered in a different way after the destruction of the temple, as also happened after 587/6 BC.[64] Guttmann[65] rightly argues that one reason why sacrifice was not revived was that the Pharisees were against renewing the power of the Sadducean priests and the Romans did not want to appoint another high priest. We shall see in the next chapter how as a result religious life began to develop in other forms.

An additional but hurtful humiliation was that from now on the two-drachma temple tax on had to be paid to the temple of Jupiter Capitolinus in Rome as the *fiscus Judaicus*. However, the tax was abolished under the Roman emperor Nerva (96-98).

From a political perspective the defeat by Rome was the most far-reaching of all. Judaea now became an independent Roman province. This new status meant that there was a fixed army of occupation in the country; this was the tenth legion, which had also taken part in the war. The headquarters of these Roman troops was Jerusalem.

The social and economic consequences were equally disturbing. Various places including Jerualem were almost completely destroyed, while a number of areas were utterly depopulated. All this and the great loss of human life had a catastrophic effect on the country. Moreover, much of the land was taken over and given to Romans or favourites of the emperor. Thus, for example, Emmaus became a fortress of 800 war veterans (cf. *BJ* VII, 217).[66]

Chapter 17

The Period between the Two Wars with Rome (74-132)

17.1 *Political developments in Rome*

As we already saw in the previous chapter, in 69 Vespasian became emperor of Rome while on his campaign in Palestine. He ruled for ten years (69-79). His accession marked the beginning of the rule of the Flavian emperors. These emperors had quite a different background from their predecessors, as they had not come from patrician houses.

When Vespasian began his reign, the financial state of the Roman empire was extremely bad. This situation had come about above all because of the extravagant expenditure of Nero. By raising taxes Vespasian was able to solve the problem. The bad discipline in the Roman army was also improved during his rule.

His son Titus ruled for only a short time (79-81) and was succeeded by his brother Domitian (81-96). Domitian, the last of the Flavians, was something of a despot, but the rule of his successor Nerva (96-98) was very different. He had a much greater social concern. During the reign of Trajan (98-117) the so-called Quietus War (see 17.4) took place. This was a rebellion of Jews above all in the Diaspora, though Palestine itself did not remain untouched. After Nerva came Hadrian (117-38), who spent a good deal of time travelling round his empire; he was particularly fond of staying in Greece. The Bar Kochba revolt or the Second Jewish War took place in his reign (see ch.18).

Above all in the time of the emperors Trajan and Hadrian the Roman administrative apparatus was well organized. Prosperity was very great in the Roman empire in the period we shall now be considering. However, wealth can hardly be said to have been evenly distributed. For the most part it lay with the emperors and the senators.[1]

17.2 *The social and economic situation in Palestine*

At the end of the previous chapter (16.7) we already saw the social and economic consequences of the First Jewish War. It is understandable that these had an effect long after 70. Thus the destruction of the temple meant that an important social and economic centre was lost for the future. Here we need only think of the many Jews in the Diaspora who no longer came to Jerusalem for festivals, though some seem to have kept up these pilgrimages for a long time to come.[2] The destruction of the temple also meant the loss of an important financial institution to Jerusalem (cf.14.4.1). Moreover, the sacrificial worship had brought with it considerable economic activity (cf.14.3.4) which had now been completely lost.

The population structure underwent just as great changes. Before the outbreak of the war Judaea had been inhabited almost completely by Judaeans, while a mixed population had settled in Galilee[3] and especially in Transjordan. After the fall of Jerusalem, the tenth legion was stationed in the city and its wider surroundings. Along with their families, these Roman occupation forces made up another group in the area. The same thing also happened in other cities and villages. Moreover, all Jewish inhabitants were expelled from cities like Caesarea. And new cities were founded. For example, Vespasian had the city of Neapolis built,[4] close to the site of ancient Shechem.

Despite the widespread devastation and the greater poverty, there were people in Judaea who still had considerable riches even after the war.[5] In a later period these included Rabbi Tarfon,[6] Rabbi Eleazar ben Azariah[7] and Rabban Gamaliel II.[8]

After a number of years there may be said to have been a recovery of economic growth in both Judaea and Galilee. Slowly and ingeniously new modes of existence were worked out.[9]

There was a slump during the reign of Trajan, after his conquest of the Nabataean kingdom in 106. The Romans used this as a base to extend the important trade route along the old so-called Via Regis, the King's Way,[10] in Transjordan and breathe new life into it, with the result that trade increasingly took this route, to the detriment of the land west of the Jordan, which as a result lost it as a source of income.

17.3 *The rabbis and religious developments*

17.3.1 *The rabbis*

After the war with Rome all that remained of the various religious groups in Judaea were the Pharisees, though alongside them a number of figures from other groups of an earlier period also made their impression on developments in the time to come. However, the Pharisees managed not only to maintain themselves as a group but also to increase their influence considerably.

A development of this kind was not least due to the fact that the group rejected important concessions from the Romans in order to develop their activities in the religious sphere. This benevolent attitude on the part of the Romans gives the impression that the Pharisees, or at least some of them, had either stood aside or had acted very cautiously during the war against Rome after 66.[11]

The name 'Pharisees' gradually disappears after 70. The members of the group which began to play such an important role in the further development of Judaism are known as rabbis. The term rabbi, regularly used in Palestine, means 'my teacher'. However, the personal suffix 'my' in this title became as it were otiose, so that rabbi became a regular term for 'teacher'. The Babylonian teachers simply bore the title rab ('teacher'). The important leaders of rabbinic Judaism were later given the honorific title rabban, 'our teacher'.[12] The usual designation for (rabbinic) scholars was 'the wise'.

This new group of rabbis or wise men thus largely originated from the Pharisees. In addition to the Pharisees, mention should also be made of the scribes, who in a former period must have formed a separate group or class (cf. also 14.4.4), but later (perhaps even shortly before 70) were incorporated into the Pharisees.

One of the most important aims of the rabbis was to introduce reforms after the fall and destruction of the temple in 70 in order to overcome the consequences of the catastrophe of 70.[13] The temple had long been to a great extent the centre of religious life. After 70 the rabbis stressed the study and adaptation of scripture to the whole of daily life. They regarded themselves as those who handed on and mediated the oral tradition, which they did by a chain passing from generation to generation. This tradition was derived from Moses and went down to the rabbis of the generation living at the time.[14] The tractate Pirke Aboth, which gives the representatives of this chain of tradition, was also the most important document from which the rabbis derived their legitimacy as bearers of the tradition and teachers.

The function of the rabbi was not a ministry but a particular form of life, the goal of which was to live according to the aims of the tradition of the Torah and to teach others to do the same. The ideal situation was that the rabbi should also earn his own living by some other means.[15]

The most important rabbis from the period that we shall be considering here were Johanan ben Zakkai,[16] Eleazar ben Hyrcanus,[17] Ishmael ben Elisha, Gamaliel II, Akiba[18] and Tarfon.[19]

17.3.2 *Jabneh (Jamnia)*

After his flight from Jerusalem, Johanan ben Zakkai obtained the assent of Vespasian to begin a school for the study of the Torah in Jabneh, a place south of Jaffa. In the time to come this place became an important centre of rabbinic Judaism and remained so until 135. Under the leadership of Johanan ben Zakkai and his successor Gamaliel II (*c.*80-120) the foundations were laid here for rabbinic Judaism.[20]

We do not know how long Johanan ben Zakkai worked in Jabneh. It is said that at a particular moment he had to resign.[21] It seems very likely that he had to cope with opposition at Jabneh. Whether his flight from Jerusalem and his more or less pro-Roman attitude were contributory factors is not clear, but it seems reasonable to suppose that there were those who held these things against him.[22] Clearly not all rabbis followed Johanan ben Zakkai to Jabneh, but went to live in other places. Thus at a very early stage there also seem to have been rabbis in Tiberias, which was later to become an important rabbinic centre.[23]

In Jabneh the Beth Din ('court of judgment'), a continuation of the Sanhedrin, was also established, but we do not know the precise date. Nor is it certain whether Johanan ben Zakkai and Gamaliel II already bore the title *naśi'* ('president') of the Beth Din.[24]

The dispute between the schools of Hillel and Shammai, mentioned in 14.4.4, seems already to have been settled by the time of Gamaliel II. Moreover, in his day the Beth Din seems again to have acquired some political significance. Such a development is understandable. After a strict rule in the first years after 70 the Romans will gradually have allowed a degree of political freedom again.

Two other important matters from the time of Gamaliel II should also be singled out for mention. First, the establishment of the canon of the Old Testament. It is often assumed that this took place about 100 during a synod at Jabneh.[25] However, there are strong indications that nothing of the kind happened so early. Books like the Song of Songs and Koheleth were still disputed, as is evident, for example, from m.Yad.III, IV. Moreover, Schäfer[26] has given good grounds for supposing that the process of the formation of the canon ('canonical' meaning 'being appropriate for use in worship') only took place in the second century, perhaps under the influence of the events of 132-135. Moreover, this process already had a long prehistory, in which a marked Pharisaic and rabbinic influence is only perceptible in the final phase.[27] Secondly, we should note the origin of the *birkat ha-minim*, the so-called 'saying against heretics' (a euphemism for a 'curse on heretics') in the Eighteen

Benedictions. The view that this was primarily a curse on Christians, inspired above all by the church fathers,[28] is untenable.[29]

Gamaliel II probably died between 100 and 120. It is certain that he was not followed directly by his son Simeon ben Gamaliel II. It has been supposed that first Tarfon acted as president of the Beth Din.[30] Another view is that after about 120 and up to the Bar Kochba revolt in 132, other schools were dominant, above all that of Akiba in the neighbourhood of present-day Tel Aviv and that of Ishmael ben Elisha in the south of Judaea.[31]

17.3.3 *The new position of the synagogue*

Only after the destruction of the temple in 70 did the synagogue come to occupy an increasingly important place in Palestine. The earliest synagogues in Palestine date from the first century AD,[32] and primarily were to be found in Galilee (cf.14.4.2). Archaeological evidence indicates that the earliest known synagogue in the south is that of Masada.[33] This synagogue was used by the Zealots in the years between 66 and 73, but was perhaps also used by others at a rather earlier stage. After 70 a situation came about in which gradually every Jewish community, not just in the Diaspora but also in Palestine, had its own synagogue. In larger communities there were often more than one synagogue. These synagogues were always the centre of spiritual life. One important factor in this connection is that Judaism had the status of a permitted religion, *religio licita*, throughout the Roman empire. This status, which was already granted by Julius Caesar, meant that Jews everywhere in the world were free to live according to their own religious laws and regulations. Claudius later also granted the Jews exemption from military service for this reason. The *religio licita* which gave the synagogue jurisdiction over its own members was of the utmost significance for Judaism.[34]

17.4 *The so-called Quietus War (115-117)*

In 115-117 we hear of revolts of Jews in the Diaspora which began in Cyrene and spread from there to Cyprus, Egypt and Mesopotamia. These revolts took place while Trajan was occupied in a campaign against the Parthians.[35] We have very few pieces of information about the course of these revolts[36] and even then they are not always trustworthy.[37]

In Mesopotamia the revolt was put down by the Roman general Lucius Quietus, so that the revolts are known as the Quietus War. Quietus went to work in an extremely barbarous way and killed thousands of Jews. When the revolt had been put down, as a reward Quietus was nominated procurator of the province of Judaea as a reward.[38]

It is not completely certain whether these revolts also spread to Palestine. Some facts seem to point in this direction.[39] The most important reason for supposing that the war affected Jews in Palestine is that it is hard to imagine that they would have remained passive while their fellow-Jews in the Diaspora were involved in the struggle. Moreover the nomination of Quietus as procurator, mentioned above, is some indication that Palestine was not completely tranquil in the period between 115 and 117. For this reason it is assumed that the status of Judaea was also changed during the Quietus war and that it was then, rather than in 135, that it became a consular rather than a praetorian province and was given the name Palestine.[40] This change implies among other things that from then on two legions, rather than one, could be stationed there. Such reinforcement of the Roman occupying forces would certainly not have come about unless there had been a pressing need.

17.5 *The most important literature from Palestine between c.1 and 135*

In the schools which came into being in Palestine after the fall of Jerusalem in 70, the rabbis and their pupils occupied themselves with studying and interpreting the (written) Torah and the oral tradition (see 17.3.1). The collection of study material which came into being in this way is known as a *mishnah* (= teaching). Those who made such a collection are called the *tanna'im* (scholars). Johanan ben Zakkai, the founder of the school in Jabneh, is regarded as the first of these *tanna'im*. All these *mishnah* collections were later given the collective name Mishnah. The final reaction of the Mishnah, in which Jehuda ha-Nasi had a hand, took place about 200. These collections were first handed down by word of mouth, but presumably they already appeared as written collections in the period with which we are concerned.[41]

As for the New Testament, only the letters of James and Jude may be assumed with any degree of probability to have been written in Palestine.[42]

Apart from these works, I should also draw attention to some important pseudepigrapha which originated in Palestine at this time. These are the Ascension of Moses (between 4 BC and AD 30), the Life of Adam and Eve (before 70), IV Ezra 3-14 (*c.*95) and the *Paralipomena Ieremiae* (beginning of the second century). The last two works were clearly written under the impact of the fall of Jerusalem in 70. For example, the author of IV Ezra (3.34-36) protests against the devastation of Judaea and Jerusalem, not because Israel is innocent but because the sins of those who devastated it were far greater.[43]

Chapter 18

The Bar Kochba Revolt (132-135)

18.1 *Causes*

18.1.1 *The political background*

Hadrian (117-138) is known as an emperor who aimed at consolidating the frontiers of the Roman empire and not seeking to extend its territory any further. For this reason he also renounced the claims that Trajan had made to Parthia (cf. 17.4). This made areas like Syria and Palestine all the more important, because they came to be near to the eastern frontier of the Roman empire.

One of the great problems in Palestine was the relationship between the Jewish and Greek inhabitants. Here the Romans adapted their old principle of 'divide and rule' in order to keep peace in the area. Another way of achieving this end was to strengthen the Roman army in the province of Arabia (the land of the Nabataeans). One factor which probably played a part here was that in the past there had often been good contacts and alliances between Judaea and Parthia. The reinforcement of the occupying forces in the province of Arabia increased the barrier between these two countries.

On his journeys through the eastern part of his kingdom, in about 130 Hadrian had also visited Palestine, and there as elsewhere set up buildings in the Hellenistic style. This happened, among other places, in Caesarea and Tiberias. The predominantly Jewish city of Sepphoris was given the name Diocaesarea, the first letters of which indicate a connection with Zeus Olympius.[1] It is clear that a great many Jews were unhappy with these developments, and were even more so when Jerusalem and religious matters were involved (see 18.1.3).

18.1.2 *The economic situation*

There are indications that the economic situation in the country again deteriorated during Hadrian's rule (cf. 17.2). In particular the position of the leaseholders seems to have become steadily more wretched. In rabbinic sources[2] there is constant mention of landowners who oppress their lease-holders and even use violence. These landowners were often Romans or agents of the Romans or the emperor. According to Applebaum,[3] these facts are confirmed by leasing contracts which have been found in the caves of Murabba'at[4] and Nahal Ḥever.[5] These contracts relate to leasing agreements between Bar Kochba and other Judaeans during the period of the revolt. Evidently they refer to land which was taken by Bar Kochba from the then owners.

All this gives the impression that bad economic conditions were also a breeding ground for the revolt in 132-135. The feeling of being exploited obviously led to increasing tension. The sending of a Roman legion from Caparcotna to Sepphoris[6] may also indicate a tense situation. Evidently only one or two provocative actions by Rome were needed for the dam to break.

18.1.3 *Direct causes*

Dio Cassius (LXIX 12,1-2) gives as a cause of the revolt the fact that Hadrian planned to rebuild Jerusalem as a Graeco-Roman city with the name Aelia Capitolina. By contrast, the reason given in the *Historia Augusta*[7] is that Hadrian had forbidden circumcision. Moreover some sources[8] seem to allude to a promise by Hadrian to rebuild the temple, a promise which he later withdrew. However, the authenticity of these last texts is so disputed that they need not be considered further.[9]

As to the first two causes, many scholars think that both the prohibition of circumcision and the plan to rebuild Jerusalem are to be seen as consequences rather than as causes of the revolt,[10] in other words that these are measures which were taken after the revolt. There is evidence in Eusebius[11] which points in this direction in connection with the rebuilding. It is difficult to come to any conclusion here because the sources I have mentioned give us too little information. However, we have seen (18.1.1) that Hadrian had Hellenistic buildings erected in various part of his kingdom. His plan to found Aelia Capitolina certainly fits in with this. Since he visited Palestine in about 130, it seems natural that this plan should have come to the fore then. So the plan for Jerusalem must have been at least one of the causes of the rebellion.[12] We have less support for presupposing a prohibition of circumcision. At all events it is going too far to see it as one of the main causes of the revolt.[13]

In addition to all this another point needs to be considered. Schäfer[14] considers the possibility that there was a group of Jews in Palestine who actively supported Hadrian's Hellenistic policy and therefore were very much in favour of changing Jerusalem into the Roman colony of Aelia Capitolina. In that case

Hadrian will have made his plans exclusively in connection with this group and may later have been completely surprised by the opposition of the Jews who were faithful to the law. The revolt of 132-135 and the prelude to it would on this view show similarities in various respects to that against Antiochus IV Epiphanes in the time of the Maccabees. The positive attitude of the Jews who were well disposed to Rome would then be expressed in *Sibylline Oracles* V, 46-50, in which, according to Schäfer, Hadrian is highly praised.

There is a very real possibility that such a group of Jews favourable to Rome did in fact exist in Palestine. It would have been made up above all of those who profited from the Roman occupation. There is no occasion to suppose that they were large in number, but they will doubtless have had the sympathy of the many non-Jewish inhabitants of Palestine. Their influence must therefore not be underestimated. Thus the existence of this group may also have played into the hands of the rebels.

Looking back on this section we get the impression that perhaps a complex of factors influenced the revolt, among which the economic ones must certainly not be lost sight of.

18.2 *The figure of Bar Kochba*

18.2.1 *Name and origin*

Thanks to the discovery of a number of documents and letters in the caves of Murabba'at and Nahal Ḥever,[15] along with a number of coins,[16] we know a few things about the Jewish leader of the revolt in 132-135. He called himself Simon ben Kosiba, but in the Christian tradition[17] he is called Bar Kochba, which means 'son of the star' (see 18.3). In rabbinic literature he is called Ben or Bar Kozeba/Koziba.[18] This name was probably interpreted as 'son of the lie'.[19]

We have no reliable historical information of any kind about the origins of Bar Kochba.

18.2.2 *Title*

On many coins Bar Kochba is designated 'prince of Israel',[20] as he also is in documents[21] and one letter.[22] The title 'prince' (*nasi*) was used in Talmudic times after 70 for the president of the Beth Din or the head of the Jewish community in Palestine. Those who bore the title in this period were descendants of Hillel. There is some dispute as to what significance the title has in connection with Bar Kochba. Schäfer[23] conjectures that in the time of

Bar Kochba it was not yet associated with descent from Hillel, so that in the case of Bar Kochba it need not have this connotation. We do not find the title messiah or king for Bar Kochba either in documents and letters or on coins. However, while this may be the evidence in Rabbinic literature,[24] it is clear that messianic expectations were bound up both with the figure of Bar Kochba and with the revolt itself (see also 18.3).

18.2.3 *Bar Kochba as leader*

We have some information about Bar Kochba which gives us a vague impression of him as leader of the rebellion.

We find the most important material in the correspondence carried on by and with him.[25] Bar Kochba shows his authority not only in the military sphere but also in social, economic and religious matters. Clearly his leadership extended to all aspects of the people's life. On the basis of the documents that have been discovered containing leases (see 18.1.2) we must assume that Bar Kochba carried out land reforms.

The regulation of religious life has a prominent place in a number of letters. Matters discussed include the raising of tithes[26] and the Feast of Tabernacles.[27] The sabbath year also seems to be significant in the leases (cf. Mur 24B, 24C, 24D). The importance attached to religious life by the rebels also emerges in the designation 'the priest Eleazar' on a number of coins.[28] This could indicate that in addition to political power, the priesthood was also restored, perhaps even in the framework of a newly established sacrificial cult.[29] Be this as it may, Eleazar must be regarded as one of the leaders of the revolution, subordinate to Bar Kochba. An identification of him with Rabbi Eleazar ben Azariah or Eleazar of Modein, an uncle of Bar Kochba, cannot be substantiated.[30]

All this information about Bar Kochba gives the impression that he was the undoubted leader of the revolt.

18.3 *The role of Rabbi Akiba and the other rabbis*

According to rabbinic sources,[31] the famous rabbi Akiba regarded Bar Kochba as the 'star of David' which was expected on the basis of Num.24.17. In this connection Akiba also called him 'king Messiah'. With this interpretation Akiba was going back to the old traditions like those in Qumran (cf. CD VII, 18-20).

This positive attitude attributed to Akiba in connection with Bar Kochba seems to go against that of other rabbis – at all events the majority of them. The designation 'son of the lie' in rabbinic literature (see 18.2.1) suggests that the rabbinic authorities were very suspicious about Bar Kochba's enterprise. Now it may well be that these sayings were only written later and therefore after the revolt, when it was already evident to what a catastrophe this revolt had led, but despite this we do not get the impression that many rabbis were very enthusiastic about the revolt, although we really have no specific details of their attitude during the years 132-135. Granted, there are the lists of the 'ten martyrs',[32] on which some rabbis from about 135, including Akiba, are mentioned, but it is very uncertain how far these lists are historically reliable. On the whole the rabbis were not inclined towards revolution, so that in his sympathy for Bar Kochba, Akiba may be regarded as an exception. It therefore seems most probable that apart from Akiba and some followers, most rabbis kept as far from the revolution as they could.

The fact that Akiba's positive attitude is described so explicitly in the rabbinic literature also argues strongly for its historical authenticity. People might have preferred to keep quiet about such a misconception on the part of one of the most important rabbis in later times.

18.4 *The course of the revolt*

18.4.1 *The scene of the struggle*

The big question is whether the whole of Palestine was affected by this revolt. There is uncertainty over Galilee, Samaria and Transjordan. Dio Cassius (LXIX 13,1) speaks of 'all Judaea', but it is conceivable that here he meant the whole land.[33] On the other hand, on the basis of an investigation into information in the Talmud, Büchler[34] has indicated that the revolt was limited to Jerusalem and its wider environs. This view of Büchler's is largely shared by Schäfer, who after a thorough investigation of all the sources[35] comes to the conclusion that the revolt was limited to part of Judaea and at most a small part of Samaria. Others, however, think that the revolt must have spread much further.[36]

Presumably Judaea was the major scene of the revolt, but that does not mean that there were no disturbances and skirmishes with the Romans in the rest of Palestine in 132-135. A more passive attitude in Galilee might perhaps be explained by the fact that even before the outbreak of the revolt a strong Roman contingent was stationed there.[37] However, that does not mean to say that no Galileans fought on Bar Kochba's side (cf. Mur.43.4).

18.4.2 *The beginning of the revolt*

On the basis of the most important sources,[38] we must assume that the revolt began in early 132.[39] The coins from the time of the rebellion also seem to point in this direction. Three kinds of coins have been found, two kinds dated after the first and second year of the revolt respectively and a group of undated coins, most of which are regarded as coming from the third year.[40] So the duration of the revolt can presumably be put at about three years. Current Roman coins were also used for the striking of these coins, the oldest of which come from 131/132. These Roman coins must have been in circulation up to the beginning of the revolt. This gives an indication that the revolt began in 132.[41]

The rebels must soon have occupied a number of fortresses (including Herodium), strongholds and caves, which served as a kind of hiding place. This can be inferred from a report by Dio Cassius (LXIX 13,1-14,1) that in a later phase the Romans recaptured fifty important fortresses from the rebels. The city of Jerusalem may also have fallen into the hands of the rebels at a very early stage, though we have no solid information about this.[42] However, some contemporaries[43] report an occupation and devastation of Jerusalem. Had the city not been in the hands of the rebels, something of this kind would not have happened.

An open battle with the Romans was carefully avoided by Bar Kochba's troops. A fierce guerrilla war was waged against them from strategic positions.[44]

At the time when the rebellion began, Tineius Rufus was procurator in this area. He and his troops could not cope with the rebels, which was why to begin with Bar Kochba and his men were successful, above all thanks to the element of surprise. The result of this successful beginning was that Bar Kochba's following rapidly increased. However, it soon became evident that these successes could only be repeated because the Romans did not have enough troops in the country. This siutation would soon change.

18.4.3 *The further development of the struggle*

At a later stage of the rebellion Hadrian ordered one of his most famous commanders, Julius Severus, to put it down. Severus pursued the tactic of hunting down the rebels and blockading them when they hid in caves. In this way they were forced to surrender to the Romans through lack of food and the like. The burial places in the caves at Nahal Ḥever show the cruel scenes which must have taken place there.[45] In this way Severus was therefore able successively to eliminate the rebels.

We have no accurate information about the precise course of events in the fight between Bar Kochba and the Romans. The letters from the Murabba'at caves mentioned above suggest that the situation gradually got worse for Bar Kochba. The last phase of the campaign involved the occupation and capture of the fortress of Bethar. This place, not far from Jerusalem,[46] was, like Engedi, an important base for the rebels. Bethar must have been very easy to defend because the fortress was surrounded on three sides by ravines, while the fourth side was a kind of fortified ditch.[47]

When the city was finally taken by the Romans, there must have been some bloody scenes, though the later descriptions are probably somewhat exaggerated.[48] Bar Kochba and Rabbi Akiba must have been among the dead.

In Jewish tradition the fall of Bethar is dated on 9 Ab (m.Ta'an IV, VI), the day of the commemoration of the destruction of the first and second temples. However, this must be a theological symbol rather than a historical recollection.

The fall of Bethar was not the final end of the revolt. There are indications[49] that the Romans took more time to eliminate centres of resistance in the caves in the wilderness of Judah.

18.5 *Consequences of the revolt*

The Roman victory over Bar Kochba and his followers must have cost them dearly. This is to be concluded from the fact that in his account of this event to the Roman senate Hadrian left out the customary formula 'all is well with me and my legions' (Dio Cassius LXIX 14,3). Moreover Judaea had suffered so much from the revolt that to all intents and purposes an important province was lost to Rome.[50]

Even more serious were the consequences for the Judaeans themselves. Countless of them were killed in battle, while after the revolt many were sold as slaves. The story even goes that the number of Judaean slaves was so great that in the market in Hebron a Jewish slave did not cost much more than a horse.[51]

Jerusalem was now a completely Gentile city under the name of Aelia Capitolina. Judaeans were forbidden to enter the city on pain of death.[52] According to Dio Cassius (LXIX 2,1), a shrine to Jupiter was built on the site of the ruined temple, but this seems far from certain.[53]

In various rabbinic sources it is suggested that during and above all after the revolt there was a religious persecution in Palestine. Circumcision, the observance of the sabbath and the teaching of the Torah are said to have been forbidden. All we can demonstrate with any certainty is a prohibition of circumcision, since later under Antoninus Pius (138-161) the rescinding of such a prohibition is recorded.[54]

After this revolt an extremely hard and difficult time dawned for the Jewish people. Deprived of their political homeland, the Torah was the only bond that held them together. History has shown just how strong this bond has been over the course of time.

NOTES

Chapter 1   Introduction

1. For the use of this term see H.Jagersma, *A History of Israel in the Old Testament Period*, London and Philadelphia 1982, 2.

2. See n.1.

3. See also Jagersma, op.cit., 1f.

4. E.g. M.A.Beek, *Das Danielbuch*, Leiden 1935, differs.

5. For a detailed account of all this see e.g. J.C.H.Lebram, 'Perspektiven der gegenwärtigen Danielforschung', *JSJ* 5, 1974, 1-33, and K.Koch (ed.), *Das Buch Daniel*, EdF 144, Darmstadt 1980.

6. Thus F.Crüsemann, 'Die unveränderbare Welt. Überlegungen zur Krisis der Weisheit beim Prediger (Kohelet)', in W.Schottroff-W.Stegemann (eds.), *Der Gott der kleinen Leute* I, Munich 1979, 80ff.

7. See e.g. J.H.Charlesworth,*The Old Testament Pseudepigrapha*, New York and London 1983; G.W.Nickelsburg, *Jewish Literature between Bible and Mishnah*, Philadelphia and London 1981; J.A.Soggin, *Introduction to the Old Testament*, ²1980, 429-73; J.T.Nelis, 'Joodse literatuur uit de periode tussen Oude en Nieuwe Testament', *BH* 2b, Kampen 1983, 118-47.

8. Cf. e.g. K.D.Schunck, *1.Makkabäerbuch*, JSHRZ I, 4, Gütersloh 1980, 291f.; Nelis, op.cit., 125f.

9. See e.g. C.Habicht, *2. Makkabäerbuch*, JSHRZ I, 3, Gütersloh 1979, 185ff.

10. For more details on this question see e.g. J.T.Nelis, *I Makkabeeën*, BOT, Roermond 1972, 16ff.; id., *II Makkabeeën*, BOT, Bussum 1975, 17-34; J.R.Bartlett, *The First and Second Books of the Maccabees*, CBC, Cambridge 1973, 14ff.; 215ff.

11. See further Schürer I, 34-7.

12. Thus e.g. also M.A.Beek, *A Short History of Israel*, London 1963, 166. For *BJ* see also H.Lindner, *Die Geschichtsauffassung des Flavius Josephus im Bellum Judaicum. Gleichzeitig ein Beitrag zur Quellenfrage*, AGAJU XII, Leiden 1972; T.Rajak, *Josephus. The Historian and His Society*, London 1983, 78ff.

13. See further Lindner, op.cit., 135-41: R.Mayer-C.Möller, 'Josephus, Politiker und Prophet', in *Josephus-Studien* (FS Otto Michel), Göttingen 1974, esp. 271-3.

14. But cf. also H.F.Weiss, 'Pharisäismus und Hellenismus. Zur Darstellung des Judentums in der Geschichte des jüdischen Historikers Flavius Josephus', *OLZ* 74, 1979, 421-33.

15. Cf. Schürer I, 57f. But see also Rajak, op.cit., 233-6.

16. For this see e.g. E.Bickerman, 'Un document relatif à la persécution d'Antiochos IV Epiphane', *RHR* 114, 1937, 188-221; id., 'Ein jüdischer Festbrief vom Jahre 124

v.Chr. (II Macc.1.1-9)', *ZNW* 32, 1933, 233-54, and I. Gafni, 'On the Use of I Maccabees by Josephus Flavius', *Zion* 43, 1978, 81-95.

17. See H.St J.Thackeray, *Josephus, The Man and the Historian*, New York 1929, 100-24.

18. For further information about Josephus see e.g. Thackeray, op.cit.; Schürer I, 43-63; A.Schalit (ed.), *Zur Josephus-Forschung*, WdF 84, Darmstadt 1973; O.Betz-K.Haacker-M.Hengel (ed.), *Josephus Studien* (FS O.Michel), Göttingen 1974; S.J.D.Cohen, *Josephus in Galilee and Rome. His Vita and Development as a Historian*, Leiden 1979; and also especially H.Schreckenberg, *Bibliographie zu Flavius Josephus*, ALGHJ I, XIV, Leiden 1968, 1979; Rajak, op.cit., and L.H.Feldman, *Josephus and Modern Scholarship (1937-1980)*, Berlin and New York 1984.

19. In this connection see F.Jacoby, *Die Fragmente der griechischen Historiker* I-III, Berlin-Leiden 1923ff.; T.Reinach, *Textes d'auteurs grecs et romains relatifs au Judaïsme*, Hildesheim 1963; M.Stern, *Greek and Latin Authors on Jews and Judaism* I-II, Jerusalem 1974, 1980.

20. See A.M.A.Hospers-Jansen, *Tacitus over de Joden (Hist.5,2-13)*, Groningen 194º.

21. For this group see also 9.4.

22. There is a good survey in e.g. G.Vermes, *The Dead Sea Scrolls. Qumran in Perspective*, London 1977, 142ff.

23. In this connection see also C.J.den Heyer, 'Het Ontstaan en de Ontwikkeling van het Nieuwe Testament', in A.F.J.Klijn (ed.), *Inleiding tot de studie van het Nieuwe Testament*, Kampen 1982, 12ff.

24. For more detail on this literature see e.g. G.F.Moore, *Judaism in the First Centuries of the Christian Era* I, Cambridge, Mass. 1958, 125-78; Schürer I, 68-118; J.Maier, *Geschichte der jüdischen Religion*, Berlin and New York 1972, 122ff.; and H.L.Strack-G.Stemberger, *Einleitung in Talmud und Midrasch*, Munich ⁷1982.

25. Cf.e.g. B.Jongeling, 'Een Aramees boek Job uit de bibliotheek van Qumran', *Exegetica* (Nieuwe reeks 3), Amsterdam 1974, 12ff.

26. See H.Lichtenstein, 'Die Fastenrolle. Eine Untersuchung zur jüdisch-hellenistischen Geschichte', *HUCA* 8-9, 1931/32, 257-31, and J.Derenbourg, *Essai sur l'histoire et la géographie de la Palestine*, Paris 1867, 439-46.

27. For the significance of the archaeology of Palestine see further e.g. H.J.Franken and C.A.Franken-Battershill, *A Primer of Old Testament Archaeology*, Leiden 1963; F.Crüsemann, 'Alttestamentliche Exegese und Archäologie. Erwägungen angesichts des gegenwärtigen Methodenstreits in der Archäologie Palästinas', *ZAW* 91, 1979, 177-93; E.Noort, *Biblisch-archäologische Hermeneutik und alttestamentliche Exegese*, Kamper Cahiers 39, Kampen 1979; and C.H.J.de Geus, 'De ontwikkeling van de Palestijnse archeologie en haar betekenis voor de bijbelwetenschap', *BH* 1, 94-109. Accounts of recent excavations can regularly be found in journals like *BA, IEJ, PEQ, RB* and *ZDPV*.

28. See Schürer I, 6-16, and the literature given there.

29. Cf. F.M.Cross, 'The Discovery of the Samaria Papyri', *BA* 26, 1963 = *BAR* 3, 227-39, and P.W. and N.Lapp, *Disoveries in Wadi ed-Daliyeh*, AASOR 41, Cambridge, Mass. 1976.

30. The papyri which are significant for Palestine can be found in *CJP* I, nos.2a, 2b, 2c, 2d, 4, 5. Cf. also P.W.Pestman (ed.), *Greek and Demotic Texts from the Zenon Archive*, I-II, Leiden 1980, esp. no.32.

31. See Y.Yadin, *Masada*, London 1966.
32. See Y.Yadin, *Bar-Kokhba. The Rediscovery of the Legendary Hero of the Last Jewish Revolt against Imperial Rome*, London 1971. Cf. also *DJD* II, 119ff.
33. *Hist* III, 9.
34. M.Noth, 'Die Geschichte des Namens Palästina' (1939), *ABLA* I, Neukirchen-Vluyn 1971, 294-308.
35. See C.H.J. de Geus, 'Idumea', *JEOL* 26, 1979-1980, 53-74; W.Schottroff, 'Die Ituräer', *ZDPV* 98, 1982, 125-52.

Chapter 2   The Beginning of the Hellenistic Period

1. For this see the detailed account in e.g. J.G.Droysen, *Geschichte des Hellenismus* I, Hamburg 1836; W.W.Tarn and G.T.Griffith, *Hellenistic Civilization*, London ³1952; R.Bichler, *Hellenismus. Geschichte und Problematik eines Epochenbegriff*, Impulse der Forschung 46, Darmstadt 1983.
2. Cf. A.H.M.Jones, *The Greek City from Alexander to Justinian*, Oxford 1940.
3. See G.J.D.Aalders, 'De Hellenistische wereld', *BH* 2b, Kampen 1983, 97.
4. Cf. P.Grimal, *FWG* 6, p.18.
5. See H.Bengtson, *FWG* 5, p.292.
6. Bengtson, op.cit., 305.
7. Ibid., 303.
8. For this see the outstanding survey in J.P.Levy, *L'économie Antique*, Que sais-je? 1155, Paris 1969, 45ff., and also M.Cary, *A History of the Greek World, 323-146 BC*, London 1972, 287-306.
9. Defended by K.Elliger, 'Ein Zeugnis aus der jüdischen Gemeinde im Alexanderjahr 332 v.Chr.', *ZAW* 62, 1950, 63-115, esp. 107-10, and M.Delcor, 'Les allusions à Alexandre le Grand dans Zach.ix.1-8', *VT* 1, 1951, 110-24.
10. *AJ* XI, 325ff.
11. b.Yoma 69a.
12. *AJ* XI, 321-5.
13. See F.M.Cross, 'Aspects of Samaritan and Jewish History in Late Persian and Hellenistic Times', *HTR* 59, 1966, 201ff.
14. See in M.Stern, *GLAJJ* I, Jerusalem 1974, 448.
15. See in H.G.Kippenberg, *Garizim und Synagoge*, Berlin and New York 1971, 46.
16. Thus e.g. F.M Cross, 'The Discovery of the Samaria Papyri', *BA* XXVI (1963) = *BAR* 3, 236f.; G.E.Wright, *Shechem*, London 1965, 181; M.Stone, *Scriptures, Sects and Visions*, New York 1980, 27. But cf. also Kippenberg, op.cit., 46f.; R.J.Coggins, *Samaritans and Jews. The Origins of Samaritanism Reconsidered*, Oxford 1975, 107f.; P.Schäfer, *Geschichte der Juden in der Antike*, Neukirchen-Vluyn 1983, 21.
17. Thus S.H.Horn, 'Shechem. History and Excavations of a Palestinian City', *JEOL* 18, 1964, 305f.; G.E.Wright, op.cit., 173; K.Jaroš-B.Deckert, *Studien zur Sichem-Area*, OBO 11a, Göttingen 1977, 47ff.; R.T.Anderson, 'Mount Gerizim: Navel of the World', *BA* 43, 1980, 218; J.Negenman, *Geografische gids bij de bijbel*, Boxtel 1981, 302.
18. See Coggins, op.cit., 110; B.Reicke, *The New Testament Era*, London 1969, 30.
19. The name 'Samaritans' only comes into use later and is therefore strictly speaking

incorrect here, as also in H.Jagersma, *History of Israel in the Old Testament Period*, London and Philadelphia 1982, 207f. In the period described here they are referred to, for example, as Shechemites.

20. As in Jagersma, op.cit., 208.
21. See *AJ* XI, 342.
22. See also V.Tcherikover, *Hellenistic Civilization and the Jews*, Philadelphia 1961, 42ff.; Kippenberg, op.cit., 56; and Schäfer, op.cit., 20.
23. See Kippenberg, op.cit., esp. 57; Coggins, op.cit., esp. 97.
24. See also M.Delcor, 'Le temple d'Onias en Egypte', *RB* 75, 1968, 188-203; Coggins, op.cit., 112; D.E.Gowan, *Bridge Between the Testaments*, Pittsburgh ²1980, 167. G.Fohrer, *History of Israelite Religion*, London 1973, 368, differs.
25. Thus e.g. Kippenberg, op.cit., 59ff.
26. Thus e.g. Coggins, op.cit., 164.
27. See e.g. Gen.12.6f; 33.18-20; Josh.24; I Kings 12.
28. See A.Alt, *Der Stadtstaat Samaria*, Berichte über die Verhandlungen der Sächsischen Akademie der Wissenschaften zu Leipzig. Phil.hist.Klasse. Band 101, Heft 5, 1954 = *KS* III, 301.

Chapter 3   The Period of the Diadochi (c.323-301 BC)

1. Cf. Diodorus Siculus XVIII, 28, 3-4.
2. Cf. Diodorus Siculus XIX, 93, 2.
3. Cf. Diodorus Siculus XIX, 93, 5-7.
4. Cf. P.Grimal, *FWG* 6, p.59.
5. Cf. e.g. O.Plöger, *Das Buch Daniel*, KAT XVIII, Gütersloh 1965, 155; M.Delcor, *Le livre de Daniel* (SB), Paris 1971, 222; A.Lacoque, *Le livre de Daniel*, CAT XVb, Neuchâtel-Paris 1976, 159.
6. Cf.E.Bickerman, *From Ezra to the Last of the Maccabees*, New York ⁶1975, 46f.
7. *Contra Apionem* I, 186-9.
8. Thus also P.Schäfer, *IJH*, 570.
9. Cf. Y.Meshorer, *Jewish Coins of the Second Temple Period*, Tel Aviv 1967, 36.
10. For the Nabataeans see e.g. J.R.Bartlett, 'From Edomites to Nabataeans: A Study in Continuity', *PEJ* 111, 1979, 53-66.
11. Cf. Diodorus Siculus XIX, 94-5.
12. Cf. Diodorus Siculus XIX, 110, 1-3.
13. See Schürer II, 146 and n.324.
14. Cf. *contra Apionem* I, 208-11; *AJ* XII, 4-6.
15. Cf. *AJ* XII, 7.
16. Cf. Letter of Aristeas 12-13.
17. Thus F.M.Abel, *Histoire de la Palestine* I, Paris 1932, 31.
18. Thus e.g. V.Tcherikover, *Hellenistic Civilization and the Jews*, Philadelphia-Jerusalem 1961, 56f.; M.Hengel, *Jews, Greeks and Barbarians*, London and Philadelphia 1980, 19.
19. See A.Schalit, *König Herodes. Der Mann und sein Werk*, Berlin 1969, 187ff.
20. See M.Hengel, *Judaism and Hellenism* I, London 1974, 20f.
21. See Schürer II, 200ff.

22. Cf. Aboth I.1.

23. *AJ* XII, 142.

24. See also in Diodorus Siculus, LX, 3,5 and on this Stern, *GLAJJ* I, 28.

25. For this question see Stern, op.cit., 31; cf. also G.Alon, 'Par'irtin. On the History of the High Priesthood at the End of the Second Temple Period', in *Jews, Judaism and the Classical World. Studies in Jewish History in the Times of the Second Temple and the Talmud*, Jerusalem 1977, 48ff.

26. *AJ* XI, 347.

27. Thus e.g. Abel, op.cit., 41.

28. On this see J.T.Nelis, *I Makkabeeën*, BOT, Roermond 1972, 211f.; M.Hengel, *Judaism and Hellenism* II, 50 n.124.

29. *AJ* XII, 43; 57. Cf. also the fact that the Simeon mentioned in Luke 2.25 is regarded as 'righteous', i.e. just.

30. Cf. m.Aboth I,2; b.Yoma 39a,b; b.Menahoth 109b.

31. See Schalit, op.cit., 190 and n.150.

32. See S.Freyne, *Galilee from Alexander the Great to Hadrian (323 BCE to 135 CE)*, Wilmington, Delaware 1980, 25.

33. See e.g. B.van Elderen, 'Nieuwtestamentische geografie', *BH* 1, Kampen 1981, 68ff.

34. See S.T.Parker, 'The Decapolis Reviewed', *JBL* 94, 1975, 437-41.

35. For all these cities see now M.Rostovtzeff, CAH VII, 192.

36. *AJ* XIII, 364.

Chapter 4   The First Half-Century of Ptolemaic Rule (301-246 BC)

1. See M.Hengel, *Judaism and Hellenism* I, London 1974, 18.

2. See M.Rostovtzeff, in CAH VII, 113ff.; H.G.Kippenberg, *Religion und Klassenbildung im antiken Judäa. Eine religionssoziologische Studie zum Verhältnis von Tradition und gesellschaftlicher Entwicklung*, Göttingen ²1981, 79.

3. Cf. C.Préaux, *L'économie royale des Lagides*, Brussels 1939, 297ff.; Rostovtzeff, CAH VII, 136ff.

4. Cf. J.P.Lévy, *L'économie antique*, Que sais-je?, no.1155, Paris 1969, 53f.

5. See W.Clarysse, 'Egyptian Estate-Holders in the Ptolemaic Period', in E.Lipiński (ed.), *State and Temple Economy in the Ancient Near East* II, Louvain 1979, 731ff.

6. See the *Chronicle of Jerome*, ed. R.Helm, GCS 47, 127f.

7. See J.Negenman, *Een geografie van Palestina*, Palaestina Antiqua 2, Kampen 1982, 108ff.

8. Cf. *EAEHL* I, p.15.

9. See Schürer II, esp. 121ff., 142ff.

10. See *EAEHL* I, p.253. For the last-mentioned cities see also A.Alt, 'Galiläische Probleme', *KS* II, Munich 1964, 384ff.

11. See Schürer II, 155f.

12. Cf.M.Stern, in H.H.Ben-Sasson, *Geschichte des jüdischen Volkes* I, Munich 1978, 233ff.

13. Polybius V 86, 10.

14. Thus A.Kasher, 'First Jewish Military Units in Ptolemaic Egypt', *JSJ* 9, 1978, 57-67.
15. Cf. Kippenberg, op.cit., 78ff.
16. Cf. Kippenberg, op.cit., 78-82, 93.
17. Cf.M.Rostovtzeff, *The Social and Economic History of the Hellenistic World* I, Oxford 1941, 278ff.
18. In this connection see *CPJ* no.6.
19. See *AJ* XII, 169f.
20. See Rostovtzeff, CAH, 130.
21. Cf. Kippenberg, op.cit., 79.
22. Edited e.g. by P.W.Pestman, *Greek and Demotic Texts from the Zenon Archive*, Papyrologica Lugduno-Batava XX A and B, I,II, Leiden 1980, and see also *CPJ* nos.1-16.
23. *CPJ*, nos 4,5.
24. See the Letter of Aristeas, 84ff., and Diodorus Siculus, XL 3.
25. See Rostovtzeff, CAH VII, 193.
26. Thus too Hengel, op.cit., 24.
27. See also F.Crüsemann, 'Hiob und Kohelet', in *Werden und Wirken des Alten Testament* (FS Claus Westermann), Göttingen 1980, 392, and also the literature mentioned in nn.90,91.
28. Cf. e.g. J.P.M.van der Ploeg, *Prediker*, BOT, Roermond-Maaseik 1953, 8ff.; H.W.Hertzberg, *Der Prediger*, KAT XVII, 4-5, Gütersloh 1963, 45ff.; A.Lauha, *Kohelet*, BKAT XIX, Neukirchen-Vluyn 1978, 3. We find a completely different view in C.F.Whitley, *Koheleth. His Language and Thought*, BZAW 148, Berlin and New York 1979, who thinks in terms of about 152 BC.
29. In this connection see Crüsemann, op.cit., 386, and the literature listed in n.69 there.
30. For all this see now also Crüsemann, 'Hiob und Kohelet', and id., 'Die unveränderbare Welt. Überlegungen zur "Krisis der Weisheit" beim Prediger (Kohelet)', in W.Schottroff and W.Stegemann, *Der Gott der kleinen Leute* I, *Altes Testament*, Munich 1979, 80-104, and the criticism of it by D.Michel, 'Qohelet-Probleme. Überlegungen zu Qoh 8,2-9; 7.11-14', *Theologica Viatorum* 15, 1979/80, 81-105.
31. See n.27.

Chapter 5 The Second Half-Century of Ptolemaic Rule (246-198 BC)

1. Cf. P.Grimal, *FWG* 6, p.157.
2. Thus e.g. M.Hengel, *Jews, Greeks and Barbarians*, London and Philadelphia 1980, 29; cf. also p.147 n.42.
3. Cf. Grimal, op.cit., 154.
4. Cf. W.W.Tarn, CAH VII, 719.
5. *AJ* XII, 159.
6. For the arguments see M.Hengel, *Judaism and Hellenism* II, London 1974, 179 n.76.
7. *AJ* XII, 159.

8. *Contra Apionem* II, 48.

9. Thus B.Mazar, 'The House of Tobiah', *Tarbiz* 12, 1941, 122 (in Hebrew). See further on the Tobiads e.g. A. Büchler, *Die Tobiaden und die Oniaden im II. Makkabäerbuch und in der verwandten jüdisch-hellenistischen Literatur* (1899), Hildesheim 1975; although on some points this is dated, it still has much useful information. Cf. also B.Mazar, 'The Tobiads', *IEJ* 7, 1957, 137-45, 229-38; V.Tcherikover, in A.Schalit, *The World History of the Jewish People*, Vol.6: *The Hellenistic Age*, Jerusalem 1972, 96ff.

10. *AJ* XII, 160-236.

11. See e.g. Tcherikover, op.cit., 98.

12. Cf. *CPJ*, nos. 2d, 4,5.

13. *CPJ*, no.2d and cf. also *AJ* XII, 233.

14. Se O.Plöger, 'Hyrkan im Ostjordanland', in *Aus der Spätzeit des Alten Testaments*, Göttingen 1971, 92ff.

15. *AJ* XII, 175ff.

16. Cf. M.Hengel, *Judaism and Hellenism* I, London 1974, 269.

17. Cf. *AJ* XII, 180-5.

18. Hengel, *Judaism and Hellenism*, 53.

19. Cf. *AJ* XII, 200.

20. Cf. *AJ* XII, 168.

21. Cf. *AJ* XII, 185-6; also *CPJ*, no.5.

22. Cf. *AJ* XII, 187ff., 206.

23. See Grimal, op.cit., 172 and Tarn, op.cit., 772ff.

24. Cf. Polybius V,34 and Tarn, op.cit., 727.

25. Cf. Polybius V, 58-61,2.

26. Cf. Polybius V, 40,1-3; 61,3-62,6.

27. Cf. Polybius V, 71, 11,12.

28. Thus e.g. Büchler, op.cit., 65f.; Hengel, *Judaism*, 8. M.Stern, *GLAJJ* I, 112f., differs.

29. For Joppa see B.Lifhitz, 'Beiträge zur palästinischen Epigraphik', *ZDPV* 78, 1962, 82f. and for Marisa F.J.Bliss and R.A.S.Macalister, *Excavations in Palestine during the Years 1898-1900*, London 1902, 62ff.

30. Cf. F.M.Abel, *Histoire de la Palestine* I, Paris 1952, 82.

31. Hengel, *Judaism and Hellenism* I, 269.

32. Cf. P.Jouguet, 'Les Lagides et les Indigènes', *RBPH* 2, 1923, 419-45, and also Abel, op.cit., 84.

33. Polybius XVI, 22a, 6.

34. In a report in *AJ* XII, 136, taken from Polybius.

35. Cf. *AJ* XII, 129-30, 139.

36. Cf. *AJ* XII, 141.

37. See Sirach 50.1. Cf. *AJ* XII, 141.

38. Cf. *AJ* XII, 138-44.

39. Cf. *AJ* XII, 133 and also Stern, op.cit., 134.

40. Cf. *AJ* XII, 136.

41. Cf. *AJ* XII, 138ff. and also 6.2.1.

Chapter 6   The Beginning of Seleucid Rule (198-175 BC)

1. See F.M.Abel, *Histoire de la Palestine* I, Paris 1952, 104.
2. Cf. Diodorus Siculus XVIII, 3; XXIX, 15; Strabo, *Geographica* VII, 223.
3. See Abel, op.cit., 105.
4. See E.Meyer, *Ursprung und Anfänge des Christentums* II, Stuttgart 1925, 127 n.21; E.Bickerman, 'La Charte séleucide de Jérusalem' (1935), *Studies in Jewish and Christian History* II, Leiden 1980, 44-85; A.Alt, 'Zu Antiochos' III. Erlass für Jerusalem', *ZAW* 57, 1939, 283-5.
5. Cf. H.Jagersma, 'The Tithes in the Old Testament', *OTS* XXI, Leiden 1981, 126f.
6. *AJ* XII, 145f.
7. Cf.E.Bickerman, 'Une proclamation séleucide relative au temple de Jérusalem' (1937), *Studies in Jewish and Christian History* II, Leiden 1980, 86-104.
8. *BJ* V, 194. Cf. also *AJ* XV, 417.
9. Cf. Acts 21.26ff.; Philo, *Leg. ad Gaium*, 31; and above all, E.Bickerman, 'The Warning Inscriptions of Herod's Temple' (1947), *Studies in Jewish and Christian History* II, Leiden 1980, 210-24.
10. See Y.H.Landau, 'A Greek Inscription found near Hefziba', *IEJ* 16, 1966, 54-70.
11. Cf. Landau, op.cit., 66 n.15.
12. See e.g. G.A.te Stroete, 'Van Henoch tot Sion', in *Vruchten van de Uithof (feestbundel voor H.A.Brongers)*, Utrecht 1974, 120-33.
13. See *AJ* XII, 197-202, 213-20; also Abel, op.cit. 107; M.Hengel, *Judaism and Hellenism* I, London 1974, 272.
14. Cf. Hengel, op.cit., 272 and *AJ* XII, 229-36.
15. Thus at least Josephus in *AJ* XII, 229ff. Cf. also O.Plöger, 'Hyrkan im Ostjordanland' (1955), in *Aus der Spätzeit des Alten Testaments*, Göttingen 1971, 90-101.
16. *AJ* XII, 228f.
17. Cf. Abel, op.cit.; V.Tcherikover, *Hellenistic Civilization and the Jews*, Philadelphia and Jerusalem ²1961, 464f. n.10; Hengel, op.cit., 25.
18. On this see E.Bickerman, 'Héliodore au temple de Jérusalem' (1939-44), in *Studies in Jewish and Christian History*, Leiden 1980, 159-91.
19. Thus e.g P.Schäfer, *Geschichte der Juden in der Antike*, Stuttgart 1983, 51f.
20. Cf. Tcherikover, op.cit., 156ff.
21. Cf. II Macc.10.11; Strabo, *Geographica* XVI 2,2, 34, and also J.T.Nelis, *I Makkabeeën*, BOT, Roermond 1972, 95.
22. Thus S.Freyne, *Galilee from Alexander the Great to Hadrian (323 BCE to 135 CE)*, Wilmington and Notre Dame 1980, 33.
23. Thus A.Alt, 'Galiläische Probleme' (1940), *KS* II, Munich ³1964, 404 and n.3. Cf. also *AJ* XII, 154, 175.
24. *AJ* XII, 156.
25. H.G.Kippenberg, *Garizim und Synagoge*, Berlin and New York 1971, 74 and n.70.
26. See now H.Stadelmann, *Ben Sira als Schriftgelehrter. Eine Untersuchung zum*

Berufsbild des vor-makkabäischen Sofer unter Berücksichtigung seines Verhältnisses zu Priester-Propheten- und Weisheitslehrertum, WUNT 2,6, Tübingen 1980.

27. Cf. Hengel, op.cit, 131; G.Sauer, *Jesus Sirach*, JSHRZ III, 5, Gütersloh 1981. T.Middendorp, *Die Stellung Jesu Ben-Siras zwischen Judentum und Hellenismus*, Leiden 1972, 141.

28. See E.Janssens, *Das Gottesvolk und seine Geschichte*, Neukirchen-Vluyn 1971, 16ff.; te Stroete, op.cit., 120-33.

29. Cf. e.g. Middendorp, op.cit., 7-34.

30. For this see e.g. A.Sisti, 'Riflessi dell'epoca premaccabaica nell'Ecclesiastico', *RivBib* 12, 1964, 215-56; Hengel, op.cit., 138f.

31. Middendorp, op.cit. For this material see now especially P.C.Beentjes, *Jesus Sirach en Tenach*, Nieuwegein 1981.

32. For this passage see Beentjes, op.cit., 176-86.

33. Thus Hengel, op.cit., 134.

34. See also J.C.H.Lebram, *Legitimiteit en Charisma. Over de herleving van de contemporaine geschiedschrijving in het jodentom tijdens de 2ᵉ eeuw v.Chr*, Leiden 1980, 7.

Chapter 7   The Prelude to the Revolt

1. For this see M.Rostovtzeff, CAH VII, 160.

2. Cf. Polybius, XXIX 27.8; Livy, XLV 12.4ff. For the relationship between Rome and the Ptolemies see also H.Heinen, 'Die politische Beziehungen zwischen Rom und dem Ptolemäerreich von ihren Anfängen bis zum Tag von Eleusis (273-168 v.Chr.)', *ANRW* I, 1, Berlin – New York 1972, 633-59.

3. See J.G.Bunge, 'THEOS EPIPHANES. Zu den ersten fünf Regierungsjahren Antiochos IV Epiphanes', *Historia* 23, 1974, 57-85.

4. Cf. V.Tcherikover, *Hellenistic Civilization and the Jews*, Philadelphia and Jerusalem ²1961, 466 n.17, and also II Macc.4.29.

5. See *AJ* XII, 238.

6. M.Hengel, *Judaism and Hellenism* I, London and Philadelphia 1974, 277.

7. Cf. E.Bickerman, *The God of the Maccabees*, Leiden 1979, 39.

8. Thus Hengel, op.cit., 279.

9. See J.A.Goldstein, *I Maccabees*, AB, New York 1976, 115 n.75.

10. See also Goldstein, op.cit., 115f.

11. Thus F.Millar, 'The Background to the Maccabean Revolution; Reflections on Martin Hengel's *Judaism and Hellenism*', *JJS* 29, 1978, 1ff. Cf. also the review of *Judaism and Hellenism* by J.C.H.Lebram in *VT* XX, 1970, esp. 505.

12. See II Macc.4.23. According to Josephus, *AJ* XII, 238, however, he was a brother of Onias III and Jason. But this is wrong, see Schürer I, 149 n.30.

13. The reading in II Macc.3.4 that he came from Benjamin is wrong. See C. Habicht, *2.Makkabäerbuch*, JSHRZ I, 3, Gütersloh 1979, 210 n.4b.

14. See *AJ* XII, 239ff.

15. Thus II Macc.4.39-42.

16. See II Macc.4.32-38; also Dan.11.22b.

17. Thus Bickerman, op.cit., 43.

18. See *AJ* XII, 239.

19. See also Hengel, op.cit., 280.

20. See *AJ* XII, 239-40.

21. See *AJ* XII, 229.

22. Thus also Tcherikover, op.cit., 187-90; E.Bickerman, op.cit., 46.

23. Thus e.g. F.M.Abel, *Histoire de la Palestine* I, Paris 1952, 119; Schürer I, 150ff.; T.Fischer, *Seleuciden und Makkabäer*, Bochum 1980, 257.

24. Thus e.g. Hengel, op.cit., 11, 280f.; Bickerman, op.cit., 45.

25. Op.cit., 187-9, followed e.g. by Goldstein, op.cit., 122.

26. The chronology is still disputed. See the literature mentioned in J.C.H.Lebram, 'König Antiochus im Buch Daniel', *VT* XXV, 1975, 737 n.3, and now also K.Bringmann, *Hellenistische Reform und Religionsverfolgung in Judäa. Eine Untersuchung zur jüdisch-hellenistischen Geschichte (175-163 v.Chr.)*, Göttingen 1983, 15ff.

27. Cf. Schürer I, 50.

28. Cf. Tcherikover, op.cit., 392ff.

29. Cf. Bickerman, op.cit., 47.

30. Cf. Polybius XXVI 1,11 and see also O.Mørkholm, *Antiochus IV of Syria*, Classica et Mediaevalia, Copenhagen 1966, and Bickerman, op.cit., 79.

31. J.G.Bunge, 'Die sogenannte Religionsverfolgung Antiochus IV Epiphanes und die griechischen Städte', *JSJ* 10, 1979, 155-65.

32. Cf. also J.C.H.Lebram, *Legitimiteit en Charisma*, Leiden 1980, 26 n.44.

33. Lebram, *Legitimiteit*, 16, 26 and also 'König Antiochus', esp. 754-61.

34. J.G.Bunge, 'Die Feiern Antiochos IV Epiphanes in Daphne in Herbst 166 v.Chr.', *Chiron* 6, 1976, 64ff. does this, but in order to connect I Macc.1.41-51 with a procession of Antiochus IV in Daphne. For this see e.g. the criticism by K.Bringman, op.cit., 35.

35. Cf. also Hengel, op.cit., 286f.

36. According to II Macc.6.2, Zeus Xenios, see below.

37. Cf. E.Bickerman, 'Un document rélatif à la persécution d'Antiochos IV Epiphane' (1937), *Studies in Jewish and Christian History* II, Leiden 1980, 105-35. Cf. also A.Alt, 'Galiläische Probleme' (1940), *KS* II, Munich ³1964, 398 n.2 and A.Schalit, 'Die Denkschrift der Samaritaner an König Antiochus Epiphanes zu Beginn der grossen Verfolgung der jüdischen Religion im Jahre 167 v.Chr. (Josephus, *AJ* XII, 258-64)', *ASTI* 8, 1970/71, 131-83.

38. See H.G.Kippenberg, *Garizim und Synagoge*, Berlin-New York 1971, 79.

39. Cf. Kippenberg, op.cit., 76.

40. Ibid., 80ff.

41. See Hengel, op.cit., 286f.; Bickerman, *God of the Maccabees*, 83f.; Bringman, op.cit., 103.

42. *Hist.* V.7.4.

43. See A.M.A.Hospers-Jansen, *Tacitus over de Joden*, Groningen 1941, esp. 156.

44. See the literature mentioned in n.41.

45. See II Macc.13.3 and especially *AJ* XII, 384.

46. See e.g. M.Delcor, *Le livre de Daniel*, SB, Paris 1973, 175-7, 201.

47. *The God of the Maccabees*, 88f.

48. Cf. K.Toki, 'The Dates of the First and Second Books of Maccabees', *AJBI* III, 1977, 69-83.

49. Cf. also Lebram, *Legitimiteit*, 17.

50. Cf. also Bickerman, *God of Maccabees*, 54.

51. C.J.den Heyer, *De messiaanse weg* I, Kampen 1983, 148.

52. Thus e.g. H.H.Rowley, *The Relevance of Apocalyptic*, London 1961, 13; D.S.Russell, *Between the Testaments*, London and Philadelphia ²1963, 93ff.; T.C.Vriezen, *The Religion of Ancient Israel*, London 1967, 266.

53. Thus G.von Rad, *Old Testament Theology* II, Edinburgh and New York 1965, 306ff. For this view of von Rad and also the views of the authors mentioned in n.52 see R.Wilson, 'From Prophecy to Apocalyptic. Reflections on the Shape of Israelite Religion', *Semeia* 21, 1981, 79-95, but he fails to recognize that there is a direct line from prophecy or wisdom to apocalyptic.

54. Thus P.A.H. de Boer, *Het oudste Christendom en de Antieke Cultuur* I, Haarlem 1951, 444-78.

55. O.Plöger, *Theocracy and Eschatology*, Oxford and Philadelphia 1968.

56. See e.g. D.S.Russell, *The Method and Message of Jewish Apocalyptic*, London and Philadelphia 1964; also J.M.Schmidt, *Die jüdische Apokalyptik*, ²1976, 277ff.

57. For this see e.g. I. Willi-Plein, *Das Geheimnis der Apokalyptik*, *VT* XXVII, 1977, 62-81.

58. See further e.g. den Heyer, op.cit., 150.

59. For details see e.g. A.S.van der Woude, *Die messianische Vorstellungen der Gemeinde von Qumrân*, Assen 1957, and also E.M.Laperrousaz, *L'attente du Messie en Palestine à la veille et au début de l'ère chrétienne*, Paris 1982, 75-333.

60. See also M.Noth, 'The Understanding of History in Old Testament Apocalyptic', in *The Laws in the Old Testament*, Edinburgh 1966 reissued London 1984, 194-214; G.I.Davies, 'Apocalyptic and Historiography', *JSOT* 5, 1978, 15-28, and above all also den Heyer, op.cit., 149ff.

61. Cf. K.Koch, *Das Buch Daniel* (EdF 144), Darmstadt 1980, 8ff. Fischer, op.cit., 140, differs; he thinks in terms of 160/159 BC.

62. Cf. Koch, op.cit., 59-61.

63. See e.g.Plöger, op.cit., 17; Hengel, op.cit., 176; A.Lacocque, *Le livre de Daniel* (CAT XVb), Neuchâtel-Paris 1976, 20ff. Delcor, op.cit., 15ff., assumes this for the second part of Daniel.

64. J.C.H.Lebram, 'Apokalyptik und Hellenismus im Buche Daniel. Bemerkungen und Gedanken zu Martin Hengels Buch über Judentum und Hellenismus', *VT* XX, 1970, 523f.

65. See 8.1.3.

66. See Lebram, 'König Antiochus'.

67. Cf. J.T.Milik, *The Books of Enoch: Aramaic Fragments of Qumran Cave 4*, Oxford 1976.

68. See M.A.Knibb, *The Ethiopic Book of Enoch*, Oxford 1979.

69. See e.g. J.M.Myers, *I & II Esdras*, AB, New York 1974, 52f.

70. Cf. Myers, op.cit., 8-15.

71. See N.Poulssen, *Judith*, BOT, Roermond 1969, 8f. According to E.Zenger, *Das Buch Judith*, JSHRZ I, 6, Gütersloh 1981, 431, however, this book was not written before 150 BC.

Chapter 8 The Maccabaean Struggle

1. See M.Hengel, *Judaism and Hellenism* I, London 1974, 56.
2. Cf.*AJ* XII, 265. But cf. also I Macc.2.1 and J.A.Goldstein, 'The Hasmonaeans: The Dynasty of God's Resisters', *HTR* 68, 1975, 53-8. In the Talmud the term 'Hasmonaean' is used exclusively, see e.g. b.Sabbat 21b.
3. Cf. Neh.5.1-13 and on it my *History of Israel in the Old Testament Period*, London and Philadelphia, 1982, 205.
4. See H.Kippenberg, *Religion und Klassenbildung im antiken Judäa*, Göttingen ²1982, 81.
5. E.Bickerman, *The God of the Maccabees*, Leiden 1979, 90f.
6. Thus also e.g. O.Plöger, *Theocracy and Eschatology*, Philadelphia and Oxford 1968; L.Finkelstein, *The Pharisees*, II, Philadelphia ³1966, 573; Hengel, op.cit., 181. H.A.Brongers, 'De chasidim in het Boek der Psalmen', *NTT* 8, 1954, 297, and others differ.
7. Cf. I Macc.2.31-32; *AJ* XII, 272.
8. Cf. I Macc.2.33-38; *AJ* XII, 274.
9. Cf. I Macc.2.41; *AJ* XII, 276.
10. See J.T.Nelis, *I Makkabeeën*, BOT, Roermond 1972, 90; J.A.Goldstein, *I Maccabees*, AB, New York 1976, 13ff.
11. Cf. I Macc. 3.13-26 and on it B.Bar-Kochva, 'Seron and Cestius Gallius at Beit Huron', *PEQ* 108, 1976, 13ff.
12. See I Macc.3.31 and e.g. also F.M.Abel, *Histoire de la Palestine* I, Paris 1952, 136f.; J.A.Goldstein, *I Maccabees*, 252.
13. The events which now follow are put in I Macc. and II Macc. in a different order. I describe them in the generally accepted order. For these problems see A.Penna, 'Le spedizioni di lisa nella versione Peshitta', *Studii Biblici Franciscani Liber Annuus* 13, 1962/63, 93-100; P.Schäfer, in J.H.Hayes and J.Maxwell Miller, *Israelite and Judaean History*, London and Philadelphia 1977, 564ff.
14. Cf. also S.Wibbing, 'Zur Topographie einzelner Schlachten des Judas Makkabäus', *ZDPV* 78, 1962, 159ff.
15. Cf. also Polybius XXI.9, and D.Mendels, 'A Note on the Tradition of Antiochus IV's Death', *IEJ* 31, 981, 53-6.
16. See e.g. O.Roth, *Rom und die Hasmonäer*, BWAT 17, Leipzig 1914, 8. T.Fischer, 'Zu den Beziehungen zwischen Rom und den Juden im 2.Jahrhundert v.Chr.', *ZAW* 86, 1974, 90-3; id., 'Rom und die Hasmonäer. Ein Überblick zu den politischen Beziehungen 164-37 v.Chr.', *Gymnasium* 88, 1981, 139ff.
17. Thus B.Z.Wacholder, 'The Letter from Judah Maccabee to Aristobulus: Is 2 Maccabees 1:1b-2:18 Authentic?', *HUCA* 48, 1977, 89-133.
18. See Nelis, op.cit., 51ff.
19. For contacts with Egypt in this period see e.g. M.A.Beek, 'Relations entre Jérusalem et la diaspora égyptienne au 2ᵉ siècle avant J.C.', *OTS* XI, Leiden 1943, 119-43.
20. Cf. I Macc.6.58ff.
21. *AJ* XII, 383.
22. *AJ* XIII, 383.
23. See M.Delcor, 'Le temple d'Onias en Egypte', *RB* 75, 1968, 188-203;

R.Hayward, 'The Jewish Temple of Leontopolis: A Reconsideration', *JJS* 33, 1982, 429-43.

24. Cf. I Macc.7.26-50; *AJ* XII, 402-12.

25. Cf. also *AJ* XII, 417ff. and Diodorus LX, 2.

26. For this treaty cf. Roth, op.cit., 3ff.; T.Fischer, *Seleukiden und Makkabaër*, Bochum 1980, 105ff.

27. See Roth, op.cit., 10; Fischer, op.cit. (n.26), 108. J.G.Bunge, *Untersuchungen zum zweiten Makkabäerbuch*, Bonn 1971, 660 n.59a and Schäfer, op.cit., 589, differ.

28. See the literature mentioned in n.16.

29. See Polybius, XXXIII, 18, 6ff.

30. For all this see I Macc.11.1-19; *AJ* XIII, 103-19.

31. For this location see H.Donner, *Einführung in die Biblische Landes- und Altertumskunde*, Darmstadt 1976, 109f.; A.Schalit, *König Herodes. Der Mann und sein Werk*, Berlin 1969, 196f.; Schürer I, 175 n.15.

32. Cf. I Macc.9.50; *AJ* XIII, 15.

33. See Nelis, op.cit., 175.

34. See I Macc.9.35f.; *AJ* XIII, 11. Cf. also *BJ* 1, 47.

35. See Jagersma, *History*, 96f.

36. In *AJ* XII, 414, 419, 434, however, Josephus states that Judas succeeded Alcimus; this is impossible because Judas had already been killed in 161 BC. Moreover, according to an early rabbinic tradition Mattathias and all his sons were high priests, but cf. J.Derenbourg, *Essai sur l'histoire et la géographie de la Palestine, d'après les Thalmuds et les autres sources rabbiniques*, Paris 1867, 58.

37. Thus H.Stegemann, *Die Entstehung der Qumrangemeinde*, Bonn 1971, 250f. This theory has been taken over with some qualifications by J.G.Bunge, 'Zu Geschichte und Chronologie des Untergangs der Oniaden und des Aufstiegs der Hasmonäer', *JSJ* 6, 1975, 1-46, and in part also by J.Murphy-O'Connor, 'Demetrius I and the Teacher of Righteousness (I Macc.X, 25-45)', *RB* 83, 1976, 400ff.

38. For this see e.g. H.Burgmann, 'Das umstrittene Intersacerdotium in Jerusalem 159-152 BC', *JSJ* 11, 1980, 135-76.

39. H.Kreissig, *Wirtschaft und Gesellschaft in Seleukidenreich*. Schriften zur Geschichte und Kultur der Antike 16, Berlin 1978, 112.

40. See Nelis, op.cit., 202.

41. Cf. I Macc.11.54ff.; *AJ* XIII, 131ff., and Diodorus XXXI, 2.4a.

42. See H.Wilrich, *Urkundenfälschung in der hellenistisch-jüdischen Literatur*, Göttingen 1924, 23-7, and also F.M.Abel, *Les Livres des Maccabées*, Paris 1949, 231-3.

43. Thus rightly Nelis, op.cit., 212. Goldstein, op.cit.(n.10), 455ff., differs.

44. Cf. A.Alt, 'Galiläische Probleme' (1940), *KS* II, Munich 1964, 389f.

Chapter 9 The Origin and Development of Some Important Groups

1. For this see e.g. J.LeMoyne, *Les Sadducéens*, Paris 1972, 67ff.; H.Mulder, *De Sadduceeën. Deconfessionalisering in bijbelse tijden*, Amsterdam 1973, 13f.

2. For a survey see J.Wellhausen, *Die Pharisäer und die Sadducäer*, Göttingen ³1967, 56ff.

3. See in *AJ* XIII, 173; XVIII, 16f.; *BJ* II, 164-6.

4. For a survey see Le Moyne, op.cit., 159-63, and H.Mulder, op.cit., 16-24.

5. See H.Jagersma, *A History of Israel in the Old Testament Period*, London 1982, 104 and 243 n.62.

6. See Le Moyne, op.cit., 163 and n.11.

7. See e.g. b.Sukkah 43b.

8. Cf. J.Jeremias, *Jerusalem in the Time of Jesus*, London ⁴1979, 154f., 193f.

9. See Schürer II, 409 n.16; also Le Moyne, op.cit., 113-15.

10. Cf. Le Moyne, op.cit., 335.

11. Ibid., 388.

12. Thus also E.M.Smallwood, *The Jews under Roman Rule from Pompey to Diocletian. A Study in Political Relations*, Leiden ²1981, 17.

13. E.Bammel, 'Sadduzäer und Sadokiden', *ETL* 55, 1979, 107-15.

14. Cf. e.g. *AJ* XIII, 298; ARNa I.5.

15. See also M.Stern, 'Aspects of Jewish Society: The Priesthood and Other Classes', in S.Safrai and M.Stern, *The Jewish People in the First Century* II, Assen 1976, 610f.

16. See further e.g. D.Flusser, 'Josephus and the Sadducees and Menander', *Immanuel* 7, 1977, 61ff.

17. See J.Neusner, *The Rabbinic Traditions about the Pharisees before 70*, Parts I, II, III, Leiden 1971.

18. Thus Schürer II, 396. According to K.Schubert, *Die jüdischen Religionsparteien in neutestamentlicher Zeit*, SBS 43, Stuttgart 1970, this relates to their separation from the Hasidaeans.

19. See m.Hag II, 7; m.Sotah III,4; Yaddayim IV, 6-8.

20. See e.g. E.Lohse, *The New Testament Environment*, London 1976, 77f.; P.R.Davies, 'Hasidim in the Maccabaean Period', *JJS* 28, 1977, 127-40; Schürer II, 400.

21. Neusner, op.cit.

22. Neusner, op.cit., Part III, 318, speaks in this connection of a 'society of table fellowship'.

23. For this see M.Smith, 'Palestinian Judaism in the First Century', in M.Davis, *Israel: Its Role in Civilization*, New York 1956, 67-81.

24. Cf. also G.Alon, 'The Attitude of the Pharisees to Roman Rule and the House of Herod', in *Jews, Judaism and the Classical World*, Jerusalem 1977, 18-47.

25. J.Neusner, *From Politics to Piety*, New York 1979.

26. Wellhausen, op.cit., 94.

27. Cf. *AJ* XIII, 297 and e.g. also J.Maier, *Geschichte der jüdischen Religion*, New York 1972, 20-3.

28. Cf. m.Aboth I, 1ff. and also E.Bickerman, 'La Chaîne de la tradition pharisienne', in *Studies in Jewish and Christian History* II, Leiden 1980, 256-69.

29. Cf.Sirach 15.1-20; 36.10-15; Ps.Sol.9.4.

30. There is a full survey in A.Adam and C.Burchard, *Antike Berichte über die Essener*, Berlin ²1972. See also C.Burchard, 'Die Essener bei Hippolyt', *JSJ* VIII, 1977, 1-41, and D.Graf, 'The Pagan Witness to the Essenes', *BA* 40, 1977, 125-9.

31. Cf *De Vita contemplativa*, 1ff., and also *Quod omnis probus Liber sit*, 75ff.; *Hypothetica* 11.1ff.

32. Cf. S.Wagner, *Die Essener in der wissenschaftlichen Diskussion vom Ausgang des 18. bis 20. Jahrhunderts*, BZAW 79, Berlin 1960, 114-27.

33. Cf.G.Vermes, *Post-Biblical Jewish Studies*, Leiden 1975, 1-9; E.M.Laperrousaz, *L'Attente du Messie en Palestine à la veille et au début de l'ère chrétienne*, Paris 1982, 47.

34. Thus e.g. F.M.Cross, *The Library of Qumran*, New York 1961, 51 n.1; M.Hengel, *Judaism and Hellenism* I, London 1974, 175.

35. See Schürer II, 559.

36. Thus e.g. Vermes, op.cit., 19ff.

37. See n.30.

38. *AJ* XIII, 171.

39. Thus e.g. by W.Bousset, *Die Religion des Judentums*, Tübingen ³1926, 457; Hengel, op.cit., 175; B.Reicke, *The New Testament Era*, London 1969, 170.

40. See also 9.3.2 and Schürer II, 257.

41. *AJ* XVIII, 21, and *Quod omnis probus Liber sit*, 75.

42. *Quod omnis probus Liber sit*, 76.

43. *Hypothetica*, 11.1.

44. *Naturalis Historia*, V.7.

45. Cf. *AJ* XVIII, 21 and *Quod omnis probus Liber sit*, 79.

46. Cf. *BJ* II, 135.

47. *BJ* II, 123 and 149-50.

48. *Quod omnis probus Liber sit*, 75, and cf. *AJ* XVIII, 19.

49. Cf. *BJ* II, 147.

50. See *AJ* XVIII, 20; *BJ* II, 120 and *Hypothetica* 11.4.

51. See *AJ* XVIII, 21; *BJ* II, 120-21; *Hypothetica*, 11.14-16, and *Naturalis Historia* 73.

52. *BJ* II, 160-61.

53. See *Quod omnis probus Liber sit*, 78.

54. Cf. *BJ* II, 141.

55. Thus e.g. A.Dupont-Sommer, *The Essene Writings from Qumran*, Oxford 1961, 39-67; M.Black, *The Essene Problem*, London 1961; J.P.M.van der Ploeg, *Vondsten in de woestijn van Juda*, Utrecht and Antwerp 1970, 61; F.M.Cross, 'The Dead Sea Scrolls and the People who Wrote Them', *BARev* 3, 1977, 1, 23-32, 51; G.Vermes, *The Dead Sea Scrolls. Qumran in Perspective*, London 1977, 125-30.

56. Thus e.g. R.North, 'The Qumran Sadducees', *CBQ* 17, 1955, 164-80. Cf. also R.Eisenman, *Maccabees, Zadokites, Christians and Qumran*, Leiden 1983, esp. 19ff.

57. Thus e.g. C.Rabin, *Qumran Studies*, Oxford 1957, 53ff.

58. Thus e.g. C.Roth, *The Historical Background of the Dead Sea Scrolls*, Oxford 1958.

59. Thus J.Murphy-O'Connor, 'The Essenes in Palestine', *BA* 40, 1977, 100-24. This view has been strongly challenged by M.A.Knibb, 'Exile in the Damascus Document', *JSOT* 25, 1983, 99-117.

60. The influence of the priest in the community was very great, especially as there is also mention among the community of a priest Messiah, see 7.5.

61. Cf. Cross, op.cit. (n.34), 57ff., 63; R. de Vaux, *Archaeology and the Dead Sea Scrolls*, London 1973, 5,18; J.Maier and K.Schubert, *Die Qumran Essener*, Munich and Basle 1973, 28f.

62. E.M.Laperrousez, *Qumran, L'établissement essénien des bords de la Mer Morte*, Paris

1976, 44ff., 93ff., differs; he thinks that the settlement was uninhabited between 67 BC and the beginning of the reign of Herod the Great.

63. For a full survey of the various views see Vermes, op.cit., 160. There is quite a different view in B.E.Thiering, *Redating the Teacher of Righteousness*, Sydney 1979, 212ff., who argues that there is enough evidence to suggest that John the Baptist is this Teacher. According to J.Starcky, 'Les Maîtres de Justice et la chronologie de Qumrân', in M.Delcor, *Qumrân. Sa piété, sa théologie et son milieu*, Louvain 1978, 249-56, the designation 'Teacher of Righteousness' does not denote a historical figure but a function.

64. One and the same person can also be indicated by these two figures, cf. Vermes, op.cit., 150; also B.E.Thiering, 'Once More the Wicked Priest', *JBL* 97, 1978, 191-205.

65. See the survey in Vermes, op.cit., 161, and also in W.H.Brownlee, *The Midrash Pesher of Habakkuk*, Missoula 1979, 95-8.

66. Thus A.S.van der Woude, 'Wicked Priest or Wicked Priests? Reflections on the Identification of the Wicked Priest in the Habakkuk Commentary', *Essays in Honour of Yigael Yadin, JJS* 33, 1982, 349-60.

67. See also Vermes, op.cit., 160.

68. See CD VI, 4-5; VII, 13-19; and also 1QpHab XI.6.

69. Thus e.g. J.T.Milik, *Ten Years of Discovery in the Wilderness of Judaea*, London 1957, 58f., 113f.

70. Thus e.g. R.North, 'The Damascus of Qumran Geography', *PEQ* 87, 1955, 34-48.

71. Thus e.g. I.Rabinovitz, 'A Reconsideration of Damascus', *JBL* 73, 1954, 11-35; A.Jaubert, 'Le pays de Damas', *RB* 75, 1958, 214-48.

72. See Vermes, op.cit., 147f.

73. See de Vaux, op.cit., 5, 18.

74. For a survey see Cross, op.cit.; Vermes, op.cit., 45-86; J.A Fitzmyer, *The Dead Sea Scrolls. Major Publications and Tools for Study*, Missoula 1977, 11ff.

75. K.H.Rengstorf, *Hirbet Qumran und die Bibliothek vom Toten Meer*, Stuttgart 1961, who sees these as the remains of the temple library which was brought there shortly before the fall of Jerualem in AD 70.

76. See *DJD* II.

77. English texts are easily available in G.Vermes, *The Dead Sea Scrolls in English*, Harmondsworth 1970.

78. Edited by Y.Yadin, *The Temple Scroll*, Jerusalem 1977 (in Hebrew)., See also J.Maier, *Die Tempelrolle vom Toten Meer*, Munich 1978; B.Jongeling, 'De Tempelrol', *Phoenix* 15, 1979, 84-99.

79. Cf. Maier, op.cit., 9f.; Jongeling, op.cit. 89. J.Milgrom, 'The Temple Scroll', *BA* 41, 1978, 105-29, himself thinks that a dating around the middle of the second century BC cannot be ruled out.

80. See D.Flusser, 'Pharisäer, Sadduzäer und Essener im Pescher Nahum' (1970), in K.E.Grozinger et al. (ed.), *Qumran*, WdF CDX, Darmstadt 1981, 134ff.

81. See also 7.5 and 8.5.3.

82. See C.Burchard, *Bibliographie zu den Handschriften vom Toten Meer*, BZAW 76, Berlin 1957; id., II, BZAW 89, Berlin 1965; W.S.Lasor, *Bibliography of the Dead Sea*

Scrolls 1948-1957, Pasadena 1958; B.Jongeling, *A Classified Bibliography of the Finds in the Desert of Judah 1958-69*, Leiden 1971.

Chapter 10   The Period of the Hasmonaean Priest-Rulers

1. See 1 Macc.13.31f.; *AJ* XIII, 218-22; Diodorus XXXIII, 28.

2. See T.Fischer, *Untersuchungen zum Partherkrieg Antiochos' VII im Rahmen der Seleucidengeschichte*, Tübingen 1970, and also 10.2.1.

3. Cf. G.F.Moore, *Judaism in the First Centuries of the Christian Era* I, Cambridge, Mass. 1958, 55 n.3. According to J.C. van der Kam, 'II Maccabees 6,7a and the Calendrial Change in Jerusalem', *JSJ* 12, 1981, 52-74, the Seleucid calendar was introduced in the time of Antiochus IV to replace the old priestly calendar.

4. See H.G.Kippenberg, *Religion und Klassenbildung im antiken Judäa*, Göttingen ²1982, 84ff.

5. M.Rostovtzeff, *The Social and Economic History of the Hellenistic World*, Oxford 1941, 1000, 1577f.

6. Kippenberg, op.cit., 91 n.71.

7. See H.Jagersma, 'The Tithes in the Old Testament', *OTS* XXI, Leiden 1981, esp.122ff.

8. Cf. *AJ* XIV, 203.

9. See S.W.Baron, *A Social and Religious History of the Jews* I, Philadelphia ²1952, 367f., and *Encyclopaedia Judaica* 15, 629f. According to S.B.Hoenig, *The Great Sanhedrin*, New York 1953, this will already have been the Sanhedrin, but this view is incorrect; see 3.4.2.

10. See e.g. J.T.Nelis, *I Maccabeeën*, BOT, Roermond 1972, 246.

11. Thus e.g. F.M.Abel, *Histoire de la Palestine* I, Paris 1952, 267; Nelis, op.cit., 247; P.Schäfer, in *IJH*, 595. For detailed comments on this letter see J.A.Goldstein, *I Maccabees*, AB, New York 1976, 493f.

12. See B.Kanael, 'The Beginning of Maccabees Coinage', *IEJ* 1, 1950, 170-5; Y.Meshorer, *Jewish Coins of the Second Temple Period*, Tel Aviv 1967, 42f; Schürer I, 190f.

13. Thus W.Wirgin, 'History from Coins', *PEQ* 104, 1972, 104-10.

14. See R.Reich, 'Archaeological Evidence of the Jewish Population at Hasmonean Gezer', *IEJ* 31, 1981, 48ff.

15. Thus Josephus, *AJ* XIII, 236f.

16. See *AJ* XIII, 237ff.; Diodorus XXXIV/XXXV 1,1-5.

17. See Schürer I, 202f. n.5.

18. Cf. *AJ* XIII, 245ff. and Diodorus XXXIV/XXXV 1, 1-5.

19. Cf. *AJ* XIII, 259ff. and also J.C.H.Lebram, 'Eerste ontmoetingen tussen Rome en de Joden', *Phoenix* 26, 1980, 94ff.; T.Rajak, 'Roman Intervention in a Seleucid Siege of Jerusalem?', *Greek, Roman and Byzantine Studies* 22, 1981, 65-81.

20. For this see M.Pucci, 'Jewish-Parthian Relations in Josephus', *The Jerusalem Cathedra. Studies in the History, Archaeology, Geography and Ethnography of the Land of Israel* 3, 1983, 13-25.

21. Cf. J.Negenman, *Een geografie van Palestina* (Palaestina Antiqua 2), Kampen

1982, 119-333. Cf. also G.Foerster, 'Concerning the Conquest of John Hyrcanus in Moab and the Identity of Samaga', *Eretz-Israel* 15, 1981, 353-5 (in Hebrew).

22. Cf. also G.Fuks, 'The Jews of Hellenistic and Roman Scythopolis', *Essays in Honour of Yigael Yadin*, *JJS* 33, 1982, 407ff.

23. Cf. *AJ* XIII, 255-258; *BJ* I, 63 and also G.Horowitz, 'Town Planning of Hellenistic Marisa: A Reappraisal of the Excavations after Eighty Years', *PEQ* 112, 1980, 95ff.

24. Cf. *AJ* XIII, 255-258; *BJ* I, 63. It is uncertain whether Megillat Ta´anit 22 also relates to this event. Cf. J.Derenbourg, *Essai sur l'histoire et la géographie de la Palestine, d'après les Thalmuds et les autres sources rabbiniques*, Paris 1867, 72.

25. See e.g. John 4.9, and also J.J.Collins, 'The Epic of Theodotus and the Hellenism of the Hasmonaeans', *HTR* 73, 1980, 91-104.

26. Thus e.g. Schürer I, 207; D.E.Gowan, *Bridge Between the Testaments*, Pittsburgh ²1980, 168; B. Reicke, *The New Testament Era*, 66; A.S. van der Woude, in *BH* IIB, 57.

27. Thus e.g. E.Campbell Jr, 'Excavations at Shechem', *BA* 23, 1960, 102ff.; G.E.Wright, *Shechem. The Biography of a Biblical City*, New York and Toronto 1965, 172, 184; P.R.Ackroyd, *AOTS*, 351; D.S.Russell, *The Jews from Alexander to Herod*, Oxford 1967, 63.

28. For these two documents see Schürer I, 204f.

29. See Schürer I, 204ff.; T.Fischer, *Seleukiden und Makkabäer*, Bochum 1980, 64-77. For the first mentioned document see also J.C.H.Lebram, 94ff.

30. Cf. M.Stern, 'The Relations between Judaea and Rome during the Rule of John Hyrcanus', *Zion*, 1961, 1-22.

31. For this letter see E.Bickerman, 'Ein jüdischer Festbrief vom Jahre 124 v.Chr. (II Macc.1.1-9)' (1933), in *Studies in Jewish and Christian History* II, Leiden 1980, 136-58.

32. Thus B.Kanael, 'Ancient Jewish Coins and their Historical Importance', *BAR* 3, 1970, 281ff.; A.Ben-David, 'When did the Maccabees begin to strike their First Coins', *PEQ* 104, 1972, 93-103; U.Rappaport, 'The Emergence of Hasmonean Coinage', *AJSR* 1, 1976, 171-86; B.Daraq and S.Kedar, 'When did the Hasmonaeans begin Minting Coins?', *Qadmoniot* 15, 1982, 29-32 (in Hebrew).

33. Thus Meshorer, op.cit., 56-9, cf. also 43ff.; Schürer II, 603ff.

34. See H.Jagersma, *A History of Israel in the Old Testament Period*, London and Philadelphia 1982, 101, 108.

35. See b.Qidd.66a.

36. See Derenbourg, op.cit., 80 n.1, 95 n.1; Schürer I, 214 n.30; cf. also b.Ber.29a. M.S.Keller, 'Alexander Jannaeus and the Pharisee Rift', *JJS* 30, 1979, 202-11, differs.

37. In this connection see also W.Baars and R.Zuurmond, 'The Project for a New Edition of the Ethiopic Book of Jubilees', *JSS* 9, 1964, 67-74.

38. See e.g. *DJD* I, 82-4; *DJD* III, 77-79, 96-98, and A.S.van der Woude, 'Fragmente des Buches Jubiläen aus Höhle XI (11QJub)', in J.Jeremias and H.Stegemann, *Tradition und Glaube* (FS K.G.Kuhn), Göttingen 1971, 140-6.

39. See also n. 3 and e.g. E.Vogt and H.Cazelles, 'Sur les origines du calendrier des Jubilées. Note sur le calendrier du Déluge', *Biblica* 43, 1962, 202-16; S. van Mierlo, *De oude kalender bij de Hebreeën en zijn verband met de lijdensweek*, Kampen 1963, 9f. and above all J. van Goudoever, *Biblical Calendars*, Leiden 1961, 62ff.

40. See G.L.Davenport, *The Eschatology of the Book of Jubilees* (SPB XX), Leiden 1971; K.Berger, *Das Buch Jubiläen*, JSHRZ II, 3 (Unterweisung in erzählender Form), Gütersloh 1981.

Chapter 11   The Reigns of the Hasmonaean Priest-Kings

1. XVI 2, 40.
2. See also M.Stern, *GLAJJ* I, 307.
3. For this see D.Mendels, 'Hecateus of Abdera and a Jewish *patrios politeia* of the Persian Period', *ZAW* 95, 1983, esp. 104, and the literature mentioned there.
4. See also 10.2.1, 10.2.4.
5. Thus Schürer I, 218. Cf. also *AJ* XIII, 319. S.Freyne, *Galilee from Alexander the Great to Hadrian (323 BCE to 153 CE)*, Wilmington and Notre Dame 1980, 43f., differs.
6. See *BJ* I, 76; Schürer I, 217f.; W.Schottroff, 'Die Ituräer', *ZDPV* 98, 1982, 134.
7. Cf.*AJ* XIII, 324ff.; *BJ* I, 86; and also G.Barkay, 'A Coin of Alexander Jannaeus from Cyprus', *IEJ* 27, 1977, 119-20.
8. Cf.*AJ* XIII, 354ff.; *BJ* I, 87.
9. See M.Stern, 'The Political Background of the Wars of Alexander Janna', *Tarbiz* 33, 1963/4, 325ff.; Schürer I, 134-221.
10. Cf.*AJ* XIII, 372ff. and also J.Derenbourg, *Essai sur l'histoire et la géographie de la Palestine, d'après les Thalmuds et les autres sources rabbiniques*, Paris 1867, 98.
11. Cf.*AJ* XIII, 375f.
12. Cf.*AJ* XIII, 380.
13. Thus e.g. J.M.Allegro, 'Further Light on the History of the Qumran Sect', *JBL* 75, 1956, 92; Y.Yadin, 'Pescher Nahum (4QpNahum) erneut untersucht', *IEJ* 21, 1971, 1ff. H.H.Rowley, '4QpNahum and the Teacher of Righteousness', *JBL* 75, 1956, 192, differs. For more detail on this question see M.Burrows, *More Light on the Dead Sea Scrolls*, London 1958, 201-3.
14. See F.E.Peters, 'The Nabateans in the Hawran', *JAOS* 97, 1977, 263-77.
15. See J.Negenman, *Geografische gids bij de bijbel*, Boxtel 1981, 171.
16. Cf.*AJ* XIII, 392.
17. Cf.*AJ* XIII, 393f. and *BJ* I, 104f.
18. See S.T.Parker, 'The Decapolis Reviewed', *JBL* 94, 1975, 437-31, and B. van Elderen, 'Nieuwtestamentische geografie', *BH* I, Kampen 1981, 68f.
19. Cf.*AJ* XIII, 397.
20. For the situation, etc., of this fortress see F.M.Abel, *Géographie de la Palestine* II, Paris ³1967, 427.
21. Thus *AJ* XIII, 406.
22. See Stern, op.cit (n.9), and also the survey by Josephus in *AJ* XIII, 395-7; also most recently Schürer I, 228 n.31.
23. See B.Mazar, *AOTS*, 227.
24. For the situation of the fortress see *BJ* VIII, 165-70.
25. See Abel, op.cit., 241f.
26. See Y.Yadin, *Masada*, London 1966, 15f.; *EAEHSL* III, esp.805f.
27. See Y.Meshorer, *Jewish Coins of the Second Temple Period*, Tel Aviv 1967, 118f.
28. See Meshorer, op.cit., 59.

29. Thus D.Jesselsohn, 'Hever Yehudim – A new Jewish Coin', *PEQ* 112, 1980, 11-17.

30. For this see J.Klausner, *The Messianic Idea in Israel from Its Beginning to the Completion in the Mishnah*, London 1956, 7-243; S.Mowinckel, *He That Cometh*, Oxford 1956; H.Cazelles, *Le Messie de la Bible*, Paris 1978; C.J. den Heyer, *De messiaanse weg* I, Kampen 1983.

31. See G.L.Davenport, *The Eschatology of the Book of Jubilees*, Leiden 1971, esp. 77.

32. See Test.Simeon VIII, 1-2 and also den Heyer, op.cit., 202ff.

Chapter 12   The Downfall of the Hasmonaean Dynasty

1. See e.g. E.Will, *Histoire politique du monde hellénistique* II, Nancy 1967, 419-34, and P.Grimal in *FWG* 7, p.148.

2. See Grimal, op.cit., 136. M.Grant, *The History of Ancient Israel*, London 1984, 221, differs.

3. Cf. Livy, *Ab urbe condita* C, and Dio Cassius XXXVI 45,3.

4. For this see also H.J.W.Drijvers, 'De Provincia Syria. Grieks Romeinse beschaving in het Nabije Oosten', *Phoenix* 26, 1980, 73ff.

5. See 11.2.6 and also J.Derenbourg, *Essai sur l'histoire et la géographie de la Palestine, d'après les Thalmuds et les autres sources rabbiniques*, Paris 1867, 96-101.

6. Cf. *AJ* XIII, 409. Cf. also *BJ* I, 111.

7. m.Hag.II, 2. But cf. J. Neusner, *The Rabbinic Traditions about the Pharisees before 70*, I, Leiden 1971, 110ff., esp. 141.

8. Thus b.Ber, 48a.

9. Cf. F.M.Abel, *Histoire de la Palestine* I, Paris 1952, 240, and Schürer I, 230.

10. Cf. *AJ* XIII, 410ff.

11. Cf. *AJ* XIII, 418 and *BJ* I, 115-16.

12. Cf. *AJ* XIII, 419-21; Strabo XVI 2,8.

13. Cf. e.g. *AJ* XIII, 427f., and also W.H.Buehler, *The Pre-Herodian War and Social Debate*, Bonn 1974, 40,53.

14. Cf. *AJ* XIII, 427.

15. Thus also Abel, op.cit., 248.

16. Cf. *AJ* XIV, 19-21.

17. Cf. *AJ* XIV, 30.

18. Cf. *AJ* XIV, 29-33.

19. Thus Josephus in *AJ* XIV, 40f., and also Diodorus Siculus in XL, 2.

20. Cf. *AJ* XIV, 34ff.

21. Cited by Josephus in *AJ* XIV, 35f. For this see K.Albert, *Strabo als Quelle des Flavius Josephus*, Würzburg 1902, 27ff.

22. For this see K.Galling, 'Die *terpole* des Alexander Jannäus', in J.Hempel and L.Rost (eds.), *Von Ugarit nach Qumran, FS O.Eissfeldt*, BZAW 77, Berlin ²1961, 49-62, and also H.E. del Medico, '*Zahab parwayim*. L'or fructifère dans la tradition juive', *VT* 13, 1963, 169-83.

23. Cf. *AJ* XIV, 45.

24. Cf. Dio Cassius XL 4,1.

25. Cf. *AJ* XIV, 58ff.; *BJ* I, 145-51 and also on this campaign Dio Cassius XXVIII, 14, 2 and Strabo XVI, 2,40.

26. See Ps.Sol 2,8 and also Tacitus, *Histories* V,9.

27. Cf. Philo, *Leg. ad Gaium* 155 and also E.M.Smallwood, *The Jews under Roman Rule*, Leiden ²1981, 2.

28. Cf. *AJ* XIV, 75f. and *BJ* I, 155f. See also G.Alon, 'The *Strategoi* in the Palestinian Cities during the Roman Epoch', in *Jews, Judaism and the Classical World*, Jerusalem 1977, 458ff.

29. See 11.2.5 and n.18 of that chapter; also H.Bietenhard, 'Die syrische Dekapolis von Pompeius bis Traian', *ANRW* II, 8, Berlin and New York 1977, 220-61.

30. Cf. V.Burr, 'Rom und Judäa im 1.Jahrhundert v.Chr. (Pompeius und die Juden)', *ANRW* I, 1, Berlin and New York 1972, 875-86; also B.Lifhitz, 'Jerusalem sous la domination romaine. Histoire de la ville depuis la conquête de Pompée jusqu'à Constantin (63 a.C.- 325 p.C.)', *ANRW* II, 8, Berlin and New York 1977, 444ff.

31. Thus e.g. M.A.Beek, *A Short History of Israel*, London 1963, 191.

32. Cf. *AJ* XIV, 158 and *BJ* I, 203.

33. Cf. *AJ* XIV, 159ff.

34. Cf. *AJ* XIV, 181-4.

35. *BJ* I, 213. But cf. *AJ* XIV, 180 and A.Schalit, *König Herodes. Der Mann und Sein Werk*, Berlin 1969, 46 n.154.

36. See Grimal, op.cit., 217ff.

37. *AJ* XIV, 302ff., 324ff.

38. See H.G.Kippenberg, *Religion und Klassenbildung im antiken Judäa*, Göttingen ²1982, 110ff.

39. Cf. *AJ* XIV, 342, 412 and 450. However, for Galilee see also E.Loftus, 'The Anti-Roman Revolts of the Jews and Galileans', *JQR* 68, 1977, 78ff.

40. Cf. *AJ* XIV, 303-69; *BJ* I, 248-373.

41. Dio Cassius, XLVIII 26,2.

42. See Y.Meshorer, *Jewish Coins of the Second Temple Period*, Tel-Aviv 1967, 60-3.

43. Cf. *AJ* XIV, 394ff.; *BJ* I, 290ff.

44. Cf. *AJ* XIV, 451ff., *BJ* I, 328ff. and also Dio Cassius XLVIII 41,4-5.

45. Cf. *AJ* XV, 8ff.

46. *AJ* XVIII, 9, 23 and *BJ* II, 118.

47. But cf. *AJ* XVIII, 4.

48. M.Hengel, *Die Zeloten*, Leiden and Cologne 1976, 92.

49. Cf. also G.F.Moore, 'Fate and Free Will in the Jewish Philosophers according to Josephus', *HTR* 22, 1929, 373.

50. In *BJ* IV, V. See e.g. *BJ* IV, 224f.; V, 5ff.

51. Cf. Luke 10.30 and J.T.Nielsen, *Het evangelie naar Lucas* I, PNT, Nijkerk 1979, 317f.

52. Thus e.g. S.W.Baron, *A Social and Religious History of the Jews* II, Philadelphia ²1952, 46-8; S.G.F.Brandon, *Jesus and the Zealots*, Manchester 1967, 26ff.; Hengel, op.cit., esp. 411.

53. K.Kohler, in *Jewish Encyclopaedia* XII, 1907, 639f. Cf. also W.R.Farmer, *Maccabees, Zealots and Josephus*, New York 1956.

54. Cf. J.Klausner, *Jesus of Nazareth*, 274.

55. G.R.Driver, *The Judean Scrolls – The Problem and a Solution*, Oxford 1965.

56. C.Roth, *The Dead Sea Scrolls – A New Historical Approach*, New York 1965.

57. M.Menken, 'De "Zeloten" ', *Vox Theologica* 45, 1975, 30-47.

58. Menken, op.cit., esp. 33ff. Cf. also T.Rajak, *Josephus. The Historian and his Society*, London and Philadelphia 1983, 86ff.

59. Menken, op.cit., 34.

60. Hengel, op.cit., 151ff.

61. Cf. also M.de Jonge, *Jezus, inspirator en spelbreker*, Nijkerk 1971, 101.

62. De Jonge, op.cit., 102.

63. Cf. *AJ* XVIII, 4ff.

64. See S.Applebaum, 'The Zealots: The Case for Revaluation', *JRS* 61, 1971, 155-70, and also H.Kreissig, *Die sozialen Zusammenhänge des judäischen Krieges*, Berlin 1970.

Chapter 13 The Reign of Herod the Great (37-4 BC)

1. There is another view e.g. in W.E.Filmer, 'The Chronology of the Reign of Herod the Great', *JTS* NS 17, 1966, 183-98, which dates the reign of Herod from 38 to 2 BC.

2. For this see Plutarch, *Vita Antonii*, LXI, 1-3.

3. For more details about these events see P.Grimal, in *FWG* 7, 226-9, and H.M.Beliën and F.J.Meijer, *Een geschiedenis van de oude wereld. Historisch overzicht*, Haarlem 1980, 264-6.

4. Cf. Beliën and Meijer, op.cit., 268.

5. Cf. Grimal, op.cit., 230ff.

6. A.Schalit, *König Herodes. Der Mann und sein Werk*, Berlin 1969, is a thorough study of the life and work of Herod. For further details see e.g. also M.Stern, 'The Reign of Herod and the Herodian Dynasty', in *CRINT* I, 216-307.

7. For a survey see Schalit, op.cit., 648ff.

8. Thus e.g. Schalit, 248f. n.11, and cf. also J.T.Nielsen, *Het Evangelie naar Matthëus* I, PNT, Nijkerk ³1978, 52 n.31.

9. For a detailed portrait of Herod see Schalit, op.cit., 605-10.

10. For him see B.Z.Wacholder, *Nicolaus of Damascus*, Berkeley and Los Angeles 1962.

11. Cf. Schalit, op.cit., 674f.

12. Cf. *AJ* XV, 305ff.

13. Cf. J.Gagé, 'L'Empéreur romain et les rois', *Revue Historique* 221, 1959, 221-60.

14. Cf. *AJ* XV, 317 and Strabo XVI, 4,23.

15. Cf. Schalit, op.cit., 146ff.

16. Cf. *AJ* XV, 187ff.; *BJ* I, 386ff.

17. Cf. *AJ* XV, 217.; *BJ* I, 396.

18. *AJ* XV, 360.

19. Cf. Schürer I, 319 n.122 and also *BJ* I, 399.

20. Cf. *AJ* XV, 380ff.; *BJ* V, 181ff.

21. Cf.b.Middoth 34a-37b. See further e.g. also R. de Vaux, 'Le temple de

Jérusalem', in *BeO*, Paris 1967, 312ff. A.Schalit, op.cit., 372-97; D.M.Jacobson, 'Ideas concerning the Plan of Herod's Temple', *PEQ* 112, 1980, 33-40.

22. Cf. *AJ* XV, 417.

23. E.Bickerman, 'The Warning Inscriptions of Herod's Temple', in *Studies in Jewish and Christian History* II, AGJU IX, Leiden 1980, 222ff.

24. H.Geva, 'The "Tower of David" – Phasael or Hippicus?', *IEJ* 31, 1981, 57-65.

25. Cf. *AJ* XV, 417. For excavations relating to the time of Herod the Great in Jerusalem see e.g., J.L.Blok-v.d.Boogert, 'Israëlische opgravingen langs de muur van de tempelberg', *Phoenix* 20, 1974, 345-50; id., 'Recente opgravingen op de westelijke heuvel van het oude Jerusalem', *Phoenix* 22, 1976, 70; *EAEHL* II, 604-8; M.Broshi, 'Along Jerusalem's Walls', *BA* 40, 1977, 12f.; B.Mazar, 'Herodian Jerusalem in the Light of the Excavations South and South-West of the Temple Mount', *IEJ* 28, 1978, 230-7.

26. Cf. *AJ* XV, 280ff.; *BJ* I, 407.

27. Cf. *AJ* XV, 292f.; *BJ* I, 403; Strabo XVI, 2.4.

28. Cf. *AJ* XV, 331f.; XVI, 136ff. Archaeological excavations seem to confirm the information in Josephus, see e.g. R.Bull, 'Caesarea Maritima: The Search for Herod's City', *BA Rev* 8.1, 1982, 25-40; R.L.Hohlfelder, 'Caesarea beneath the Sea', *BA Rev* 8.1, 1982, 42-7, and id. *et al.*, 'Sebastos, Herod's Harbor at Caesarea Maritima', *BA* 46, 1983, 133-43. For the significance of Caesarea see especially L.I.Levine, *Caesarea under Roman Rule*, SJLA 7, Leiden 1973; B.Lifhitz, 'Césarée de Palestine, son histoire et ses institutions', *ANRW* II, 8, 490-518.

29. Cf.M.Kochavi, 'The History and Archeology of Aphek-Antipatris: A Biblical City in the Sharon Plain', *BA* 44, 1981, 75-86.

30. M.Broshi, 'The Cities of Eretz-Israel in the Herodian Period', *Qadmoniot* 14, 1981, 70-9.

31. Cf. E.Netzer, 'The Hasmonean and Herodean Winter Palaces at Jericho', *Qadmoniot* 7, 1974, 27-36, and id., 'Recent Discoveries in the Winter Palaces of Second Temple Times at Jericho', *Qadmoniot* 15, 1982, 21-9.

32. Cf. Schürer II, 1979, 104.

33. Thus according to *BJ* I, 416.

34. Thus according to *BJ* I, 87.

35. See *BJ* I, 419.

36. For this fortress see E.Netzer, *Greater Herodium*, Qedem Monographs of the Institute of Jerusalem 13, Jerusalem 1981.

37. For all these fortresses see also F.M.Abel, *Géographie de la Palestine* II, Paris 1967, 172, 242, 350, 371; *EAEHL* II, 502-10 (Herodium) and III, 792-816 (Masada). Also Schalit, op.cit., 341ff., and Y.Tsafrir, 'The Desert Forts of Judaea in Second Temple Times', *Qadmoniot* 8, 1975, 41-53.

38. Cf.Schalit, op.cit., 271.

39. Cf. J.Jeremias, *Jerusalem in the Time of Jesus*, London [4]1979, 124f.

40. Cf. *AJ* XVII, 205, 308 and *BJ* II, 85f.

41. Cf I Kings 12.1-4 and on this H.Jagersma, *A History of Israel in the Old Testament Period*, London and Philadelphia 1982, 127f.

42. Cf. *BJ* III, 55f. and on it H.G.Kippenberg, *Religion und Klassenbildung im antiken Judäa*, Göttingen [2]1982, 116.

43. Cf. *AJ* XIV, 450.
44. See F.Herrenbrück, 'Wer Waren die Zöllner?'. *ZNW* 72, 1981, 178-94.
45. Cf. *AJ* XV, 365.
46. Schalit, op.cit., 274ff.
47. See Schalit, op.cit., 276 n.439.
48. See Schürer I, 416ff.
49. Thus also Schürer I, 420ff. J.T.Nielsen, *Het evangelie naar Lucas* I, PNT, Nijkerk 1979, 67ff., differs.
50. N.Avigad, 'How the Wealthy Lived in Herodian Jerusalem', *BA Rev* 2,4, 1976, 23-35.
51. Cf. e.g. *BJ* I, 153.
52. Cf. *AJ* XV, 5.
53. Cf. *BJ* I, 358.
54. See e.g. b.BB 3b-4a and the Ascension of Moses 6.2.
55. See Schalit, op.cit., 734.
56. Cf. *AJ* XVII, 149ff.; *BJ* I, 648ff.
57. *AJ* XV, 368ff.; XVII, 42.
58. See Schürer I, 394ff.
59. For these two figures see e.g. Schalit, op.cit., 768-70.
60. Cf. also *AJ* XV, 3-4.
61. *AJ* XIV, 386f.
62. Cf. also Schalit, op.cit., 689f.
63. Cf. *AJ* XV, 50ff.; *BJ* I, 435ff.
64. Cf. *AJ* XVI, 361ff.; *BJ* I, 538ff.
65. See also n.1.
66. *AJ* XVII, 168ff.; *BJ* I, 656.
67. See Schalit, op.cit., 638ff., and especially D.J.Ladouceur, 'The Death of Herod the Great', *Classical Philology* 76, 1981, 25-34.
68. See Matt.22.16; Mark 3.6; 12.13.
69. *AJ* XIV, 450; also *BJ* I, 319 and 351.
70. Schalit, op.cit., 479f. and n.1127.
71. Thus Bickerman, 'Les Hérodiens', *RB* 47, 1938, 184ff.
72. Thus also rightly Schalit, op.cit., 479.
73. See e.g. R.H.Charles, *The Apocrypha and Pseudepigrapha of the Old Testament In English*, II, *Pseudepigrapha*, Oxford 1913, 163-281; J.H.Charlesworth, *The Old Testament Pseudepigrapha*, New York and London 1983, 5-90.
76. See also Charles, op.cit., 625-52.
75. See e.g. J.A.Sanders, *The Psalms Scroll of Qumran Cave 11*, DJD IV, Oxford 1965.
76. See Charles, op.cit., I, *Apocrypha*, 569-95.
77. Published by S.Schechter, *Documents of Jewish Sectaries, Vol.I: Fragment of a Zadokite Work*, Cambridge 1910.
78. See now P.R.Davies, *The Damascus Covenant. An Interpretation of the 'Damascus Document'*, JSOT Suppl.Series 25, Sheffield 1983, esp. 202ff.
79. For a survey of the various studies of the Damascus Document see H.Bardtke, 'Literaturbericht über Qumran VIII. Teil', *TR* NF 39, 1974, 189-221; Davies, op.cit., 5-47.

Chapter 14   The Period from the Death of Herod the Great to Agrippa I
(c. 4 BC to AD 41)

1.Cf. *AJ* XVII, 206f.; *BJ* II, 1ff.

2. For the pilgrimages to Jerusalem see S.Safrai, *Die Wallfahrten im Zeitalter des Zweiten Tempels*, Neukirchen-Vluyn 1981.

3.Cf. *AJ* XVII, 250ff.; *BJ* II, 39ff.

4. The name of this king and of his family appear on an inscription found in Petra, cf. N.I.Khary, 'A New Dedicatory Nabataean Inscription from Wadi Musa', *PEQ* 113, 1981, esp. 21.

5.Cf. *AJ* XVII, 271ff.; *BJ* II, 56ff.

6. H.Guevara, *La resistencia Judia contra Roma en la época de Jésus*, Meitingen 1981, differs.

7. According to Luke 3.1 Philip ruled over Trachonitis and Ituraea.

8. For this division see *AJ* XVII, 317ff.; *BJ* II, 93ff.

9. Cf. Strabo XVII, 1,13.

10. Cf. also Matt.2.22; *AJ* XVII, 342; *BJ* II, 111.

11.Cf. *AJ* XVII, 342f.; *BJ* II, 111f.

12. Cf. P.Winter, *On the Trial of Jesus*, Berlin and New York [2]1974, 13ff.

13.Cf. *AJ* XVIII, 26; Dio Cassius LV, 27.6.

14. For a detailed account of him see J.P.Lémonon, *Pilate et le gouvernement de la Judée, Textes et monuments*, Paris 1981.

15. For the significance of this city see now K.Beebe, 'Caesarea Maritima: Its Strategic and Political Significance to Rome', *JNES* 42, 1983, 195-207. In the excavations there an inscription has also been discovered with the name of Pilate, see K.R.Veenhof, 'Nieuwe Palestijnse Inscripties', *Phoenix* XI, 2, 1965, 260.

16. For the situation of these areas see Schürer I, 336-8 n.2. For Ituraea see especially W.Schottroff, 'Die Ituräer', *ZDPV* 98, 1982, esp.132.

17. Cf. *AJ* XVIII, 106f.

18. For a detailed account see H.W.Hoehner, *Herod Antipas*, Cambridge 1972.

19. Cf. *AJ* XVIII, 114 and also G.E.Wright, 'Herod's Nabataean Neighbor', *BA* 41, 1978, 123.

20. For the problems see Schürer I, 346 n.24.

21. Cf. H.Kippenberg, *Religion und Klassenbildung im antiken Judäa*, Göttingen [2]1982, 125.

22. See Mark 12.14 par.

23. Cf. Tacitus, *Annals* II, 42 and also E.M.Smallwood, *The Jews under Roman Rule from Pompey to Diocletian*, Leiden [2]1981, 160.

24. Cf. F.Herrenbrück, 'Wer waren die "Zöllner" ', *ZNW* 72, 1981, 189 n.66; 191. See also 5.3.

25. Cf.M.Stern, 'The Province of Judaea'. in *CRINT* I, 1, 133 and L.Schottroff-W.Stegemann, *Jezus van Nazareth – de hoop van de armen*, Baarn 1982, 24.

26. Cf. Herrenbrück, op.cit.,184.

27. Cf. Luke 3.13 and b.Sanh 25b.

28. See S.Applebaum, 'Economic Life in Palestine', *CRINT* I, 2, 631-700 and also Josephus, *Vita* 47, 58.

29. Cf. Kippenberg, op.cit., 152.

30. Thus e.g. J.R.Armenti, 'On the Use of the Term Galileans in the Writings of Josephus Flavius', *JQR* 72, 1981/82, 45-9 and L.H.Feldman, 'The Term Galileans in Josephus', *JQR* 72, 1981/2, 50-2.

31. See J.T.Milik, *DJD* II, 122f.

32. See Applebaum, op.cit., 659; Kippenberg, op.cit., 147.

33. See e.g. Mark 12.1-12 and M.Hengel, 'Das Gleichnis von den Weingärtnern Mc.12,1-12 im Lichte der Zenonpapyri und die rabbinische Gleichnisse', *ZNW* 59, 1968, 1-39.

34. See H.L.Strack and P.Billerbeck, *Kommentar zum Neuen Testament aus Talmud und Midrasch* IV, 2, Munich 1969, 698, also J.Klausner, *Jesus of Nazareth*, London, 1925, 182f. and J.Helderman, 'De vrijkoop in het Nieuwe Testament met name in Mc 10:45 par', *Vox Theologica* 34, 1964, 90f. S.Safrai, 'Home and Family', *CRINT* I, 2, 751 differs.

35. Thus M.Stern, 'Aspects of Jewish Society: The Priesthood and other Classes', *CRINT* I, 2, 628.

36. Cf.S.Krauss, *Talmudische Archäologie* II, Leipzig 1911, 253-311; Klausner, op.cit., 177; Applebaum, op.cit., 576, 680-5; *AJ* XX, 54.

37. See H.Jagersma, *History of Israel in the Old Testament Period*, London and Philadelphia 1982, 120, 137.

38. See M.Elat, 'The Monarchy and the Development of Trade in Ancient Israel', in E.Lipiński (ed.), *State and Temple Economy in the Ancient Near East* II, Louvain 1979, 529, and also Hos.12.8.

39. See e.g. Matt.22.5; Luke 19.13-15; Josephus, *Vita* 70ff.

40. Thus e.g. F.Buhl, *Die sozialen Verhältnisse der Israeliten*, Berlin 1899, 7f.

41. See e.g. E.Otto, *Jerusalem – die Geschichte der Heiligen Stadt*, Stuttgart 1980, 147.

42. Cf. S.Safrai, 'The Temple', in *CRINT I*, 2, 865-9.

43. Cf. Safrai, op.cit., 880.

44. Ibid., 898.

45. See P.Billerbeck, 'Ein Tempelgottesdienst in Jesu Tagen', *ZNW* 55, 1964, 1-17 and Schürer II, 292ff.

46. Cf. J.Maier, 'Tempel und Tempelkult', in J.Maier and J.Schreiner (eds.), *Literatur und Religion des Frühjudentums*, Gütersloh 1973, 380, and the literature mentioned in n.25.

47. See m.Taʿanit IV, I and VII, II. Cf. also Luke 1.22.

48. See the different contributions in Lipiński, op.cit.

49. See V.Tcherikover, *Hellenistic Civilization and the Jews*, Philadelphia and Jerusalem ²1961, 155ff.

50. See S.Krauss, *Synagogale Altertümer*, Hildesheim ²1966, 2ff.; K.Hruby, *Geschichtliche Entwicklung einer Institution*, Zurich 1971, 21ff.; J.Gutman (ed.), *Ancient Synagogues: The State of Research*, Chico 1981, 1ff; L.I.Levine (ed.), *Ancient Synagogues Revealed*, Jerusalem 1981; M.Dothan, *Hammath Tiberias. Early Synagogues and the Hellenistic and Roman Remains*, Jerusalem 1983.

51. Thus e.g. C.H.Kraeling, *The Synagogue. Part I of Final Report VIII on the Excavations at Dura Europos*, Yale and London 1956, and Schürer II, 426.

52. Thus e.g. Hruby, op.cit., 19; M.Hengel, 'Proseuche und Synagoge', in *Tradition und Glaube* (FS K.G.Kuhn), Göttingen 1971, 158ff.

53. Cf. J.T.Nielsen, *Het evangelie naar Lucas* I, Nijkerk 1979, 147.

54. Cf. P.Schäfer, 'Der synagogale Gottesdienst', in J.Maier and J.Schreiner (eds.), *Literatur und Reliigon des Frühjudentums*, Gütersloh 1973, 391; J.J.Petuchowski, 'The Liturgy of the Synagogue: History, Structure and Contents', in W.S.Green (ed.), *Approaches to Ancient Judaism* IV, Chico 1983, 1-64, and also Luke 4.16ff.

55. Cf. Hengel, op.cit (n.52), 165 n.30.

56. See C.Houtman, 'Ezra and the Law', *OTS* XXI, Leiden 1981, 91-15.

57. Cf. Schäfer, op.cit., 394.

58. Cf. *AJ* XIV, 167 and also John 11.47; Acts 22.30.

59. See Schürer II, 212.

60. For a list of high priests at this time see Schürer II, 230.

61. For this see H.G.M.Williamson, 'The Origins of the Twenty-four Priestly Courses; A Study of 1 Chronicles XXIII-XXVII', in J.A.Emerton (ed.), *Studies in the Historical Books of the Old Testament*, SVT XXX, Leiden 1979, 251-68.

62. See also Schürer II, 247ff.

63. Cf. J.Jeremias, *Jerusalem in the Time of Jesus*, London ⁴1979, 181ff.

64. Cf.H.Gese, 'Zur Geschichte der Kultsänger am zweiten Tempel' (1963), in *Vom Sinai zum Sion*, Munich 1974, 147-58.

65. See P.A.H. de Boer, 'De godsdienst van het Jodendom', in J.H.Wassink, W.C.van Unnik and C. de Beus (eds.), *Het oudste Christendom en de antieke cultuur*, I, Haarlem 1951, 484ff.; Schürer II, 322ff.

66. See J.Neusner, *The Rabbinic Traditions about the Pharisees before 70*, I and III, Leiden 1971, pp.184-340 and 255ff. respectively. Also Schürer II, 363f.

67. See Neusner, op.cit., I,II, III and also A.J.Avery-Peck and J.Neusner, 'Die Suche nach dem historischen Hillel', *Judaica* 38, 1982, 194-214.

68. Thus S.Safrai, 'Religion in Everyday Life', *CRINT* I, 2, 793-84.

69. See L.L.Grobbe, 'Orthodoxy in First-Century Judaism: What are the Issues', *JSJ* 8, 1977, 149-53; N.J.McElency, 'Orthodoxy in Judaism of the First Christian Century. Replies to David E.Aune and Lester L.Grobbe', *JSJ* 9, 1978, 83-8.

70. Cf. J.Finegan, *Handbook of Biblical Chronology*, Princeton 1964, 238ff.

71. See e.g. A.F.J.Klijn, *De wordingsgeschiedenis van het Nieuwe Testament*, Utrecht and Antwerp ³1971, 59.

72. Cf.e.g. John 20.30; 21.25. For the traditions about Jesus see introductions to the New Testament and A.F.J.Klijn, *Wat weten wij van Jezus van Nazareth*, 's Gravenhage 1962; G.Vermes, *Jesus the Jew*, London and Philadelphia 1973; id., *Jesus and the World of Judaism*, London and Philadelphia 1983; and now especially E.P.Sanders, *Jesus and Judaism*, London 1985.

73. D.Flusser, *Jesus*, London 1969, 16f., and W.Schneemelcher, *Das Urchristentum*, Stuttgart 1981, 45, differ.

74. See e.g. Schneemelcher, op.cit., 56f.

75. For this problem see Smallwood, op.cit., 168 n.82 and also J.van Goudoever, *Biblical Calendars*, Leiden 1961, 161, 223ff.

76. H.Baarlink, *Anti-Judaisme in hed oudste Evangelie*, Kampen 1979, 16, rightly stresses that this indicates a common basis to Jesus and the Pharisees.

77. See Matt.22.23-33; Mark 12.18-27; Luke 14.20,27-40 and cf. also m.Sanh. XI, 1.

78. According to Flusser, op.cit., 54, the seven 'Woes' of Jesus in Matt.23.13-35 must be seen in this light. For the problems of this pericope cf. also K.Schubert, *Jesus im Lichte der Religionsgeschichte des Judentums*, Vienna 1973, 5ff.; W.S.Duvekot, *Kunnen wij Jezus kennen?*, Kampen nd., 125f.

79. For the relationship of Jesus to the Pharisees. cf. also H.Merkel, 'Jesus und die Pharisäer', *NTS* 1967/68, 194-208 and U.Luz, 'Jesus und die Pharisäer', *Judaica* 38, 1962, 229-46.

80. Thus e.g. by A.Dupont-Sommer, *The Essene Writings from Qumran*, Oxford 1961, 371ff.

81. For this material see also e.g. Schubert, op.cit., 105ff; K.Maier and K.Schubert, *Die Qumran-Essener*, Munich 1973, 124ff.; G.Vermes, *The Dead Sea Scrolls. Qumran in Perspective*, London 1977, 212ff.; J.H.Charlesworth (ed.), *John and Qumran*, London 1972.

82. Thus e.g. by S.G.F.Brandon, *Jesus and the Zealots*, Manchester 1967; P.Lehmann, *The Transfiguration of Politics: Jesus Christ and the Question of Revolution*, New York and London 1975.

83. See e.g. M.Hengel, *Was Jesus a Revolutionist?*, Philadelphia 1971; M.de Jonge, *Jezus. Inspirator en spelbreker*, Nijkerk 1971, 107ff.; Schubert, op.cit., 111ff.; Winter, op.cit., 69.

84. Cf. e.g. Matt.5.38f.; 26.52.

85. For this trial see e.g. J.Blinzler, *Der Prozess Jesu*, Regensburg ²1960; H. van der Kwaak, *Het proces van Jezus*, Assen 1969; Winter, op.cit.,; J.Imbert, *Le procès de Jesus*, Que sais-je? 1896, Paris 1980, and also Lémonon, op.cit., 173-203.

86. Cf.e.g.Klijn, op.cit. (n.71), 72f.

87. Thus Flusser, op.cit.,56; Merkel, op.cit., 196f. differs.

88. *AJ* XX, 199-203 and see D.M.Rhoads, *Israel in Revolution 6-74 CE. A Political History based on the Writings of Josephus*, Philadelphia 1976, 92.

89. See S.Rosenblatt, 'The Crucifixion of Jesus from the Standpoint of Pharisaic Law', *JBL* 75, 1956, 315-21, and Schubert, op.cit., 142ff.

90. Thus Blinzler, op.cit., 109ff.; van der Kwaak, op.cit., 47f.; Imbert, op.cit., 33ff.

91. See Winter, op.cit., 127ff.; Schürer II, 221ff.; Lémonon, op.cit., 74ff.

92. L.Dequeker, *Geschiedenis van het Jodendom en het Zionisme*, Louvain 1982, 31.

93. Cf. also H.Koester, *Introduction to the New Testament* II, Philadelphia and Berlin 1984, 76. E.g. G.J.D.Aalders, *Het Romeinse imperium en het Nieuwe Testament*, Kampen 1938, 128ff., differs.

94. See n.82.

95. See Klijn, op.cit., 36.

96. For this passage see Schottroff-Stegemannn, op.cit., 37f. and C.H.Lindijer, *De armen en de rijken bij Lukas*, 's-Gravenhage 1981, 48ff.

97. Cf. Schottroff-Stegemann, op.cit.

98. Cf. Schottroff-Stegemann, op.cit., 37ff., and Lindijer, op.cit.

99. For the parables see e.g. J.Jeremias, *The Parables of Jesus*, London and New York ³1972, and E.Linnemann, *Parables of Jesus*, London and New York 1966.

100. Koester, op.cit., II, 80ff.

Chapter 15   The Period from Agrippa I to the Beginning of the First Jewish
War (AD 41-66)

1. Thus H.M.Beliën and F.J.Meijer, *Een geschiedenis van de Oude Wereld. Historisch overzicht*, Haarlem 1980, 286.

2. Cf. Tacitus, *Annals* III, 23-25.

3. See Beliën and Meijer, op.cit., 304, and also H.Koester, *Introduction to the New Testament* I, 310f..

4. Cf. Tacitus, *Annals* XV,44.

5. For him see also S.Perowne, *The Later Herods. The Political Background of the New Testament*, London 1958, 58ff.

6. See *AJ* XVII, 252, but cf. Schürer I, 352 n.41.

7. See *AJ* XVIII, 261ff.; *BJ* II, 184ff., Tacitus, *Histories* V,9,7 and P.Bilde, 'The Roman Emperor Gaius (Caligula)'s Attempt to Erect his Statue in the Temple of Jerusalem', *Studia Theologica* 32, 1978, 67-93.

8. See *AJ* XIX, 265ff.; *BJ* II, 206ff.

9. See J.P.Lémonon, *Pilate et le gouvernement de la Judée, Textes et monuments*, 1981, 137ff.

10. Thus e.g. Koester, op.cit., I, 397.

11. See *AJ* XIX, 331; m.Bikk.III, IV, though it is not certain whether here in the Mishnah the reference is to Agrippa I or II.

12. See J.Meyshan, 'The Coinage of Agrippa I', *IEJ* 4, 1954, 186-200; Y.Meshorer, *Jewish Coins of the Second Temple Period*, Tel-Aviv 1967, 78-80, 138-41.

13. See also E.W.Hamrick, 'The Third Wall of Agrippa I', *BA* 40, 1977, 18-23 and E.M.Smallwood, *The Jews under Roman Rule from Pompey to Diocletian. A Study in Political Relations*, Leiden ²1981, 561f.

14. Cf. *BJ* V, 45; VI, 237.

15. See *AJ* XX, 118ff.; *BJ* II, 232ff. According to Tacitus, *Annals* XII, 54, however, at this time Cumanus was openly procurator of Galilee while Felix was governor of Samaria and perhaps also Judaea. For this difference between Josephus and Tacitus see Schürer I, 459 n.15.

16. See *AJ* XX, 160ff.; *BJ* II, 254ff.

17. Cf. also Tacitus, *Histories* V, 9; *Annals* XII, 54.

18. See *AJ* XX, 189ff.

19. See *AJ* XX, 360ff.

20. The former Bethsaida, cf. Schürer II,171f.

21. See *AJ* XX, 159; *BJ* II, 252.

22. Thus e.g. M.Stern, 'The Reign of Herod and the Herodian Dynasty', in *CRINT* I, 301 n.3 and S.Freyne, *Galilee from Alexander the Great to Hadrian (323 BCE to 135 CE)*, Wilmington and Notre Dame 1980, 77.

23. Thus e.g. by Schürer II, 573 n.8 and P.Schäfer, *Geschichte der Juden in der Antike*, Stuttgart 1983, 129.

24. Op.cit., 77.

25. See *AJ* XX, 145.

26. See Meshorer, op.cit., 143-53.

27. Tacitus, *Annals*, XIII, 7.

28. Cf. J.Derenbourg, *Essai sur l'histoire et la géographie de la Palestine, d'après les Thalmuds et les autres sources rabbiniques*, Paris 1867, 252-4.

29. See *BJ* VII, 96ff.

30, For details see Smallwood, op.cit., 572-4.

31. Cf. also S.Applebaum, 'Judaea as a Roman Province: The Countryside as a Political and Economic Factor', *ANRW* II, 8, 355-96.

32. For this place see F.M.Abel, *Géographie de la Palestine* II, Paris 1967, 154, and also Schürer II, 134.

33. See W.Schneemelcher, *Das Urchristentum*, Stuttgart 1981, 86ff.

34. See e.g. Gal.2.9.

35. See Schneemelcher, op.cit., 91ff.

36. See J.Jeremias, *Jerusalem in the Time of Jesus*, London ⁴1979, 130 n.19.

37. See H.J.Klauck, 'Gütergemeinschaft in der klassischen Antike, in Qumran und im Neuen Testament', *RQ* 1, 1982, 47-79.

38. See Smallwood, op.cit., 217 and especially B.Reicke, *The New Testament Era*, London , 245f.

39. Cf. Schneemelcher, op.cit. 95f.

40. According to N.Walter, 'Apostelgeschichte 6.1 und die Anfänge der Urgemeinde in Jerusalem', *NTS* 29, 1983, 387, this group consisting of Hellenists from the Diaspora was responsible for the foundation of an independent organization of the followers of Jesus.

41. E.g. by the time of Acts 15.13ff.

42. Thus e.g. by Schürer II, 498; Reicke, op.cit., 212; Koester, op.cit., II, 200, but see his hesitation on 315.

43. Thus e.g. by H.Mulder, *Geschiedenis van de palestijnse kerk*, Kampen nd, 43ff.; Smallwood, op.cit., 298 n.18, and Schneemelcher, op.cit., 52, 164.

Chapter 16 The First Jewish War (66-74)

1. Cf. also D.M.Rhoads, *Israel in Revolution 6-74 BC*, Philadelphia 1976, esp. 150ff.

2. As H.Kreissig, *Die sozialen Zusammenhänge des jüdischen Krieges*, Berlin 1970, does.

3. U.Rappaport, 'The Relations between Jews and non-Jews and the Great War against Rome', *Tarbiz* 47, 1978, 1-14.

4. Thus also rightly P.Bilde, 'The Causes of the Jewish War according to Josephus', *JSJ* 10, 1979, 179-202, and see also T.Rajak, *Josephus. The Historian and His Society*, London 1983, esp.78ff.

5. See M.Hengel, *Die Zeloten*, Leiden and Cologne 1976, 349ff., and R.A.Horsley, 'Banditry and the Revolt against Rome AD 66-70', *CBQ* 43, 1981, 409-32.

6. Cf. also J.A.Soggin, *A History of Israel. From the Beginnings to the Bar Kochba Revolt AD 135*, London 1984, 327.

7. Cf.C.Roth, 'The Pharisees in the Jewish Revolution of 66-73', *JSS* 7, 1962, 63ff.

8. See e.g. *BJ* II, 411.

9. See also K.Toki, 'Der literarische Character des Bell.Jud.II, 151b-153', *AJBI* 7, 1981, 53-69.

10. Thus also P.Schäfer, *Geschichte der Juden in der Antike*, Stuttgart 1983, 136.

11. Cf. also M.Goodman, 'The First Jewish Revolt: Social Conflict and the Problems of Debt', *Essays in honour of Yigael Yadin, JJS* 33, 1982, 417-27.

12. Cf. *BJ* II, 449ff. and also Meg.Taʿan. 14.

13. Cf. M.Gischon, 'Cestius Gallus' Campaign in Judaea', *PEQ* 113, 1981, 39-62.

14. See L.Kadman, *The Coins of the Jewish War of 66-73 CE*, Corpus Nummorum Palestinensium III, Jerusalem 1960, and Y.Meshorer, *Jewish Coins of the Second Temple Period*, Tel Aviv 1967, 88f.

15. See C.Roth, 'The Constitution of the Jewish Republic of 66-70', *JSS* 9, 1964, 295-319.

16. For this place see F.M.Abel, *Géographie de la Palestine* II, Paris 1967, 366.

17. Cf. *BJ* II, 573f. and *Vita*, 188.

18. For the disputes between Josephus and John of Gischala see now also U.Rappaport, 'John of Gischala: From Galilee to Jerusalem', *Essays in Honour of Yigael Yadin, JJS* 33, 1982, 479ff.

19. S.Freyne, 'The Galileans in the Light of Josephus' Vita', *NTS* 26, 1979/80, 397-413.

20. Cf. *BJ* II, 558; III, 1ff. and Dio Cassius LXIII 22,1.

21. Cf. *BJ* II, 127ff.

22. For this see A.Schalit, 'Die Erhebung Vespasians nach Flavius Josephus, Talmud und Midrasch. Zur Geschichte einer messianischen Prophetie', *ANRW* II,2, Berlin and New York 1975, 208-27.

23. Cf. G.Schmitt, 'Die dritte Mauer Jerusalems', *ZDPV* 97, 1981, 153-70.

24. Cf. Meshorer, op.cit., 90.

25. Cf. *BJ* V, 25f. and Tacitus, *Histories*, V, 12.

26. *BJ* IV, 366f.

27. Cf. *BJ* III, 307ff.

28. A road was probably made between Caesarea and Scythopolis in this period, cf. B.Isaac, 'Milestones in Judaea, from Vespasian to Constantine', *PEQ* 110, 1978, 47. But see also J.Negenman, *Een geografie van Palestina*, Kampen 1982, 130.

29. Cf. *BJ* IV, 503ff. and on this O.Michel, 'Studien zu Josephus', *NTS* 14, 1967/68, 402-8.

30. For this event see in more detail e.g. S.J.Salderini, 'Johanan ben Zakkai's Escape from Jerusalem. Origin and Development of a Rabbinic Story', *JSJ* 6, 1975, 189ff.; J.W.Doeve, 'The Flight of Rabban Yohanan ben Zakkai from Jerusalem', in *Uebersetzung und Deutung (feestbundel voor A.R.Hulst)*, Nijkerk 1977, 50f., and P.Schäfer, 'Die Flucht Johanan b.Zakkais aus Jerusalem und die Gründung des Lehrhauses in Jabne', *ANRW* II 19,2, Berlin and New York 1979, 43-101.

31. See e.g. b.Git.56a-b, ARNa 4, ARNb 6, Midrash Rabba Lam.I, 31 and Midrash Mishle 15.31.

32. A. Momigliano, CAH X, 861.

33. Cf. *BJ* IV, 377ff.

34. Doeve, op.cit., 58.

35. Cf. *BJ* V, 41ff. and Tacitus, *Histories*, V, 1.

36. Cf. *BJ* V, 41ff. and Tacitus, *Histories*, V, 12.

37. See M.Ottoson, 'Fortifikation och Tempel. En studi i Jerusalem topografi', *Religion och Bibel* 38, 1979, 26-39.

38. Cf. Luke 19.43 and *BJ* V, 499ff.
39. Cf. *BJ* VI, 68ff.
40. Cf. *BJ* VI, 94 and m.Ta῾an IV, VI.
41. Cf. *BJ* VI, 241 and 254ff.
42. See also E.M.Smallwood, *The Jews under Roman Rule from Pompey to Diocletian. A Study in Political Relations*, Leiden ²1981, 325.
43. *BJ* VI, 343ff.
44. For the siege and fall of Jerusalem see also Dio Cassius LXV, 4-7.
45. See. e.g. *EAEHL* II, 607-10; E.Otto, *Jerusalem – die Geschichte der Heiligen Stadt*, Stuttgart 1980, 163f., and A.S.Kaufman, 'The Eastern Wall of the Second Temple of Jerusalem Revealed', *BA* 44, 1981, 108-15.
46. *BJ* VI, 433f.
47. Cf. *BJ* VII, 163 and *EAEHL* II, 509ff.
48. Cf. *BJ* VII, 190ff.
49. See S.Loffreda, 'Le terme erodiane di Macheronte', *Bibbia e Oriente* 23, 1981, 105-14.
50. See Y.Yadin, *Masada*, 140ff., 164ff. and also A.N.Zadoks and Josephus Jitta, 'Judea in Romeinse tijd: Masada en Herodion', *Hermeneus* 42, 1970, 43f.
51. See Yadin, op.cit., 212ff.
52. See I.A.Richmond, 'The Roman Siegeworks of Masada Israel', *JRS* 52, 1962, 142-55, and Yadin, op.cit., 226ff.
53. *BJ* VII, 319ff.; thus also Yadin, op.cit., 224ff.
54. Or in any case part, see S.J.D.Cohen, 'Masada, Literary Tradition, Archaeological Remains, and the Credibility of Josephus', *Essays in honour of Yigael Yadin, JJS* 33, 1982, 385-405.
55. Thus I.Jacobs, 'Eleazar ben Yair's Sanction for Martyrdom', *JSJ* 13, 1982, 183-6.
56. Yadin, op.cit., 193ff.; Smallwood, op.cit., 338, differs.
57. Thus e.g. F.M.Abel, *Histoire de la Palestine* II, Paris 1952, 42 and N.G.Yoss, 'Massada', *Conscience et liberté* 24, 1982, 40ff.
58. See W.Eck, 'Die Eroberung von Masada und eine neue Inschrift des L.Flavius Silva Nonius Bassus', *ZNW* 60, 1969, 282ff. and id., *Senatoren von Vespasian bis Hadrian*, Munich 1970.
59. Thus also e.g. Soggin, op.cit., 331, but cf. B.Reicke, *The New Testament Era*, London 1969, 289f.n.24.
60. Thus righly Schäfer, op.cit. (n.10). For the consequences of the fall of Jerusalem see now also H.Mulder, *De verwoesting van Jerusalem*, Amsterdam 1977, 59ff.
61. M.Noth, *History of Israel*, London ²1960, 447.
62. Thus rightly R.Rendtorff, 'Das Ende der Geschichte Israels' (1972), *GS* I, Munich 1975, 272.
63. According to I Clem.41.2-3 and Diognetus 3, however, this continued to exist. See also Schürer I, 501f.
64. See H.Jagersma, *History of Israel in the Old Testament Period*, London and Philadelphia, 184.
65. A.Guttmann, 'The End of the Jewish Sacrificial Cult', *HUCA* 38, 1967, 137-48.
66. See also B.Isaac, 'Judaea after 70', *JJS* 35, 1984, 44-50.

Chapter 17 The Period between the Two Wars with Rome

1. Cf e.g. H.M.Beliën and F.J.Meijer, *Een geschiedenis van de Oude Wereld. Historisch Overzicht*, Haarlem 1980, 301-3; H.Koester, *Introduction to the New Testament* I, Berlin and Philadelphia 1982, 322ff.

2. Cf.b.BB 75b.

3. Cf. S.Freyne, *Galilee from Alexander the Great to Hadrian (323 BCE to 135 CE)*, Wilmington and Notre Dame 1980, 101ff.

4. Cf. *BJ* IV, 449.

5. See A.Büchler, *The Economic Conditions of Judaea after the Destruction of the Second Temple*, London 1912. But cf. also S.Applebaum, 'Economic Life in Palestine', in *CRINT* I, 2, 697.

6. Cf.b.Ned.62a.

7. Cf.b.BM V, VIII.

9. See S.Zeitlin, *The Rise and Fall of the Judaean State. A Political, Social and Religious History of the Second Commonwealth* III, Philadelphia 1978, 238ff.

10. See e.g. Num.20.17 and J.Negenman, *Een Geografie van Palestina*, Kampen 1982, 118ff.

11. See also J.Neusner, *A Life of Yohanan ben Zakkai. Ca.1-80 CE*, SPB 6, Leiden ²1970, 166ff.

12. Cf. Schürer I, 325ff.; G.Stemberger, *Das klassische Judentum. Kultur und Geschichte der rabbinischen Zeit*, Munich 1979, 83, and P.Schäfer, *Geschichte der Juden in der Antike. Die Juden Palästinas von Alexander der Grossen bis zur arabischen Eroberung*, Stuttgart 1983, 147.

13. Cf.C.Thoma, 'Auswirkungen der jüdischen Krieges gegen Rom (66-70/73 n.Chr.) auf das rabbinische Judentum', *BZ* 12, 1968, 30ff., 186f.

14. See W.Bacher, *Tradition und Tradenten in den Schulen Palästinas und Babylons*, Berlin 1966, 25ff.

15. Cf. Stemberger, op.cit., 88-90.

16. For him cf. Neusner, op.cit.

17. For him see J.Neusner, *Eliezer ben Hyrcanus. The Tradition and the Man* I, II, Leiden 1973.

18. For him cf. S.Safrai, *The Life and Teaching of Rabbi Akiva Ban Yosef*, Jerusalem 1970 (in Hebrew).

19. For him see J.Gereboff, *Rabbi Tarfon, the Tradition, the Man and Early Rabbinic Judaism*, Missoula 1979; G.F.Willems, *Rabbi Tarfon. Le père de tout Israël (env.50-135 ap.J.C.)*, Brussels 1983.

20. See J.Neusner, 'The Formation of Rabbinic Judaism. Yavneh (Jamnia) from AD 70 to 100', in *ANRW* II, 19,2, Berlin and New York 1979, 3-42.

21. Cf. also Neusner, op.cit. (n.11), 225.

22. Thus Neusner, op.cit., 215, and Schäfer, op.cit., 154. But cf. also G.Alon, 'Rabban Johanan B.Zakkai's Removal to Jabneh', in *Jews, Judaism and the Classical World*, Jerusalem 1977, 269ff.

23. See H.T.de Graaf, *De Joodsche Wetgeleerden in Tiberias van 70-400 n.C.*, Groningen 1902.

24. Cf. Schäfer, op.cit., 154f.

25. Thus e.g. Zeitlin, op.cit., 203, and D.Barthélemy, in *Le canon de l'Ancien Testament*, Génève 1984, 25ff.

26. P.Schäfer, 'Die sogenannte Synode von Jabne', *Judaica* 31, 1975, 54-64.

27. See M.Smith, *Palestinian Parties and Politics that Shaped the Old Testament*, New York 1971.

28. See Schürer II, 462f. n.164.

29. See D.J.van der Sluis et al., *Elke Morgen Nieuw. Inleiding tot de Joodse gedachtenwereld aan de hand van het Achttiengebed*, Neukirchen-Vluyn 1978, 258ff., and also Schäfer, op.cit. (n.12), 154.

30. Thus G.Alon, 'The Patriarchate of Rabban Johanan Ben Zakkai', in *Jews, Judaism and the Classical World* (n.22), 321ff., and Willems, op.cit., 14.

31. Cf. e.g. Stemberger, op.cit., 18; Schäfer, op.cit. (n.12), 155.

32. See e.g. E.M.Meyers, 'Ancient Synagogues in Galilee: Their Religious and Cultural Setting', *BA* 43, 1980, esp. 100.

33. Y.Yadin, *Masada*, London 1966, 181ff.

34. Cf.A.M.Rabello, 'The Legal Condition of the Jews in the Roman Empire', *ANRW* II, 13, Berlin and New York 1980, 662-762.

35. Cf. F.A.Lepper, *Trajan's Parthian War*, Oxford 1948.

36. Cf. A.Fuks, 'The Jewish Revolt in AD 115-117', *JRS* 52, 1962, 98-104, and also M.Pucci, *La rivolta ebraica al tempo di Traiano*, Pisa 1981.

37. Cf. CPJ, nos.435-450, and Dio Cassius, LXVIII, 32,1-3.

38. Cf. E.M.Smallwood, *The Jews under Roman Rule from Pompey to Diocletian*, Leiden ²1981, 550.

39. Cf. Smallwood, op.cit., 424ff.

40. See M.Avi-Yonah, 'When Did Judaea become a Consular Province?', *IEJ* 23, 1973, 209-13. M.Grant, *History of Ancient Israel*, London 1984, 246, differs and suggests 135.

41. See H.L.Strack and G.Stemberger, *Einleitung in Talmud und Midrasch*, Munich ⁷1982, 127ff.

42. See A.F.J.Klijn, *De wordinsgeschiedenis van het Nieuwe Testament*, Utrecht and Antwerp 1971, 166, 177.

43. Cf. also M.E.Stone, 'Reactions to the Destruction of the Second Temple', *JSJ* 12, 1981, 200ff.

Chapter 18   The Bar Kochba Revolt (132-135)

1. See B.Lifhitz, 'Sur la date du transfer de la legio VI Ferrata en Palestine', *Latomus* 19, 1960, 110f., and P.Schäfer, *Der Bar Kokhba-Aufstand*, Tübingen 1981, 48 n.80. Schürer II, 176, differs.

2. See S.Applebaum, *Prolegomena to the Study of the Second Jewish Revolt (AD 132-135)*, Oxford 1976, 10ff.

3. See Applebaum, op.cit.,14.

4. See Mur. 24A-F.

5. See Y.Yadin, 'Expedition D – The Cave of the Letters', *IEJ* 12, 1962, 249ff. n.42.

6. See Lifhitz, op.cit., 110f.

7. HA Hadr.14, 2.

8. BerR 64,10 and Barnabas 16.4.

9. See Schäfer, op.cit., 29ff.

10. Thus e.g. H.Mantel, 'The Causes of the Bar Kokhba Revolt', *JQR* 58, 1968, 224ff., and Schäfer, op.cit., 38ff., 195ff. Schürer I, 537; E.M.Smallwood, *The Jews under Roman Rule from Pompey to Diocletian*, Leiden 1981, 431; and J.A.Soggin, *A History of Israel. From the Beginnings to the Bar Kochba Revolt, AD 135*, London 1984, 335, differ.

11. *HE* IV, 6, 1-4.

12. Cf. also A.Oppenheimer, 'The Bar Kokhba Revolt', *Immanuel* 14, 1982, 11.

13. As does M.D.Herr, 'The Causes of the Bar Kokhba War', *Zion* 43, 1978, 1-11.

14. Schäfer, op.cit., 46ff.

15. See e.g. Y.Yadin, *Bar Kokhba. The Rediscovery of the Legendary Hero of the Last Jewish Revolt against Imperial Rome*, London 1971, 28ff., 128ff., *DJD* II, 124ff., and cf. also J.A.Fitzmyer, *The Dead Sea Scrolls. Major Publications and Tools for Study*, Missoula, Montana 1977, 48.

16. See Y.Meshorer, *Jewish Coins of the Second Temple Period*, Tel-Aviv 1967, 92ff.

17. See e.g. Eusebius, *HE* IV, 6, 2.

18. See e.g. b.BQ 97b and b.Sanh 93b.

19. Thus e.g. Schäfer, op.cit., 52. But cf. M.A.Beek, *A Short History of Israel*, London 1963, 214, who rightly rejects such a view.

20. See Meshorer, op.cit., 94ff.

21. Thus *Mur* 24b, 24c, 24e and 24i.

22. Cf. Yadin, op.cit (n.15), 124.

23. Schäfer, op.cit., 73.

24. Cf. b.Sanh 93b and j.Ta'an 68d.

25. These letters are written in Aramaic, Hebrew or Greek.

26. See Yadin, op.cit., 129, and also W.J.van Bekkum, 'Enkele brieven uit de period van Bar-Kochba (132-135 n.Chr.)', in K.R.Veenhof (ed.), *Schrijvend Verleden*, 123 n.7.

27. See Yadin, op.cit., 128ff.; van Bekkum, op.cit., 123 no.10.

28 See Meshorer, op.cit., 159ff.

29. Thus e.g. J.Maier, *Grundzüge der Geschichte des Judentums in Altertum*, Darmstadt 1981, 107.

30. Cf. Schäfer, op.cit., 173ff.

31. See P.Schäfer, 'Rabbi Aqiva und Bar Kokhba', in *Studien zur Geschichte und Theologie des rabbinischen Judentums*, AGJU 15, Leiden 1978, 65-121; id., 'Rabbi Aqiva and Bar Kokhba', in W.S.Green (ed.), *Approaches to Ancient Judaism* II, Chico 1980, 113-30.

32. See e.g. G.F.Willems, *Rabbi Tarfon. Le Père de Tout Israel (env.50-135 ap.J.C.)*, Brussels 1983, 101ff.

33. Thus e.g. Smallwood, op.cit., 442.

34. A.Büchler, 'Die Schauplätze des Bar Kochba Krieges und die auf diesen bezogenen jüdischen Nachrichten', *JQR* 16, 1903/04, 143-205.

35. Schäfer, op.cit. (n.2), 103ff.

36. Thus e.g. Schürer I, 545; Applebaum, op.cit., 35; Smallwood, op..cit., 442f.

37. See also Oppenheimer, op.cit., 69f., and the literature mentioned in his nn.35, 36.

38. Cf. Dio Cassius LXIX 12,2 and also the sources mentioned in Schäfer, op.cit.(n.2), 18ff.
39. Milik, *DJD* II, 125ff., differs.
40. See Schäfer, op.cit (n.2), 85ff.
41. Cf. Meshorer, op.cit., 92ff., 159ff., and also B.Kanael, 'Notes on the Dates Used during the Bar Kochba Revolt', *IEJ* 21, 1971, 39-46.
42. Cf. Schäfer, op.cit (n.2), 78ff.
43. Justin Martyr, *Dialogue with Trypho*, 108,3; Appian, *Bellum Syriacum* 50.
44. Cf. Dio Cassius LXIX, 12,3 and also A.Kloner, 'Underground Hiding Complexes from the Bar Kokhba War in the Shephelah', *BA* 46, 1983, 210-21.
45. Cf. Yadin, op.cit. (n.15), 60-5.
46. Cf. F.M.Abel, *Geógraphie de la Palestine* II, 276.
47. Yadin, op.cit., 193.
48. Schäfer, op.cit., 178f.
49. See Applebaum, op.cit., 53ff.
50. Cf. Dio Cassius LXIX, 14,2.
51. Cf. Corpus Christianorum, Series Latina LXXIV, 307, and LXXVa, 851.
52. Thus Justin Martyr, *Dialogue with Trypho*, 16, and Eusebius, *HE* IV, 6,3.
53. See Schürer I, 554 n.186.
54. Cf. *Digesta Justiniani* XLVIII 8, 11, 1.

CHRONOLOGICAL TABLES

I. The Time of Alexander the Great and the Diadochi

The campaigns of Alexander the Great in the Near East (*c.* 333–323 BC)
The struggle between the Diadochi (*c.* 323–301 BC)

II. Ptolemaic Rule (*c.* 301–198 BC)

Ptolemies		Seleucids	High Priests in Jerusalem	
Ptolemy I Soter 323–283 BC		Seleucus I 312–280 BC	Onias I Simeon I Eleazar	
Ptolemy II Philadelphus 283–246 BC	First Syrian War 274–272 BC	Antiochus I 280–261 BC	Manasseh	Zeno's journey 261–258 BC
	Second Syrian War 260–253 BC	Antiochus II 261–246 BC	Onias II	
Ptolemy III Euergetes 246–221 BC	Third Syrian War 246–241 BC	Seleucus II 246–226 BC		Joseph the Tobiad
		Seleucus III 226–223 BC		
Ptolemy IV Philopator 221–204 BC	Fourth Syrian War 221–217 BC	Antiochus III 223–187 BC	Simeon II *c.* 220–190 BC	
Ptolemy V Epiphanes 204–180 BC	Fifth Syrian War 202–198 BC			

III. The Rule of the Seleucids (*c.* 201–142 BC)

Ptolemies		Seleucids	High Priests in Jerusalem	
Ptolemy V 204–181 BC	Defeat by Rome at Magnesia 188 BC	Antiochus III 223–187 BC	Onias III *c.* 190–174 BC	Conflict with Simon, the captain of the temple

Ptolemies		Seleucids	High Priests in Jerusalem	
Ptolemy VI 181–145 BC		Seleucus IV 187–175 BC		
	Campaigns against Egypt, 170–168 BC	Antiochus IV Epiphanes 175–164 BC	Jason 175–172 BC	
		Antiochus V 164–162 BC	Menelaus 172–162 BC	Judas the Maccabee
		Demetrius I 162–150 BC	Alcimus 162–159 BC	Jonathan 161–142 BC
			Intersacerdotium 159–152 BC	
		Alexander Balas *c.* 150–145 BC	Jonathan 152–142 BC	
Ptolemy VII 145 BC		Demetrius II *c.* 145–138 BC		
Ptolemy VIII 145–116 BC		Antiochus VI *c.* 145–142 BC		
		Trypho *c.* 142–138 BC		

IV. The Time of the Hasmonaeans (142–63 BC)

Ptolemies		Seleucids	Hasmonaeans
Ptolemy VIII 145–116 BC		Antiochus VII 138–28 BC	Simon 142–135/34 BC
	Conquest of Idumaea and subjection of the 'Samaritans'	Demetrius II 128–125 BC	John Hyrcanus 135/34–104 BC
Ptolemy IX 116–107 BC	Conquest of Ituraea great expansion of territory	Antiochus IX 119–95 BC	Aristobulus I 104–103 BC
Cleopatra III 107–101 BC		Demetrius III 95–87 BC	Alexander Jannaeus 103–76 BC
Ptolemy X 101–88 BC		Antiochus XII *c.* 86–84 BC	
	Hyrcanus II high priest 76–67 BC		Salome Alexandra 76–67 BC
	Syria becomes a Roman province in 64 BC		Aristobulus II 67–63 BC
	Pompey conquers Jerusalem in 63 BC		

V. The Period from *c.* 63 BC to 4 BC

Rulers in Rome	Some Roman Governors in Syria	Authorities in Palestine	
Triumvirate Pompey, Crassus and Caesar, 60–53 BC	Scaurus, 65–62 BC Gabinius, 57–55 BC	Antipater, procurator *c.* 55–43 BC	Hyrcanus II, high priest 63–40 BC
	Crassus, 55–53 BC		
Caesar, dictator 45–44 BC	Cassius, 53–51 and 44–42 BC	Hyrcanus II, ethnarch 47–40 BC	
Triumvirate of Antony, Lepidus and Octavian, 43–36 BC		Phasael governor of Judaea and Herod of Galilee, 43–40 BC	
		Antigonus, king and high priest 40–37 BC	
Octavian (Augustus) sole ruler 27 BC–AD 14		Herod, king 37–4 BC	
		Aristobulus III, high priest in 35 BC	
		Boethus, high priest *c.* 24–4 BC	

VI. The Period between 4 BC and AD 44

Roman emperors	Judaea & Samaria	Galilee & Peraea	North Transjordan
Augustus 27 BC–AD 14	Archelaus, ethnarch 4 BC–6	Herod Antipas, tetrarch 4 BC–AD 39	Philip, tetrarch 4 BC–AD 34
	Procurators: 6–41 Coponius, 6–9 Ambibulus, 9–12		
Tiberius 14–37	Rufus, 12–15 Valerius Gratus 15–26		
	Pilate 26–36		Under Syrian rule 34–37
	Marcellus 36		
Caligula 37–41	Marullus 37–41		Agrippa I king 37–44
Claudius 41–54	Agrippa I king 41–44	Agrippa I king 40–44	

VII. The Period from 44–66

Roman emperors	Procurators in Palestine		
Claudius 41–54	Cuspius Fadus 44–46	Emergence of Theudas *c.* 45	
	Tiberius Alexander 46–48	Famine *c.* 46	*c.* 49–92/93 Agrippa II
	Ventidius Cumanus 48–52	Conflict between Galileans and Samaritans in *c.* 52	*c.* 49 King of Chalcis *c.* 53 enlarged with the addition of the former tetrarchy of Philip
Nero 54–68	Felix 52–60	Arrest of Paul in Jerusalem, 58	and in *c.* 54/55 with parts of
	Festus 60–62		Galilee and Peraea
	Albinus 62–64	Death of James, 62	
	Florus 64–66		

VIII. The Period from 66–135

Roman emperors	Important Events in Palestine	
Nero 54–68	First Jewish War 66–72	Vespasian conquers Galilee (67), Peraea and part of Judaea (68)
Galba 68–69		
Otho, Vitellius 69		
Vespasian 69–79	Bassus, governor *c.* 71–73	Siege and fall of Jerusalem 70
	Silva, governor *c.* 73–81	Fall of Masada 74 Period of Jabneh *c.* 74–132 Johanan ben Zakkai *c.* 74–80
Titus 79–81		
Domitian 81–96		Gamaliel II *c.* 80–120
Nerva 96–98		
Trajan 98–117	Quietus, governor *c.* 117	Quietus War 115–117
Hadrian 117–38	Bar Kochba revolt 132–135	Fall of Bethar 135

INDEX OF MODERN SCHOLARS

INDEX OF NAMES

INDEX OF BIBLICAL REFERENCES